R - - 2004

iew of Asi

THE POSTWAR
CONSERVATIVE VIEW OF ASIA

LTCB International Library Selection No. 8

THE POSTWAR CONSERVATIVE VIEW OF ASIA

How the Political Right Has Delayed Japan's Coming to Terms With its History of Aggression in Asia

WAKAMIYA YOSHIBUMI

Deputy Managing Editor
The Asahi Shimbun

LTCB International Library Foundation

Transcription of Names

The Hepburn system of romanization is used for Japanese terms, including the names of persons and places. Long vowels are not indicated. Chinese terms are romanized using the pinyin system. The Wade-Giles system is used, however, for certain place-names outside mainland China. The romanization of Korean terms follows the McCune-Reischauer system. Russian terms are transliterated using the system of the U.S. Board on Geographic Names.

With regard to Japanese, Chinese, and Korean personal names, we have followed the local custom of placing the family name first.

This book was originally published in Japanese
by Asahi Shimbun Publishing Co. under the title
Sengo hoshu no Ajia kan
© 1995 by Wakamiya Yoshibumi
English translation rights arranged with The Asahi Shimbun
© 1998 by LTCB International Library Foundation

First English edition published December 1999
by LTCB International Library Foundation
1-8, Uchisaiwaicho 2-chome, Chiyoda-ku, Tokyo 100, Japan
Tel: 03-5223-7204   Fax: 03-5511-8123

Translation and Production by The Chogin Business Service Co., Ltd., Tokyo

Printed in Japan
ISBN 4-924971-07-3 C1331 Y3000E

CONTENTS

PART III

PIECES OF THE PAST IN RETROSPECT

Chapter 14 The Political History of Japan's Apology Diplomacy

Part IV

The Emperor's Road to China

Part V

Report: The Post-Cold War Era as Seen in the Korea–Japan Forum

Part VI

In Prospective Perspective:
How Will Japan View Asia Tomorrow?

Introduction

In the fall of 1998, with the turn of the century just around the corner, Japan received two distinguished Asian heads of state as official guests, only weeks apart: President Kim Daejung of the Republic of Korea and President Jiang Zemin of the People's Republic of China. Their statements and actions during their brief stays were as different as day and night.

Given the bitter experience of colonial rule and aggression by Japan in the first half of the 20th century, which was shared by Korea and China alike, Kim Daejung proposed a historical reconciliation and went out of his way to please the Japanese, while Jiang Zemin threw a wet blanket on the evanescent euphoria of Japan–China friendliness and harped instead on his host's history of aggression, to the consternation of many Japanese observers.

VIP's idiosyncrasies do not go far enough to account for such a drastic difference. The political community in Japan in recent years has been marked by the sharp contrast between, on the one hand, the sincere contrition of successive recent prime ministers, who have expressed regret or remorse for Japan's past wrongs of colonial rule and aggression in Asia, and on the other hand, the apparently unending series of highly publicized gaffes by die-hard rightists tied to the governing conservative party, who seem to be intent on prettifying or justifying the very same course of history as if deliberately to rub their victims the wrong way. At the risk of oversimplification, we may infer that Kim Daejung chose to take Japan's official expressions of remorse at face value, while Jiang

1

Zemin was wary of Japanese attempts to justify past misconduct. The leaders' contrasting reactions throw into sharp relief the contrasting threads from which contemporary Japan's view of Asia is woven.

Kim Daejung presidency and its symbolism as a process of democratization in his country, the rise of North Korea as a threat to both Japan and South Korea, the weight of Japan's substantial contributions to the settlement of South Korea's economic crisis, and diverse other factors affecting Japan–Korea ties must have contributed to the flexibility and softening of Kim's stance towards Japan. Jiang Zemin's dour severity, on the other hand, stems from his frustration at the rise of a new nationalism in China, the consolidation of US–Japan security arrangements, Taiwan's rising status in the international community, and Japan's increasing political conservatism, among other irritants. Sequelae of the cold war in Asia continue to distort and darken our perceptions of our Asian neighbors and their perceptions of us.

*   *   *

I was in Seoul to cover the visit of Defense Agency Director Yamashita Ganri to the Republic of Korea in the summer of 1979. It was my first trip ever to an Asian country outside of Japan, and I remember having rather mixed feelings, the haunting reminder of Japan's past colonial rule salved by my almost overwhelming sense of proximity and affinity to the Koreans. Compounding these feelings were both an unsettling awareness of the military dictatorship's looming presence and authority and, above all, a palpable sense of the tension between Korea's South and North, a tension that is next to unfathomable within the peaceful confines of today's Japan. Only months later, news of President Park Chunghee's assassination was to splash across the headlines.

And the very next year, in September 1980, I found myself on the other side of the divide, in Pyongyang, the Democratic People's Republic of Korea (North Korea), this time in the entourage led by Fujii Katsushi of the North Korea Mission of the Liberal

Democratic Party's Asian–African Society. Not only was I given a chance to encounter the "Great Don" Kim Ilsung in person, but I toured Panmunjeom from the other side of the border from my tour of about a year ago.

"There is an act of Providence in all this," I said to myself, and I applied for, and was granted, a paid leave of absence for one year beginning in September 1981 to learn the Korean language at the Korean Language Institute of Yeonsei University in Seoul. In that one short year, I had experiences of all sorts, seeing, for example, the capital city officially nominated to host the next Olympic Games. Yet what struck me most during my sojourn was the vehemence with which the Korean people voiced their anti-Japanese feelings in the wake of the so-called "Textbook Controversy" of 1982.[1]

Though I have had many overseas assignments, my jaunts since then have mostly sent me to Korea, China, Southeast Asia, and the Middle East, with European or North American destinations few and far between. My coverage of political affairs in Japan has therefore focused mostly on Asian relations. A short list of major events I witnessed and reported on first hand includes the first official visit to Japan of an incumbent President of Korea in 1984 (when all ears were fairly twitching to hear exactly what Emperor Akihito would say in his formal Imperial greetings to the South Korean head of State). The next year (1985) saw China respond irately to Nakasone Yasuhiro's visit to Yasukuni Jinja (Yasukuni Shrine) in his official capacity as prime minister. Education Minister Fujio Masayuki then forfeited his job in 1986 for a recalcitrant attempt to justify Japan's annexation of Korea. Finally, in 1992, under the Miyazawa cabinet, Emperor Akihito paid a long-anticipated formal visit to China, while in the same year Tokyo sent a Self-Defense Forces contingent overseas to take part in United Nations peacekeeping operations in Cambodia. Later, as a news reporter-turned-editorial writer, on several occasions since April 1993 I have had to editorialize gloomily on insensitive and provocative statements parroted by die-hard Old Guard politicians over the turn of the half-century since the end of the war.

An apparently unending chain of such dreary incidents has set me thinking about the changes in Japanese politicians' perceptions of Asia. Japan's deeply rooted traditional obsession with getting itself 'out of Asia into the West' endures, but so does the illusion of 'the Greater East Asia Co-Prosperity Sphere' and the yearning to build a "Greater Asia." While failing to outgrow their predisposed contempt for Asia and feigning to ignore the deep scars that Japan left on Asia, postwar Japanese rightists seem unable to live down their guilty sense of debt to Asia, unable at the same time to stop hankering after another chance at dalliance with the rest of Asia.

Consistent on the one hand with its prewar background, Japan's view of Asia has been substantially affected in the postwar years by the cold war: postwar politics in Japan has arguably developed along double historical axes, the "vertical axis" being Japan's accountability for colonial rule and aggression and its consequences, the "horizontal axis" being East–West confrontations in the context of the cold war.

Now that the horizontal axis has crumbled, "the age of Asia" is being heralded with much fanfare. Japan is at a crossroads now, one as crucial to its future as its modernization was to it during the Meiji era at the very end of the 19th century, but Japanese politicians seem not to be clearly aware of having lost their bearings. Their view of Asia is still in turmoil and shock from Japan's defeat.

I have tried in this work, in one way or another, to trace and make sense of what conservative Japanese political leaders—who have been in power throughout the postwar years with negligibly minor interludes—have said and done, and to coax from their observable behavior a coherent picture of their view of Asia.

*   *   *

The Japanese version of the present work was published in 1995, the 50th anniversary of the end of the Pacific War. The proposed Diet resolution to mark that anniversary became politicized over questions of its language, and I penned these pages as a storm of controversy was raging over whether Japan should express "regret" or "remorse" or attempt to justify its wartime behavior, as described in detail in Part I.

The English version is appearing now, four years later, and I cannot avoid being struck by a series of momentous changes that have taken place in the meantime, all of direct relevance to the theme of this book.

On the Korean peninsula, Chairman Kim Ilsung has been succeeded by his son Kim Jongil; North Korea, with its prolonged food crisis, suspected development of nuclear weapons, and testing of ballistic missiles, is a pariah in the international community. In contrast in South Korea, Korean history resolutely turned a page when the long-time anti-establishment leader Kim Daejung of worldwide fame, whose kidnapping brought some discredit and suspicion also upon Japan, was democratically elected President of the Republic of Korea.

No less dramatic has been the evolving Chinese situation. Hong Kong reverted to China in 1997, while in 1996 in Taiwan, President Lee Tenghui assumed office as the result of Taiwan's first direct presidential election. Tension has mounted between China, still set upon enforcing reunification, and Taiwan, increasingly eager to flex its formidable economic muscles. China has resorted to brinkmanship by carrying out missile maneuvers off the coast of Taiwan, presumably as a diversionary tactic and warning to check Taiwan's moves toward independence.

Prompted by such rising tensions in the Asian situation, Japan and the United States have proceeded in 1999 to redefine their security arrangements, effectively expanding the range of Japan's support for American forces should they be called to the front from their bases in Japan.

Changes have also taken place beyond the security front. The Asian currency and monetary crisis that erupted in 1997 badly hurt Thailand, Indonesia, Korea, and other regional economies, and Japan did not escape unscathed. The widely touted "the age of Asia," has apparently vanished into thin air.

These dramatic events might have been incorporated into the new English edition, but limitations of time and effort have been such that revisions and additions have been kept to the minimum. In any event, the Japanese political community's view of Asia has remained essentially unaltered. With the minor additions here and there including coverage of the visits to Japan of Kim Daejung and Jiang Zemin in Chapter 14, the present English edition is a translation of the 1995 Japanese version.

I will be more than gratified if my readers find this exercise to shed some light on the all-important theme of "Asia and Japan."

December 1999

PART I

THE FIFTIETH END-OF-WAR ANNIVERSARY RESOLUTION OF 1995 AND ITS SHORTCOMINGS

Putting years of antagonism behind them, Premier Kishi of Japan and President Chiang Kaishek of Taiwan united in the cause of anti-communism. They were on such good terms that after he stepped down, Kishi was a guest of honor at Chiang's exclusive villa. (August 1961)

© Asahi Shimbunsha

LOOSE ENDS, FIFTY YEARS AFTER THE WAR

Herewith is the full text of the resolution adopted by the House of Representatives on June 9, 1995, on the occasion of the fiftieth anniversary of the end of World War II:

> On the occasion of the fiftieth anniversary of the end of World War II, this house offers its sincere condolences to those who fell in action and victims of wars and similar actions all over the world.
>
> Solemnly reflecting upon many instances of colonial rule and aggressive acts in the modern history of the world, and recognizing that Japan carried out such acts in the past, inflicting pain and suffering upon the people of other countries, especially in Asia, the members of this house express a sense of deep remorse.
>
> We must transcend the differences over historical views of the past war and learn humbly the lessons of history so as to build a peaceful international society.
>
> This house expresses its resolve, under the banner of eternal peace enshrined in the Constitution of Japan, to join hands with other nations of the world and to pave the way to a future that allows all human beings to live together.[1]

The resolution, titled "Resolution to Learn from the Lessons of History and to Renew our Commitment to Peace," was based on an agreement by the parties (the Social Democratic Party of Japan, the Liberal-Democratic Party, and the New Party Sakigake) composing the coalition government headed by Murayama Tomiichi, and as such, it was intended to have epoch-making significance as an expression of remorse over the past by the highest organ of state power.

It did not. Due to heavy opposition from within the ranks of the LDP and from the Shinshinto (New Frontier Party), the version eventually adopted was much watered down by the time it was put to a vote: the oblique allusion to European and American imperialism ("many instances of colonial rule") effectively defused Japan's accountability, and "aggression" in the draft version was replaced with "aggressive acts." The insertion of "differences over historical views of the past war" and other retouching reduced the whole statement to a rather ambivalent, far-from-straightforward expression of regret. Worse still, committee-level talks between the government and the opposition went awry, and the opposition Shinshinto (New Frontier Party) members all abstained at voting time. It was an anomalous turn of events for a Diet resolution. "Shameful, Grievous, Unbearable" read the *Asahi Shimbun*'s editorial lambasting it on June 23. Literally, it spoke for my agonized state of mind.

In its making, from conception to adoption, the resolution had allowed one politician after another to make public statements exemplifying (without the speaker's ever realizing it) the conundrum: "When will the Japanese ever learn?" As a news reporter on political affairs with responsibility especially for Asian affairs, I for one found the fiftieth anniversary of the end of the war to be a shaky and ambiguous milestone.

© Asahi Shimbunsha

The 50-Year Post-War Diet Resolution was adopted on June 9, 1995. Nearly half of the House of Representatives' members abstained.

Diehards' gaffes die harder

The opposition to the Diet resolution was a grim reminder of a whole series of controversial statements by cabinet ministers over the years. Take for instance Okuno Seisuke, who spearheaded the opposition to the resolution in the Liberal Democratic Party. As Director General of the National Land Agency in the Takeshita cabinet in 1988, he declared, "It was the Caucasian race that colonized Asia. . . . If anybody was the aggressor, it was the Caucasians. It is nonsense to call Japan the aggressor or militaristic."[2] How he refused to retract and had to be ousted is still fresh in our memory. He would repeat his view of the past war as one of "Asian liberation" in no mistakable terms:

> Manchukuo was established under the banner of the "Union of Five Races." The idea was to establish a republican system comprising the Japanese and Koreans, and then Manchurians, Hans, and Mongolians.
>
> There was then a shift in focus as war broke out with the

Americans, and the main thrust was to create a "Greater East Asia Co-Prosperity Sphere."[3] Stability in Asia is what it was all about. The people of Asia, long colonized by whites, needed to be liberated to give them stable livelihoods. Another banner, if you will. Eventually we were defeated, but Asian nations all became independent.[4]

Okuno was not the first to forfeit a cabinet post by making offensive remarks in a similar vein:

I still think it is wrong to define [the Greater East Asia War] as a war of aggression. . . . Because Japan was in danger of being crushed, the country rose up to ensure its survival. We also sincerely believed in liberating Asia's colonies and establishing the Greater East Asia Co-Prosperity Sphere. . . . The objective of the war itself was a justifiable one, which was permissible in principle in those days. . . . I think the Rape of Nanking is a fabrication.[5]

The next *faux pas* was made by justice minister Nagano Shigeto of the Shinseito (Born-Again Party) in an interview published by the *Mainichi Shimbun* in May 1994, a matter of days after the new Hata cabinet got under way. A former chief of staff of the Ground Self-Defense Forces, he was forced to resign because of this statement, only to assert himself later as one of the leaders of the Shinshinto (New Frontier Party) group that vehemently opposed the fiftieth anniversary resolution. Inconsistent in his political views, he had apologized when he relinquished his cabinet post less than a year before.

In August 1994, shortly after Murayama Tomiichi took over a shaky helm from the short-lived Hata cabinet, Sakurai Shin of the Liberal Democratic Party, director general of the Environment Agency in the new cabinet, made another gaffe, which also cost him his job:

I do not think Japan intended to wage a war of aggression. . . . It was thanks to Japan that most nations in Asia were able to throw off the shackles of colonial rule under European domination and to win independence. As a result, education also spread substantially, . . . and Asia as a whole was energized for dramatic economic reconstruction.[6]

It is as if the same reel of a recorded tape were being played over and over again, airing the 'Asian liberation' view of history in the conservative camp.

Embittered by the episode, prime minister Murayama Tomiichi distributed to new appointees upon reshuffling of his cabinet in August 1995 copies of his own keynote address in which he articulated his perceptions of the war, seeking to persuade them to be discreet in their utterances—but all in vain! Asked about his view of the war in his first press conference in office, Education Minister Shimamura Yoshinobu lost no time in making a senseless statement. "The expression 'war of aggression' is open to question in many ways," he protested and went on to declare:

Two-thirds of the present population were born after the war. We are entering an age of complete innocence of that war, and it makes little sense to keep harping on the past and apologizing for one particular incident after another. . . . Doesn't it take two to wage a war, that is, mutual use of aggression?[7]

Taken to task for his impropriety, he acquiesced the very next day and lamely rephrased much of what he had said, but his statement was criticized harshly in the South Korean and Chinese press.

Only two months earlier, while a heated controversy raged in the House over the exact wording of notions like "aggression" and "colonial rule," yet another politician, this one a veteran with much more political clout than his colleagues, had dropped another bombshell. After a speaking engagement in his home district of Utsunomiya on June 3, 1995, about three months before his death, Watanabe Michio, who had successively held the portfolios of deputy prime minister, minister of foreign affairs, and other offices, gave a press conference where, to judge from notes taken by an *Asahi Shimbun* reporter, he expressed himself in the following vein:

> We should see to it that the proposed resolution not violate the spirit of the [Liberal-Democratic] Party. . . . As for Japan–Korea relations, Japan governed Korea for 36 years, but you would look in vain for any reference in print to "colonial rule." Both sides have now recognized the legitimacy of the annexation treaty, agreed that there would be no reparations to be paid but cooperative financing to be provided—substantial amounts in economic cooperation for reconstruction, and that's exactly what we've been providing. (Reconstructed from statements he made during his lecture)

> The Japan–Korea Agreement has been worked out on the assumption that the annexation treaty was a peacefully concluded international agreement. . . . You mention "colonial policy," but the annexation was completed peacefully, a different matter from colonization by the use of force. (Reconstructed from statements he made during the press conference)

Hence there was no need, according to Watanabe's reasoning, to mention colonization or aggression in the text of the proposed Diet resolution. And that, he said, was "the spirit of the Party." This sparked an angry protest from Korea. Students threw Molotov cocktails at the Japan Cultural Center in Seoul, and the *Dong-A Ilbo* newspaper blasted Japan in its editorial:

> Our nation is shocked the more deeply because [Watanabe's] preposterous nonsense was made, of all conceivable times, on the fiftieth anniversary of our Independence. His sophistry is nothing short of deliberate and malevolent abuse designed to eradicate the historic self-esteem of the 70 million Korean people.[8]

I happened to visit Seoul immediately after this incident, and with the fatalistic resignation of a summer insect flying into a flame to its death, I felt a cold sweat come over me as I was bombarded with questions from the Korean press about the background of "Watanabe's nonsense" and its repercussions in Japan.

Watanabe's blunder had multiple antecedents. Nine years earlier, in 1986, Fujio Masayuki, education minister in the cabinet of Nakasone Yasuhiro, contributed an essay to the *Bungei Shunju* monthly magazine where he argued:

> Japan's annexation of Korea rested on mutual agreement both in form and in fact. As such, the Korean side also bears some responsibility for it. . . . Can we be sure that China or Russia would not have meddled in the Korean peninsula if Japan had not annexed it?[9]

Anxious at that time to improve Japan–Korea relations, prime minister Nakosone reportedly blanched when he read this and demanded that Fujio renege, but Fujio agreed neither to retract nor to resign voluntarily, preferring to be sacked.

The subject of 'Japan's annexation of Korea' being so controversial, and Fujio's blunder having raised such a commotion in the recent past, it is hard to comprehend why Watanabe (an ex-foreign minister!) should have seen fit to repeat the same *faux pas*. Even his notorious proclivity for saying the wrong thing would be a poor excuse and fail to exonerate him in this case. Such thoughtless comments by politicians who are untypical of Japan's current frame of mind receive the same treatment in the Korean media as a major scandal, rekindling the smoldering flames of anti-Japanese resentment. There is no point in whipping a dead horse, as they say, but Watanabe's guilt is undeniable and his responsibility grave.

The "Asian liberation" view of history lingers

Watanabe's statement contained multiple elementary errors. Korea in the prewar years was nothing short of a colony. Indeed, there may be "no reference in print to 'colonial rule,'" but that is only cosmetics of form having nothing to do with the substance. It changes not a whit of the fact that one country was deprived of its independence and ruled by another politically, economically, militarily, and culturally. Even Korea's ethnically distinctive language, script, and personal names were suppressed. And the people were subjected to countless forms of harsh discrimination never experienced by the Japanese. If this was not a case of colonization pure and simple, what else is?

His contention that the annexation was based on "a peacefully concluded international agreement" is equally absurd. The circumstances leading to the Japan–Korea Annexation Treaty of 1910 have been discussed in detail in Unno Fukuju's *Kankoku heigo* (Annexation of Korea)[10] and elsewhere. From the assassination by a Japanese of Min Bi, the Li dynasty queen, in 1895 to Japan's threats of force to exact an agreement on the Japan–Korea Protection Treaty (Second Japan–Korea Agreement) to the subsequent usurpation of Korea's diplomatic rights, there is not a shadow of a doubt that the process culminating in Korea's annexation was advanced by force as a whole. The government of the Republic of Korea even today maintains that "Korea was blackmailed into the annexation treaty, which was thus invalid from the very outset." In the postwar negotiations leading to the Japan–Korea Treaty of 1965,[11] the Korean position conflicted of course with the Japanese claim that the annexation treaty was valid in terms of international law at that time. The two parties' differences over the treaty's status had eventually to be shelved in favor of a compromise and the adoption of vaguer language describing the treaty as "deemed to be no longer valid." Yet regardless of whether the annexation treaty was valid or invalid in legalistic terms, the still yawning gap between the two countries' perceptions of its validity indicates how far from "peacefully" the annexation was carried out.

"Economic cooperation for reconstruction," as Watanabe put it, is also interpreted as such by the Japanese, while the Koreans regard it as a payment to settle their rightful claim for damages during the colonial years. Watanabe's statement reads as if the Korean side had agreed to the way the Japanese wanted to interpret these sensitive terms, and represents a woefully mistaken perception of the facts. Watanabe later reneged at least on "peacefully," but the fiasco again brought into bold relief just how provincial and impoverished is Japanese politicians' view of Asia.

Fully fifty years after the war, it is flabbergasting to observe a political climate that leaves old hard-liners free of qualms about the war's objective having been "Asian liberation." Hayashi Kentaro, a typically conservative historian who served a term in the House of Councilors as a Liberal Democrat, was convinced that "the Russo–Japanese War (1904–05) was a defensive war of racial self-determination," but even he had to admit that the fifteen-year war beginning with the Manchurian Incident (1931) "could not be described as anything short of aggression," and explicitly rejected any rationale for the Asian liberation view of the war.[12] Nor is there any denying, apart from the exact magnitude of the atrocities, the reality of the Rape of Nanking. That no affirmative appraisal of the Greater East Asia war is objectively tenable has been conclusively demonstrated by historical evidence culled from military archives and other sources, as discussed in detail for example by Kuroha Kiyotaka in his *Taiheiyosenso no rekishi* (The history of the Pacific War).[13]

If it had indeed been a war for the liberation of Asia, why did-n't the Japanese begin by liberating Korea and Manchuria? Why do people in North and South Korea even now celebrate August 15 as the day of their "Liberation" (or of the "Restoration of Light [Independence]") and the Chinese celebrate their 'victory in the anti-Japanese war'? There is no explaining away such realities. The Korean opposition leader (now President) Kim Daejung happened to be visiting Japan when Okuno made his reckless and inaccurate statement that Japan did not wage war against Asia; his terse comment was: "Let's leave it to the people of Asia to decide who fought against whom."

Let us now think about Chiang Kaishek, the President of Taiwan (the Republic of China), the 20th anniversary of whose death came around in April 1995. He had fought against the Japanese army in mainland China, only to be driven later from the continent by the Communist Party to Taiwan, where he assumed leadership of the Kuomintang (nationalist Chinese forces). During the war, he exposed the fraudulence of the "Greater East Asia Co-Prosperity Sphere" and joined hands with the Americans. Yet, once the war was over, he preached "Virtue in Return for Vice": his generosity in letting Japanese troops go home in safety and in waiving reparation claims was highly appreciated and gratefully acknowledged by conservative politicians in Japan. When normalization of diplomatic relations with China obliged Japan to sever its ties with Taiwan, right-wing members of the Liberal Democratic Party loudly and vehemently opposed what they termed "an act of treachery against Generalissimo Chiang." Today, the same men have no scruples about claiming that "the Greater East Asia War was a war of Asian liberation." Exalting Chiang Kaishek for his anti-communism while shutting their eyes to his anti-Japanese past hardly seems the right way to return their acknowledged debt of gratitude to him. It is sheer opportunism, a thin veil over their contempt for Asia.

In brief, if the war had really been waged for Asia's liberation, Japan's defeat should have meant Asia's defeat as well. If it had been a just war against European and American imperialism, defeated Japan might have been engulfed in the jaws of imperialism. I do not intend here to defend imperialism—be it European, American, or of whatever stamp—, but the mere fact of Japan's restoration as an independent state after only six years of postwar occupation and the winning of independence by one Asian country after another after the war must be duly recognized for what they are. Is it not the case that, as Japan was launching itself headlong into a war of Asian liberation, the once-imperialistic powers of Europe and America were undergoing a metamorphosis, while Japan and Germany grievously failed to note the sea change in the tide of the times?

WAS THE ISSUE EVER REALLY SETTLED?

One of the arguments against the fiftieth anniversary resolution was that the International Military Tribunal for the Far East (Tokyo Tribunal), the San Francisco Peace Treaty, and war reparations to

Asian countries have settled all related matters under law, and because prime ministers and other high Japanese officials have offered their apologies time and again, there is no longer any need to remake these apologies. Apart from a few pending cases requiring separate treatment, it is true that the case is virtually closed in legal terms. Particularly in recent years, Japan's prime ministers have taken every opportunity to present their apologies to Asian countries. I acknowledge that it is not conducive to constructive diplomacy for prime ministers to apologize constantly and to be always on the defensive. It is high time that Japan's relations with Asia matured sufficiently to obviate the need to make opening statements of contrition before any serious discussions about the future can begin.

Yet is it not true that every recorded statement of formal apology and legal form of settlement has been received with suspicions of duplicity, as repeatedly over the years subsequent statements and incidents have contradicted Japan's apologies? The pattern has been demonstrated by one cabinet minister after another, by their gaffes, as described above; by the so-called "Textbook Controversy" of 1982, in which, under pressure, the word "invasion" was replaced by "advance" in high-school history textbooks in order to receive the Ministry of Education's approval; by prime minister Nakasone Yasuhiro's bravado in paying an official visit as prime minister to Yasukuni Shrine (a Shinto sanctuary sacred to the memory of the war dead, including those executed as Class A war criminals) in 1985. The glib arguments aired by conservatives in the Diet sessions before the 1995 resolution were nothing but another round of denials and counterproductive maneuvers.

Whatever statements of contrition prime ministers may have made to express their deepest apologies, they have been belied by the bad company of subsequent gaffes, as noted pointedly by former prime minister Lee Kuan Yew of Singapore. Widely acknowledged for his pragmatic leadership in Asia, Lee gave the keynote speech at the "Fiftieth End-of-War Anniversary Symposium on the Future of Asia and the World" sponsored by the *Asahi Shimbun*, where he explained in no uncertain terms why the most abject apologies by successive Japanese prime ministers have failed to re-solve the misgivings of Asian nations. In sharp contrast to the can-didness of the Germans, he said, an endless string of loose-cannon statements by right-wing politicians in Japan has aroused anxiety. Yet he offered hope: "Once such disharmony is muted, it will be easy to build relations of trust."[14]

The resolution's proponents thought that the fiftieth anniversary of the war's end might be the best possible time to break the vicious circle and that a resolution by the highest organ of state power would be the best means to achieve that end. From the government coalition, not only the Social Democratic Party and the New Party Sakigake, but even such prominent members of the Liberal Democratic Party as Kono Yohei, its president, and Kato Koichi, chairman of the Political Affairs Research Committee, espoused the idea. From the opposition Shinshinto (New Frontier Party), chairman Kaifu Toshiki in his opening interpellation in January 1995 called for a resolution in a similar vein, just as chairman Hata Tsutomu of the Shinseito (Born-Again Party) had done earlier, in April 1994, upon stepping down after a brief stint as prime minister. Even the Communist Party, which eventually opposed the resolution on the grounds that its watered-down wording "puts cosmetics on the past," was in favor of adopting a resolution for this purpose. Neither government nor opposition party leaders dreamed that the proposal would face such implacable opposition.

The resolution's opponents in the Liberal Democrats and the New Frontier Party were supported, or to be more exact, goaded, by a powerful lobby: under strong pressure from the Japan Association of the Bereaved Families of the War Dead, they contended that describing the war as a war of aggression would be tantamount to saying that the war dead had spilled their blood for nothing. If such a description were upheld, they protested, the souls of the departed war heroes would be unable to rest in peace. In his book *Seiken dakkairon* (To win back the seat of power), Hashimoto Ryutaro, chairman of the Association of Bereaved Families and soon to take over as president of the Liberal Democratic Party and prime minister in September 1995, deplored "how those who live today and cherish the memory of their deceased kinsfolk would feel if they were to be told, 'That was a war of agression after all.' "[15]

Once in the vanguard of those advocating official worship by cabinet ministers at Yasukuni Shrine, Hashimoto was Chairman of the LDP Political Affairs Research Committee in September 1993, when, during the party convention's "talk session," panelists were asked to state their views on the war. I happened to be there, covering the proceedings for my newspaper, and the clashes that followed are still fresh in my memory. When LDP president Kono Yohei explicitly admitted, "It was a wrongful act of militarism, of imperialism," Hashimoto rebutted,

> If so, what alternatives did our nation's leaders have in those times? . . . The course that our country eventually opted for— whatever better options may in hindsight appear to have existed—I cannot bring myself to dismiss curtly as a war of aggression.[16]

As minister of international trade and industry in the Murayama cabinet, Hashimoto found himself caught in a dilemma between allegiance to his current boss and his position as chairman of the Association of Bereaved Families. While acknowledging the facts of Japan's invasion of Asia and colonial rule, he had to make a show of resisting the notion that the Pacific war was categorically a war of aggression. On several occasions, his evasive, round-about turns of phrase provoked the displeasure of China and South and North Korea. Eventually he went out of his way to persuade the Association of Bereaved Families to go along with the resolution, a compromise that was among the reasons why its final wording was so ambiguous and noncommittal.

Although Hashimoto appears to be justified when saying that bereaved families understandably would not like to be told that the war was an act of aggression, dispassionate reflection reveals the sheer absurdity of this argument. If all wars cause deaths, all wars must be justified *ex post facto* or the dead will have died in vain. This is objectionable on the one hand because it equates the plights of those (Japanese) whom we hold accountable for the war with the plights of the conscripts who fell through no fault of their own. And to invoke the same line of reasoning to justify the hostilities initiated by Japan means, *a fortiori*, that if the sacrifice of Japanese lives was justified by the noble cause for which they fought (not aggression), the non-Japanese killed in the alleged "war of Asian liberation" spilled their blood in vain because they were not fighting for the same "noble cause" as the Japanese. To put it bluntly, the "sacrifice-in-vain" argument leads nowhere.

Together with other right-wing organizations, the Association of Bereaved Families assembled a National Committee for the Fiftieth End-of-the-War Anniversary chaired by the professional right-wing ideologue Kase Shunichi and mounted a signature-collecting Campaign Against the Apologetic Resolution to put pressure on the elected members of both Houses. Japan's electoral system had recently been changed, and as political analysts pointed out, quite a few incumbent members of the House of Representatives curried the Association's favor and stooped to sign the petition, afraid of losing even a single vote to their opponents in the next election, the first under the newly established small constituency system.

UNFINISHED COLD WAR BUSINESS

To my way of thinking, the resolution was unfinished business from the cold war, left over and never settled because of the East-West conflict. For years, Japan had managed to shelve and ignore the painful subject of its accountability to Asia thanks to the cold war situation prevailing in Asia. But once the cold war was over, the Japanese had to face squarely and reflect on their country's past misconduct.

Beginning in the Meiji years in the late 1890s, Japan had sought to extend its presence into Asia. The nature of its military aggression was flagrantly in evidence in the fifteen-year war touched off by the Manchurian Incident. That Japan's ambition of asserting itself in Asia was frustrated by its military defeat ought to be interpreted as evidence that Japan was defeated not only by Britain and the United States but also by other Asian nations. Yet in the immediate postwar years, the majority of Japanese doubtlessly felt that they had been beaten solely by the Anglo-American alliance. They had to believe this, for in no other wise could the "Asian liberation" view of the war persist, as it has persisted to this day, nor could Japan's specious denial of colonial rule over South and North Korea have been repeated over the years.

The International Military Tribunal for the Far East did rule on Japan's accountability for the Pacific war, but it never ruled on Japan's Asian expansionism. During the trials, Korea's colonization was not addressed at all, and of the leaders responsible for the invasion into China, those who had been reluctant to make war on Britain and the United States escaped prosecution from the outset. Ugaki Issei and Yonai Mitsumasa, for instance, who were rated as pacifists by Chief Prosecutor Joseph B. Keenan, were penalized neither for having defended the Manchurian Incident as a "war for survival and self-defense" nor for having advocated war on China.[17] Yoshida Shigeru's stance was ambivalent, too. After a stint as Consul General in Hoten (present-day Shenyang) before the war, Yoshida served as Vice Minister of Foreign Affairs in Tanaka Giichi's cabinet and consistently promoted a high-handed China policy. He clearly sensed at that time that "it is with the Europeans and the Americans that Japan should keep company, and it stands to reason for Japan to rule Asia in collaboration with them."[18] Though Japan's subsequent invasion of China went counter to the collaboration he envisaged and therefore disconcerted Yoshida, there is no denying the substantial role that Yoshida played in paving the way for Japan's invasion of Asia.

Once the war was over, thanks to his exemption from prosecution, it was Yoshida who laid down the rails, as it were, for the "pro-American" orientation of Japan's postwar politics. In Japan's postwar political community, Yoshida's view of Asia was hardly unique: Hatoyama Ichiro, later to beat Yoshida in a bid for the prime ministership, shared his views on Asia. As a matter of fact, with the rare exception of Ishibashi Tanzan, a major figure in the

press since before the war who was consistently opposed to territorial expansion into Asia, virtually all conservative politicians who
played leading roles in postwar politics in Japan shared perceptions
of Asia that inherited certain characteristic and problematic traits
of the dominant Japanese prewar view of Asia.

The lot of Kishi Nobusuke is a prime example: once a high-
ranking official in Manchukuo, he was imprisoned by the Tokyo
Tribunal for a time as a suspected Class A war criminal for his
involvement as a cabinet minister under Tojo Hideki in the declaration of war on the United States. Yet he somehow escaped
prosecution and soon walked free. China's emergence as a communist power, instabilities in Asia (notably the outbreak of the
Korean War), and other extensive impacts of the cold war structure set the background against which Kishi's release, despite his
indelible responsibility for the "Greater East Asia Co-Prosperity
Sphere," clearly indicated a policy shift by the occupier, the
Supreme Commander for the Allied Powers (SCAP), from democratization to anti-communism. That the same man eventually
climbed to the top of the greasy pole was but one instance of
cases where Japan's war responsibilities, particularly the onus of
reflection on Japan's invasion of Asia, were left undefined or forgotten amidst cold war rivalries and tensions.

It was to China and Korea that Japan should have felt the
deepest obligation, but this was swept under the rug when all of
mainland China and the northern half of the Korean peninsula
subsequently turned communist. Their status as cold war enemies
gave Japan, now throwing in its lot with the West, a very convenient excuse to forget its accountability for its past conduct.
Thanks to all-out US support for Japan as its "factory in Asia"
and a bastion of anti-communism, the cold war in progress allowed the Japanese economy to rebuild itself in the bargain.
Massive, sudden surging demand for military materiel created by
the war in Korea gave the Japanese economy a big boost, allowing it to jump-start its economy into rapid economic growth.
While the rest of Asia was in the grip of hostilities and wracked
by cold war tensions, Japan enjoyed the double, nay, triple bless-

ing of economic recovery, exemption from war responsibility, and avoidance of bloodshed and sacrifice under the shelter of the "peace constitution."

Japan's good fortune is all the more conspicuous when compared with the fate of its neighbors. Chiang Kaishek, who exposed the fraudulence of the "Greater East Asia Co-Prosperity Sphere" and waged war against Japan, was later defeated by the Communist Party of China and took refuge in Taiwan, which was later expelled from the United Nations. China and Taiwan have yet to come to terms regarding their respective legitimacy claims. The Korean people, subjected by colonial rule to years of humiliation, had hardly begun to enjoy their newly regained liberty before their country was split down the middle by the US and the USSR and they found themselves mired in internecine warfare. Theirs was arguably the cruelest lot, they the most harshly treated by the cold war. In stark contrast to divided nations like Korea, Japan was saved from partitioning of its territory by sheer luck. Yet to what extent have Japan's politicians been aware of their good fortune?

Framed against the backdrop of these events, I think of the fiftieth end-of-the-war anniversary resolution as unfinished business from the cold war: if the cold war had not followed World War II, Japan would have had to settle its neighbors' claims earlier. Though the chill of the cold war has not yet left Asia completely, the climate has definitely changed, both in form and in substance. The peace and friendship treaty between Japan and China has been in effect for decades by now, and China's open-door policy is in full swing. The end of the US–USSR confrontation has spelled the end of the Japanese presumption of American indulgence and generosity in the economic arena: bilateral trade conflict has erupted, as has been so often noted. And so is it in political affairs as well, as most of us have yet to learn.

Japan can no longer afford to shy away from involvement in hot international conflicts, as shown by its discreet decision, made despite divided public opinion, to dispatch Self-Defense Forces troops to join United Nations peace-keeping operations abroad, and by its bid to win a permanent seat in the UN Security Council. Japan's moves must be carefully calibrated to mitigate Asia's wariness and win its wholehearted support. Its motives must remain above suspicion. Our country must leave no skeletons in its closet, lest their discovery expose us to contempt.

In May 1995, while controversy raged in the Diet over the proposed "apologetic" resolution, the international community was shocked by China's resumption of nuclear tests in the wake of the indefinite extension of the Nuclear Non-Proliferation Treaty. On visiting China in June, Kaifu Toshiki of the Shinshinto (New Frontier Party) lodged a protest against China's act of defiance in his talk with Jiang Zemin, General Secretary of the Chinese Communist Party. Jiang simply shrugged it off. When Kaifu went on to ask for China's support for Japan's bid to win a permanent seat in the UN Security Council, Jiang frowned, saying the idea was "complicated by Japanese perceptions of the war," and went on:

> We understand that some Japanese feel guilty and genuinely sorry for the crimes committed by Japan's militarists in the past. But it's also true that others have erroneous perceptions of the damage inflicted on Asia and China in World War II. You should learn from the proverb: "The front wheels set an example for the rear wheels." When it comes to perceptions of the war, the Germans have shown how to win credibility.[18]

China went ahead and performed another round of nuclear tests in August. When the Japanese government again filed a strong protest, even hinting at cuts in its grant aid, China cited the fiftieth anniversary resolution as irrefutable evidence that "in Japan there are still, indisputably, recalcitrant elements who do all they can to distort history and glorify invasion."[19]

In this exchange, Japan's reproof of China for its nuclear program was in effect countered with a sarcastic reminder: "Are you really entitled to complain?" As if provoked by the haggling over the fiftieth anniversary resolution and Watanabe's gaffe, South Korean President Kim Youngsam also spoke out, exhorting Japan to reflect in an exclusive interview with *Asahi Shimbun* President

Nakae Toshitada: "To glorify the past with falsehoods or to ignore it is not in Japan's best interest."[20] Both China and South Korea undeniably enjoy playing Japan's past as their trump card in diplomatic talks. Yet regrettably, Japanese politicians have none but themselves to blame for their vulnerability.

FOR ALL ITS IMPERFECTIONS, BETTER THAN THE FORTIETH

However emasculated, the fiftieth end-of-the-war anniversary resolution was nonetheless, in my opinion, of some, even considerable, significance. This is true in the sense that, even watered down, a Diet resolution would have been inconceivable ten years, not to speak of twenty years, earlier. What was on the political agenda in the summer of 1985? It was in that fortieth anniversary year that prime minister Nakasone Yasuhiro ventured to defy public opinion by visiting Yasukuni Shrine in his official capacity as prime minister, provoking China's wrath. Described in greater detail below, Nakasone's attiude was both clear and one-sided:

> It was the fortieth anniversary of the end of the war, . . . and I was firmly resolved to mark the occasion as a Japanese and as Japan's prime minister by worshipping at Yasukuni Shrine in my official capacity and taking cognizance of both the bereaved families and the spirits of our fallen heroes.[21]

His exaltation was completely devoid of any concern for the victims elsewhere in Asia, and naturally this provoked a backlash. By comparison, the fiftieth anniversary resolution was, finally, motivated by a concern, albeit impuissant, to see Asia in proper perspective. For this reason, the controversy it sparked was more open-minded than the political climate at the fortieth.

The resolution's very adoption reflected a gradual change in the Japanese political community's perceptions of Asia. Difficult as the situation was due to successive cabinet ministers' gaffes, from the moment of the resolution's passage, statements by prime ministers and their high-ranking associates became increasingly articulate in their reference to notions like aggression and colonial rule—a noteworthy change from their predecessors, who had almost always flinched from using explicit language. Words like "remorse," "contrition," and "apology" became standard fare, at long last. Take Kaifu Toshiki in Singapore, for example:

> I express our sincere contrition for past Japanese actions which inflicted unbearable suffering and sorrow upon a great many people of the Asia-Pacific region. (May 1991)

Or Miyazawa Kiichi in Korea:

> Let me apologize from the bottom of my heart for the unspeakable pains inflicted [on the "comfort women"]. (January 1993)

Or Hosokawa Morihiro in Korea over "colonial rule":

> I hereby express genuine contrition and offer my deepest apologies for my country, the aggressor's, acts. (November 1993)

The annual memorial service for the war dead held on August 15 every year at Chidorigafuchi Park, just a few minutes' walk from Yasukuni Shrine, also changed. In 1993, both prime minister Hosokawa and Speaker of the House Doi Takako won popular support by explicitly offering condolences not just to the Japanese but, for the first time, to the war's victims in Asia as well. And on August 15, 1995, prime minister Murayama Tomiichi published a comment in which he admitted Japan's "aggression and colonial rule" to have been "a wrongful national policy" and issued a "heartfelt apology." Murayama belonged to the left-wing Social Democratic Party; Kono Yohei, president of the conservative Liberal Democratic Party and deputy prime minister and foreign minister of the ruling coalition, expressed his strong support for Murayama's statement, which had received official approbation at a cabinet meeting. The changing course of these events may reasonably be taken to reflect a change in the perceptions of the nation as a whole. Murayama's statement has since been quoted by subsequent LDP cabinets (Hashimoto, Obuchi) as the definitive version of the apology and has effectively served its purpose as such.

Yet the fact remains that the Diet consensus formulated in the fiftieth anniversary resolution was something of an anticlimax. After years with an inherited unhealthy prewar view of Asia, postwar Japanese politics took a step in the right direction—albeit limited in many ways—with the fiftieth anniversary resolution. The inescapable conclusion is that Japan's perceptions of Asia, in particular the dominant view of Asia in the conservative camp, were still in a developmental phase.

PART II

"The Wrongs Committed by Ito Hirobumi": On the Trail of an Apology and a Cover-Up

Granted an audience with President Rhee Syngman (left), special envoy Yatsugi Kazuo apologized for "the wrongs committed by Ito Hirobumi" as he conveyed a message from Prime Minister Kishi. . . . Between them stands Kim Dongjo, who witnessed their encounter. (May 1958)

THE PRIME MINISTER'S MESSAGE: SPECIAL ENVOY YATSUGI'S UNTOLD TALE

"I wish to atone for the wrongs committed by Ito Hirobumi."

In 1958, at a time when Japan–Korea negotiations were deadlocked, Yatsugi Kazuo, Kishi's special personal envoy, brought the above-cited personal message from prime minister Kishi Nobusuke to Korean president Rhee Syngman. I had never even heard of this episode until I stumbled upon it in *Kan-Nichi no wakai* (Korea–Japan Reconciliation: Seoul's Negotiator Recalls Normalization Talks) by Kim Dongjo,[1] a veteran Korean diplomat engaged for years in the Japan–South Korea reconciliation negotiations, later Korean ambassador to Japan and then foreign minister.

Kim Dongjo's record of the 14 long years of bilateral talks leading to normalization of bilateral ties relates the delivery of special envoy Yatsugi's apology in great detail. At first, as I read his account, I could not believe my own eyes. To my knowledge, Japanese foreign minister Shiina Etsusaburo's statement on his arrival at Seoul's Kimpo Airport in February of 1965 was the earliest newsworthy act of apology by Japan for its colonial rule over Korea that I had heard of until I read Kim Dongjo's book. Shiina read a prepared statement in which he declared, as the protracted negotiations were finally drawing to a close, "We feel great regret and deep remorse over the unhappy phase in the long history of

33

relations between our two countries." I, for one, did not know that Shiina's comment had been antedated by seven years, that is, in 1958, by none other than prime minister Kishi (albeit through a special envoy), who offered atonement for "the wrongs committed by Ito Hirobumi."

Yet however early the first apology may have come, gaffes were like the other side of the coin to the apologies and had often embroiled the two nations in acrimony, driving a wedge between them time and time again. The widely reported "Kubota comment" is typical.

During the third round of Japan–Korea diplomatic normalization talks in 1953, Kubota Kanichiro, who headed the Japanese negotiating team, declared: "Japanese rule over Korea was not entirely without positive benefits," citing the construction of railway lines and port facilities in Korea during the colonial era. This statement was meant to weaken and offset the Korean negotiating position on rights of property and rights of claim (based on estimates of aggregate outstanding balances in postal savings accounts, wages paid to forced laborers, pension entitlements, and so on). But the Korean side found this remark so egregiously offensive that the talks were suspended for the next four-and-a-half years.

Thus it was not until April 1958, under the Kishi cabinet, that talks were resumed. The breakthrough came as Japanese fishermen who had been detained for alleged violation of the "Rhee Syngman Line" (a sea area declared off-limits to Japanese fishing boats by Korea in 1952, ostensibly to conserve fishing resources) were released on May 17, bringing about a thaw in Japan–Korea relations. According to *Kan–Nichi no wakai*, it was Yatsugi Kazuo who had served as the pivotal behind-the-scenes mediator.

Born in 1899 in Saga prefecture, the young Yatsugi Kazuo led a wanderer's life until he organized the Labor Conditions Research Service in 1925 and arbitrated a series of major labor disputes at Noda Soy Sauce Co., Kyodo Printing Co., Nippon Gakki Co., and other blue-chip companies. In the process he cultivated extensive personal connections with influential people of both right and left wings of the political spectrum. In 1933 he teamed up with Army staff officers to establish the National Policy Institute, attracting a coterie of bureaucrats, academics, social reformers, and politicians to join him. He relaunched his business after the war and became widely known as a political maverick, a fixer, a wire-puller—in short, an altogether mysterious man of action in behind-the-scenes politics. He was on close terms with Kishi, and had good personal connections in both Taiwan and Korea. In the absence of normal diplomatic ties with Korea, Kishi lacked formal channels of communication. A man with Yatsugi's credentials, however unconventional, must have seemed like a providentially placed pawn in his game.

Yatsugi's track record as an arbitrator was duly acknowledged, and he visited Korea on May 19 as the prime minister's special envoy. His status could not, of course, be officially endorsed in formal diplomatic terms: under the circumstances, Yatsugi was designated as a "special personal envoy," with Foreign Ministry officials looking askance at his send-off and following developments with mixed feelings. Yet because Yatsugi was carrying a personal letter from the prime minister, the Korean president accepted him as a proxy for Kishi, who wanted to visit Korea in person.

Yatsugi was given an audience with the Korean president in Seoul the very day he arrived. In attendance was the aforementioned Kim Dongjo, vice minister for Foreign Affairs and the man who later wrote *Kan-Nichi no wakai* (Korea–Japan Reconciliation). Yatsugi handed the President a personal letter and a hand-written scroll from Kishi with the uplifting motto: "Abide by One's Original Purpose to the Last." He began by saying, "The entire Japanese people are deeply moved, Mr. President, by your decisive step to release the Japanese fishermen," and went on:

> Had it not been for your leadership, Mr. President, it is believed in Japan that Korea would have turned communist long ago. As he sent me off as his special envoy, Prime Minister Kishi told me to convey his warmest greetings to President Rhee Syngman, the great champion of anti-communism in Asia and the entire free world, and to express his wish for a summit meeting either in Seoul or in Tokyo. . . .
>
> Coming as he does from the same province (the fief of Choshu, Yamaguchi prefecture) as Ito Hirobumi, who soured the contem-

porary history of bilateral exchanges between Korea and Japan, Prime Minister Kishi is regretful for the wrongs committed against Korea, and is making every effort to set them right. It is his sincere wish, Mr. President, that you will understand his feelings and show him the magnanimity of your spirit by re-establishing Korea–Japan relations.[2]

The latter paragraph is, of course, the key passage. The first prime minister of Japan and the first Resident-General of the Great Korean Empire, Ito Hirobumi not only came from the same province as Kishi (many years ahead of him, of course), but was also a major political figure and symbol of modern Japan. When Japan proceeded high-handedly to establish its suzerainty over Korea beginning with the assassination of Queen Min of the Korean Li dynasty in 1895, it was none other than Ito Hirobumi, then Special Ambassador to Korea, who exacted from the Koreans an agreement on the Japan–Korea Protection Treaty (Second Japan–Korea Agreement) robbing Korea of its rights of diplomatic representation. He overcame King Kojong's resistance by warning: "The government of Japan has already made its decision: by refusing to cooperate, you will only leave your country in greater jeopardy and cause more hardship." He forced the King to agree to the treaty at a cabinet meeting convened under military guard and chaired by Ito himself.

Ito's assassination by the Korean martyr An Joongkoon at Harbin Station in 1909 was followed by the annexation treaty of 1910. For a time after the end of World War II, Ito's face was depicted on the 1,000-yen bill. Though Ito is assumed to have been opposed to complete annexation of Korea, Koreans regard him as the symbol of Japanese imperialism, and An Joongkoon as a national hero with a tragic fate.

For Yatsugi Kazuo to speak of "the wrongs committed by Ito Hirobumi" as part of Kishi's personal message must have sounded like a clincher to Rhee Syngman, champion of the anti-Japanese cause. Rhee stared hard at Yatsugi and replied, "More than any other politician in Japan, I think, prime minister Kishi has an understanding of Korea and of the special nature of Korea–Japan relations of the greatest breadth, and he has distinguished himself from his peers in his efforts to build friendly relations between the two countries."[3]

Vanishing Records

Yet despite this praise for Kishi, Rhee did not immediately comply with the Japanese prime minister's call for a summit meeting. Instead, he asked Japan first, as a gage of its good faith, to support South Korea staunchly in its standoff with the Democratic People's Republic of Korea (North Korea). As Yatsugi was taking leave, Rhee sent for Kim and told him to hold a press conference for Yatsugi, saying that "the Korean nation should be informed" of Kishi's message referring to the wrongs committed by Ito. Yatsugi was unsure what to do when this was explained to him, but agreed with some misgivings to meet the press.

Was this account true? I looked for confirmation in *Kishi Nobusuke kaikoroku* (Memoirs of Kishi Nobusuke).[4] The reference there to Yatsugi's visit as a special envoy read as if the idea had been broached but had not materialized. In another book, *Kishi Nobusuke no kaiso* (Reminiscences of Kishi Nobusuke),[5] a series of heavily edited dialogues between Kishi and Yatsugi, Yatsugi recalls the circumstances of his visit to Korea as Kishi's special envoy, but says nothing about the vitally important message he is supposed to have conveyed. Nor is any trace of it to be found in the Ministry of Foreign Affairs' records. "I don't know anything about it," said Wada Tsutomu, seconded from the Ministry of Foreign Affairs and secretary to the prime minister from soon after Yatsugi's visit to Korea. I rooted around for confirmation and asked my senior and retired colleagues who had covered political affairs at this time whether they had heard about it, but as far as they could remember, they knew nothing of it.

Yet if the press conference had in fact been held, it must certainly have been newsworthy. After a dogged search for evidence, I was rewarded by the discovery of a news item in the *Asahi Shimbun*. At that time, the Asahi had no special correspondent of its own in Korea; it therefore carried a Reuters dispatch on May 22, 1958, translated into Japanese and headlined "Regretful for Korea's Annexation, Mr. Yatsugi Says":

> (Keijo, 21st, Reuters) Prime Minister Kishi, for the first time, formally expressed regret to Korea for Japan's past annexation of Korea. Yatsugi Kazuo, Kishi's special envoy to Korea, made a prepared statement as follows at a press conference today:

> "Prime Minister Kishi feels strongly that the wrongs committed by Duke Ito Hirobumi in Japan–Korea relations should be atoned for. The Prime Minister is also very regretful for the serious damage inflicted on Korea by acts of the Japanese military. He has been making his best efforts in all sincerity to build friendly relations between the two countries, and is determined to pursue these efforts. When I conveyed this message to President Rhee Syngman, he expressed deep trust in Prime Minister Kishi and told me that the future of our friendly bilateral relations depended on Prime Minister Kishi's integrity."

(Incidentally, it embarrasses me now that, more than ten years after the end of the war and restoration of Korea's independence, the *Asahi Shimbun* when it printed this Reuters dispatch was still using the colonial-era Japanese name, "Keijo," for the capital city of Seoul.) In any event this small article establishes that, Yatsugi did apparently read his prepared statement to the press. The "mistakes (*ayamari*) committed by Duke Ito Hirobumi" in the dispatch are presumably meant to translate "wrongs (*ayamachi*)" in Yatsugi's Japanese text. That Kishi "is very regretful for . . ." is quoted verbatim, so that the Reuters wording, "for the first time, formally expressed regret . . ." is most likely correct and accurate. Less than a column long, this small item was apparently too small to attract attention. Few readers, if any, noted the crucial reference to a first formal expression of regret.

On the very same day, the *Asahi Shimbun* gave three rows to coverage of Yatsugi's press conference on his return to Tokyo. Making no mention at all of "wrongs" or of "regret," it merely underscored how the Japanese prime minister and the Korean president sought to cultivate relations of mutual trust. Apparently, in his Tokyo press conference, Yatsugi kept his lips sealed about the explicit reference to Ito Hirobumi and the wrongs he committed in Korea, and the Japanese press corps was in no position to know anything about what Yatsugi had said in Seoul only a few hours before. The Reuters dispatch was relegated to a negligibly small corner, presumably because Yatsugi had been so tight-lipped in Tokyo. Also, given the fishermen's plight, Japan's Fourth Estate might well have been hostile to apologetic overtures by Japan to Korea at that time.

Uncertainties about Kishi's message continued to nag me. My visit to Korea in June 1995 to cover the 30th anniversary of the Japan–Korea Treaty of 1965 gave me a chance to investigate. First I searched through back issues of Korean newspapers and found that Yatsugi's press conference had been covered substantially by the *Dong-A Ilbo* (three columns) and the *Chosun Ilbo* (four columns). According to the *Chosun Ilbo*'s account, Yatsugi's statement was to the following effect:

> Prime Minister Kishi is regretful for the wrongs committed against Korea by Japanese militarists in the past. He is determined to make his best and sincerest efforts to improve Korea–Japan relations. I have just conveyed to President Rhee Syngman Prime Minister Kishi's determination to continue doing so.
>
> President Rhee Syngman in turn has stated that, of all politicians in Japan, he trusts Prime Minister Kishi in particular, and that the future of Korea–Japan relations depends on Prime Minister Kishi's integrity.
>
> Coming as he does from the same province as Ito Hirobumi, Prime Minister Kishi feels obliged to strive to atone for the wrongs committed by Ito, his predecessor [*of nearly two generations ago*].

Though slightly different in wording, the tenor of this account is virtually identical to Yatsugi's prepared statement reported in the Reuters dispatch. While the *Chosun Ilbo* carried a subheading reading, "Regretful for Sins of Japanese Military Against Korea," the *Dong-A Ilbo* did not feature Kishi's expression of regret in the headline. Both papers refrained from sensationalism, presumably because the message had been delivered neither by the prime minister in person nor by any official envoy. When I asked Chairman Kwon Okie of the *Dong-A Ilbo* about this, he remembered seeing a newspaper photo showing Yatsugi bent over before President Rhee Syngman, making the deepest possible bow, but the Korean press apparently sensed something shady about Yatsugi's absence of proper diplomatic status and was not ready to be taken in by such an adulatory gesture, Kwon Okie told me.

KISHI'S STRATEGY AND MISCALCULATION

After my return to Japan, I investigated the matter further. In the interim, Yatsugi's visit to South Korea had apparently had spreading repercussions in Japan. The August 5 issue of the now defunct weekly *Nipponshuho* carried an article with the title "The Monster Who Kowtowed to Rhee Syngman" criticizing Yatsugi's speech and actions. Japanese public opinion in those days was still under the spell of the pre-war view of Asia and had been generally sympathetic to the provocative comment by Kubota Kanichiro in 1953 (mentioned at the beginning of this part); the Japanese were angry at the seizure of Japanese fishing boats for alleged violations of the Rhee Syngman Line and generally felt that the very thought of offering apologies to Korea was demeaning. What did Kishi himself think about Yatsugi's speech and actions? The minutes of the Diet's proceedings show how brazenly Kishi denied it. Pressed hard by a Socialist Party Diet member in the House of Representatives' budget committee meeting on June 24, 1958, one month after Yatsugi's visit to South Korea, Kishi acknowledged that Yatsugi

Kazuo had been sent as his personal envoy, but flatly denied having anything to do with the language of Yatsugi's statement:

> I am not familiar with what Mr. Yatsugi said in Keijo. All I did was ask him to convey my intentions to President Rhee Syngman and to sound out Korean VIPs about theirs. That's what I meant to say. Whatever view Mr. Yatsugi expressed was stated as his personal view, not mine. . . .
>
> That is a private point of view, Mr. Yatsugi's own personal opinion. I have never said anything of the sort to Mr. Yatsugi, nor entrusted him with any such thing.

All things considered, it is hard to imagine that Kishi, an ultra-nationalist and advocate of Greater Asianism in the past and a high-ranking official in Manchukuo and then a cabinet minister in the Tojo cabinet, should have felt deeply regretful for "wrongs committed by Ito." Was the whole thing, then, just concocted by Yatsugi? I had a chance to meet Kim Dongjo, now aged seventy-six, while I was in Seoul and to ask him. He assured me it could not have been a fabrication, because Kishi himself had previously spoken to Kim about Ito Hirobumi.

On his way back from the United States in February 1957, Kim, then a director in the Korean Foreign Office, made a stop in Tokyo and, through the mediation of Yatsugi Kazuo, met Kishi in utmost secrecy. (This was immediately after Kishi assumed office as prime minister. Yatsugi had had the good sense to arrange a meeting between Kim and Kishi upon learning that Kim was slated soon to become vice minister.) At this meeting, Kishi mentioned Ito Hirobumi by name, saying in effect that he was "deeply sorry for past wrongs," and asked Kim to convey to the president his determination to break the deadlock in Japan–Korea relations. As described in detail in Kim's *Kan-Nichi no wakai* (Korea–Japan Reconciliation), Kishi also emphasized the close geographic and historical ties between Yamaguchi prefecture and Korea, and went so far as to say, "I think there is a strain of Korean blood in my lineage."[6] Given such an adumbration, Kim recalled, he was not at all surprised fifteen months later to hear Yatsugi deliver Kishi's message and refer specifically to Ito Hirobumi.

This testimony certainly lends credibility to the Ito Hirobumi story. It is hard to imagine that, for all his practiced audacity, Yatsugi would make up a story of this kind on his own. It is possible that he remembered what Kishi had said and repeated it virtually verbatim, on his own initiative, to the Korean president, but it is considerably more probable that Kishi deliberately instructed him to speak for him in this way.

With bilateral relations still in abeyance, Korea was the odd man out on Kishi's itinerary when, only the previous year in 1957, he had made the rounds of Taiwan and Southeast Asian countries, presenting himself prominently as an advocate of an Asian anti-communist alliance. This must be why he suggested, by proxy, a Japan–Korea summit to Rhee Syngman. I now speculate that Kishi wanted to have his true sentiments conveyed *sotto voce*. Though a nationalist, Kishi was also enough of a strategist to have no qualms about making overtures of exactly this sort.

When I broached the subject to Hara Yoshihisa, who authored *Kishi Nobusuke* after a long series of interviews with Kishi, he said he had never heard of such a statement, but added:

> Kishi had begun laying the groundwork for overhauling the US–Japan Security Treaty and was eager to consolidate a foothold in Asia. So he must seriously have been eager to score a breakthrough in Japan–Korea relations. If he did in fact mention Ito by name, it was certainly a deliberate and strategic allusion. Yatsugi Kazuo was just the kind of handyman to be entrusted with such a sensitive message.[7]

I could not agree with him more. His fancy tickled by the allusion, Rhee went out of his way to extol Kishi in the only way he could as a confirmed Japanophobe. To that extent, Kishi's ploy worked—but only partially. Presumably it was Rhee's distrust of the Japanese that prompted him to call a press conference for Yatsugi on the spot and without a moment's delay—one-upmanship by an old fox every bit as wily as Kishi. The Japanese prime minister's miscalculation was that he wanted his message to be conveyed in some kind of telepathic tacit understanding, but it ended up being brought out into the open, committing him to his words as delivered by Yatsugi.

As Kim recalls the scene, the request for a press conference put Yatsugi in a bind. He protested: "If the story leaks out to the press, it may cause trouble for the prime minister and trigger yet another dispute." He gave in, however, when told that his appearance at the press conference would "be preferable to the Korean side unilaterally issuing a statement." For the sake of accuracy, they agreed on a prepared comment to be read at the press conference. Using notes he had taken of the conversation, Kim first drafted an English version for the foreign press corps, then translated it into Japanese for Yatsugi's approval. The Korean side evidently had the upper hand throughout the episode, and Yatsugi was trapped, with no way to back out.

And there was further fillip to Kishi's miscalculation: his strategy failed to alter, in one great diplomatic *coup*, the course of Japan–Korea relations, a change that would have redounded to Kishi's credit. Rhee's response to Kishi's request for a bilateral summit was guarded at best, but about Japan–North Korea relations, he made his wishes quite clear. But very soon, Japan–South Korea talks soured again over the repatriation of North Korean residents of Japan. A victim of Rhee's one-upmanship, Kishi's ambition was frustrated. In his *Kishi Nobusuke kaikoroku* (Memoirs of Kishi Nobusuke), the former prime minister is openly critical of Rhee Syngman's Japanophobia and makes no mention of the controversial message. The whole affair must have been a bitter pill for Kishi to swallow.

I also learned that, upon his return from Seoul, Yatsugi contributed an article to the quite respectable but generally conservative monthly *Bungei Shunju* (in the July 1958 issue, published in early June), reporting on his meeting with the Korean president. "I conveyed to him Prime Minister Kishi's message," wrote Yatsugi, thus confirming the fact of a message by proxy, and went on to elaborate on its content to the effect that "[Kishi] has long been regretful for the trouble caused by the imperialistic rule of the Japanese military clique," and that "owing to unavoidable circumstances in the Far East political arena at that particular point in time, Ito Hirobumi had no choice but to carry through the annexation plan. His deeds caused a great deal of trouble to Korea, and in hindsight, turned out to be not in the best interests of Japan either." With his domestic readership in mind, Yatsugi was now more talkative, amplifying his prepared statement in Seoul, for instance, by adding "owing to unavoidable circumstances in the Far East political arena at that particular point in time," presumably in an attempt to attenuate the possible impact of such disclosures on Kishi's political prospects.

Kishi, in Diet hearings, as we saw, had flatly denied making any apology. Fifteen years later, in his autobiography, *Waga ronin-gaiko o kataru* (The story of my maverick diplomacy),[8] Yatsugi Kazuo again mentioned his meeting with Rhee Syngman, but said not a word about the apology. Kishi of course would not have liked him to say anything about it. The first expression of regret by a Japanese prime minister was thus deleted from the history books and effaced from people's memory.

Japan's expressions of regret for its past have been inarticulate and evasive on many occasions; the fiftieth anniversary resolution of the Diet is only one example. The consignment of Kishi's message to oblivion seems to be symbolic of the fate of such equivocation and duplicity. Yet the evolution of Japanese public opinion must be viewed taking one more factor into account: the indifference of the left. The Socialist Imazumi Isamu who grilled Kishi about Yatsugi's message in the House of Representatives budget committee meeting said, among other things:

> Korea hasn't asked Japan to apologize for the annexation. For a Japanese prime minister to send a mere maverick . . . and make every imaginable concession as a conciliatory gesture that is not even being asked for—that, I submit, is not what the Japanese people are asking for either.

That was a Japan Socialist Party member verbally attacking Kishi in 1958 for being conciliatory to the Koreans! *O tempora! O mores!* (In drafting the fiftieth anniversary resolution of 1995, the same party insisted on a "clearly expressed" apology for colonizing Korea.)

The Japanese press's coverage of Yatsugi's press conference statement in Seoul and Kishi's subsequent denial was subdued, as I pointed out above. There were no screaming headlines, none of the dramatic politicization of the issue that might be expected today; the conservative camp was not alone to blame for insensitivity: the "progressive" opposition and the press were equally guilty, equally unwilling to say sorry.

PART III

PIECES OF THE PAST IN RETROSPECT

© Asahi Shimbunsha

Prime Minister Tanaka Kakuei and Premier Zhou Enlai normalized diplomatic relations between Japan and China in September of 1972. When they emerged with an agreement after intensive bargaining, Chairman Mao Zedong greeted them with the words: "You've finished quarreling now, haven't you?"

Chapter 1

The Tokyo Tribunal and Why Kishi Nobusuke Wasn't Hanged

IDYLLIC MANCHUKUO

At an international symposium held in November 1994, former Premier of Singapore Lee Kuan Yew pointed out that Asians' wariness of Japan was justified by Japanese right-wing politicians' repeated *faux-pas* (as I mentioned in Part I) [page 19]. At the same symposium, he commented as follows:

> The de-nazification process in Europe left no stone unturned. In Asia, by contrast, the communist takeover in mainland China followed by the Korean war prevented a thoroughgoing purge of those really responsible for World War II. And that is why relics from the past have managed to creep back into the mainstream.[1]

I remember how raptly I listened to Lee and how completely I agreed with his analysis. The term he used, "relics from the past," is clearly a scantily veiled reference to Kishi Nobusuke and his ilk. For Lee Kuan Yew, Kishi was the epitome of Japan's prewar and postwar political "continuity"—Japan's failure, in other words, to perform a thorough political housecleaning after the war.

Before the war, Kishi was a career bureaucrat in the Ministry of Commerce and Industry; soon after its foundation, he was sent to Manchukuo, where he controlled the country's development from a top-ranking official's desk; he was directly involved in the opening of hostilities in the Pacific as a cabinet minister in the Tojo cabinet; he won a seat in the House of Representatives in the

"Yokusan [All-Out National Support]" election of 1942 (the 21st general election, in which over 80 percent of the seats were taken by candidates recruited by Tojo). Yet not only was Kishi exonerated of all blame for his role after Japan's defeat, he also had the unbelievable luck to climb all the way to the top of the greasy pole while his erstwhile colleagues looked on in blank amazement. Even after he stepped down, he exerted considerable political influence for many years. Hence his sobriquet, "the Monster of Showa." (Showa is the era name of Hirohito's reign, 1926–89.)

Central to his survival and success was a change in occupation policy by the Supreme Commander for the Allied Powers. Initially, SCAP arrested and imprisoned Kishi as a Class A war criminal; later, it let him go scot-free, without even indicting him, soon even allowing him to resume his political activities. (And Kishi was not alone, not by a long shot: in the course of the Tokyo Trials, many Class A war crime suspects were eventually released without indictment or trial, including Kodama Yoshio, the right-wing "don," known for running clandestine operations during the war in China.)

Elder brother of ex-prime minister Sato Eisaku, Kishi was born in the old family of the Satos in Yamaguchi prefecture in November 1896. (The different last name is due to the widespread Japanese practice of adoption within a clan to ensure male succession and continuity of the family name; Nobusuke was born a Sato, but being the second-born son, he was adopted by a close relative on his father's side of the family named Kishi who had no son.) Spurred by its victory the previous year in the Sino–Japanese War of 1894–95, Japan was just beginning to secure a foothold for expansion into Asia. Yamaguchi prefecture had been the feudal era fief of the Choshu clan. This clan's leaders played a leading role in the Meiji Restoration (in which the Shogun, Japan's *de facto* ruler for centuries, was deposed and direct imperial rule was restored). Kishi grew up under the strong influence of Yoshida Shoin and his disciples like Ito Hirobumi, Kido Takayoshi, Inoue Kaoru, and other famous royalists of the Restoration period. Kishi was also related to the diplomat Matsuoka Yosuke, the foreign minister who steered Japan out of the League of Nations.

The process of Kishi's personal development overlaps perfectly with that of Japan's imperialistic nationalism and its aspirations to rank with the great powers of Europe and America: the Russo–Japanese war of 1904–05 broke out when Kishi was eight years old; Japan occupied Port Arthur and triumphed in the Battle of the Japan Sea, filling the nation with euphoria and setting the stage for a triumphal victory, when he was nine years old; the South Manchuria Railway Company was founded when he was ten; Japan annexed Korea when he was a junior high school boy of thirteen; the First World War (1914–18) broke out and Japan presented China with the Twenty-One Demands, an act of open interference in China's affairs, while he was enrolled in the elite First Senior High School in Tokyo (a sure stepping stone for admission to the Imperial University of Tokyo).

It is not hard to imagine to what extent Kishi's character building was crucially molded by the times and circumstances of his adolescence. It is against this historical and clan background that Kishi's reference to "the wrongs committed by Ito Hirobumi" related in the last chapter was laden with deep implications.

At the Imperial University of Tokyo, Japan's most prestigious university and the gateway to coveted careers, Kishi put himself under the tutelage of the ultra-nationalist Professor Uesugi Shinkichi, and was otherwise strongly influenced, he admits, by Kita Ikki's "Draft Principles of State Reconstruction (later 'Bill for Reconstructing Japan')" and the "Greater Asianism" of Okawa Shumei (who was later to be arrested as a Class A war criminal, put on trial at the Tokyo Tribunal, and released on grounds of mental illness). Upon graduation, he entered the Ministry of Commerce and Industry, serving there until October 1936, when he was appointed to a high-ranking government position in the newly founded Manchukuo. In one of his interviews with Hara Yoshihisa from 1980 to 1982, Kishi reminisces: "In those days I had no idea about the Greater East Asia Co-Prosperity Sphere. But these notions and my decision to go to Manchuria were undeniably based on Mr. Okawa's thinking."[2] In Hara's words, "A skeletal theory of nationalism based on Kita Ikki's model was forming in his mind, i.e., one of state socialism integrating internal reconstruction and external expansion; this skeleton was further fleshed out by Okawa's Greater Asianism."[3]

While at the Ministry of Commerce and Industry, Kishi was very closely involved in Manchuria, and on being sent there he answered the hopes of the Kanto Army (long stationed in Manchuria and now in virtual control), rapidly rising to the position of deputy director of the industrial and general affairs departments and effectively becoming the man in command of Manchukuo. The chief of staff of the Kanto Army at the time was Itagaki Seishiro (later appointed army minister), succeeded by Tojo Hideki, the prime minister-to-be. While in Manchuria, Kishi made friends with them and other Army strongmen and strengthened his position. In stark contrast to Itagaki and Tojo, military men who were later convicted and hanged as Class A war criminals after the war, Kishi turned his stint in Manchuria into the first decisive step in a meteoric career as a big-time bureaucrat-turned-politician.

The deception-ridden realities of the puppet state of Manchukuo are described in great detail by Yamamuro Shinichi in his *Kimera—Manshukoku no shozo* (Chimera: A portrait of Manchukuo).[4] Yamamuro notes that Kishi waxes lyrical on Manchuria in his memoirs, *Aa Manshu* (Oh Manchuria), published in 1965, calling it "the hope of East Asia . . . radiant with the ideals of racial harmony and a realm of peace and prosperity."[5] Strange, is it not, that he could write this without even the slightest hint of a bad conscience?

A Class A war criminal

Kishi was still stationed in Manchuria when hostilities broke out between Japan and China. He returned to Japan in 1939 and received the portfolio of commerce and industry in the Tojo cabinet formed in October 1941. Tojo was a confirmed advocate of war with the United States, and his accession to power meant that the opening of hostilities was only a question of time. Kishi took part in the process.

To illustrate how far back the process began, let us turn back the clock about a decade: when Kishi visited the United States in 1930 as a Ministry of Commerce and Industry official, he was flabbergasted at America's economic might. In one of his interviews with Hara, he says:

> I had the feeling that, if it should ever come to war, we Japanese would be cornered and would have no choice but to surrender totally to the United States or to annihilate ourselves. . . . Somehow or other, we would have to restrain them from advancing this way and, by whatever means we could, secure our vital supplies of oil from Indonesia and other resources from elsewhere in Southeast Asia and continental China.[6]

Shocked as he was at the vast gap in strength between the United States and Japan, Kishi evidently had foremost in his mind, as early as in 1930, the possibility of war with the United States and presumed that Asia was destined to supply vital resources to Japan. Eleven years later, he was personally involved in declaring war against the United States.

Soon after receiving the portfolio of commerce and industry, he was busy reorganizing the industrial sector in anticipation of wartime economic controls when the surprise attack on Pearl Harbor was launched on December 8. The next year he ran in the "Yokusan" general election as an incumbent cabinet minister and a recommended candidate, and won the seat in the House of Representatives that he had long and fervently wished for.

In November 1943, as the fortunes of war were turning slowly but steadily for the worse, Kishi assumed the additional office of vice-minister of the newly organized Munitions Ministry, reporting directly to prime minister Tojo, who concurrently held the portfolio of munitions. One of Kishi's duties was to boost aircraft production. It is true that, in the closing days of the Tojo cabinet, Kishi joined the anti-Tojo faction and schemed secretly for Tojo's removal, but such was his record of aggressive economic controls in Manchuria and of personal involvement in the opening of hostilities against the United States that he was in a position of inescapable responsibility and accountability for his previous collaboration with Tojo and the military clique.

A famous episode is told by Kishi's daughter Abe Yoko (the late foreign minister Abe Shintaro's widow) in her *Watashi no Abe Shintaro* (Abe Shintaro as I remember him). In summary, it goes like this:

> Just before Kishi was imprisoned on suspicion of being a Class A war criminal, Sugi Toshisuke, who came from Yamaguchi prefecture and was his former teacher at the First Senior High School, sent him as a parting gift a *tanka* (Japanese poem of thirty-one syllables) by Yoshida Shoin:
>
> > No man has two lives
> > But it is his name that thrives
> > A fame that never dies.
>
> The suggestion presumably was that Kishi should not hold his life dear but choose the way to honorable death. To which Kishi replied with a tanka of his own:
>
> > Ere seeking immortal fame,
> > I'd rather live to make for justice a claim
> > That the hereafter may remember.[7]

In sum, he was convinced of the justice of the sacred war and was ready to present his case squarely before the Tokyo War Crimes Tribunal.

The prosecution was busy collecting evidence against Kishi. The Waldorf Report, for example, branded him as a "Manchuria gangster" and "warmonger." His influence in Manchuria, his involvement in the opening of hostilities in the Pacific, and his intimate ties with the military were all closely scrutinized. Eventually, however, Kishi was not indicted and had the good fortune to be released. Though the exact reasons for this clemency are unknown, it is certain that the cold war's shadow loomed menacingly over the trial proceedings.

The Nuremberg trials, which passed severe judgement on the war crimes of Nazi Germany, were concluded in October 1946; the Tokyo Tribunal took two more years before closing in November 1948. In the interim, the confrontation between the United Sates and the Soviet Union manifested itself indelibly. The tide in the power occupying and ruling Japan, the Supreme Command Allied Powers, was now evidently turning favorable to the nurture of anti-communist forces and backing away from the emasculation of Japan's traditional conservative forces.

NO COLD WAR, NO ACQUITTAL

I have already quoted, more than once, Hara Yoshihisa's *Kishi Nobusuke*, a minutely researched piece of documentary work; it includes frequent references to a prison diary that Kishi kept while at Sugamo. They give us a vivid picture of Kishi and his mind wavering between the bitterness of being wronged and the fond hope of being set free. Kishi experienced the humiliation of imprisonment more often than he liked to recall—having his personal belongings inspected and confiscated while standing stark naked before his jailers, being ordered to sweep the ceiling of his cell clean and having the dust fall in his eyes and hurt them, leaving him sleepless, and so on.

Yet in less than a year after the end of the war, Kishi was encouraged by the intensifying confrontation between the United States and the Soviet Union. His diary entry of August 11, 1946, records how he and his fellow inmates agreed unanimously and hoped fervently that the US–USSR confrontation would provide a good opportunity for rehabilitating Japan, and how he "felt elated for the first time in many months."

The Communist Party was consolidating its hold over China and Kim Ilsung had founded the Democratic People's Republic of Korea (North Korea) astonishingly early (namely, on August 11,

1948), Kishi put on record an astoundingly bold proposal in his diary. In order to prevent the Communist Party's reign in China, which "would lead to the spread of communism across East Asia," he argued, the United States should deploy its own troops to put down Mao Zedong and his soldiers—and the same American troops should include Japanese volunteers!

While registering his surprise at Kishi's surrealistic conception of a "Japanese volunteer army" for the great cause of anti-communism in Asia, Hara probes Kishi's psyche and suggests how, for Kishi, a good opportunity to rehabilitate Japan was coterminous with a good opportunity to rehabilitate himself.

Seven defendants, including Tojo Hideki, having already been sentenced to death, Kishi at this time was painfully anxious what his verdict would be. But his apprehension was mixed with a fervent hope for release. Significant changes were in the making inside SCAP (Supreme Commander for the Allied Powers). There was keen rivalry between GS (Government Section), the Civil Administration Bureau, headed by General Courtney Whitney, and G2 (Intelligence Section), Department 2 of the General Staff Office, headed by Charles A. Willoughby. The former was committed to promoting democratization programs; the latter was in charge of intelligence and security and bent on fighting communism. Eventually it became evident that G2 was gaining ground. It was literally the chance of a lifetime for Kishi.

The coalition government of the Democratic, Socialist, and National Alliance Parties with Ashida Hitoshi at the helm was toppled in October 1948 after the "Showa-Denko" bribery scandal. It is now widely believed that G2 wanted Yoshida Shigeru's Liberal Party to be in power and that a G2 "conspiracy" was involved in the scandal. The course of events represented a radical shift in the US occupation policy, from a democratization stance endorsing the coalition governments of Katayama Tetsu and Ashida Hitoshi to an anti-communist stance designed to contain the USSR and China.

Earlier (that is, in April 1947), G2 had sent to the supreme commander, General Douglas MacArthur, a recommendation obliquely urging him to release Kishi. Though the recommendation was expressed in the conditional, words to the effect of "should sufficient evidence to convict be lacking," it clearly conveyed G2's hope that Kishi would be released. That Kishi had done a turnabout and joined the anti-Tojo faction in the last days of the war was apparently to be counted in his favor now. Although there is not found anywhere in Kishi's prison diary even the slightest hint of a deal cut with G2, it is a known fact that an odd assortment of visitors with G2 connections were in frequent contact with Kishi behind bars. Later, after Kishi's release and successful comeback in politics, he came under suspicion of having received secret funds from the Central Intelligence Agency (CIA). Whether this suspicion is founded or not, it is certain that Kishi's mystery-cloaked release was not unrelated to the ongoing cold war, and that subsequently Kishi as a postwar political leader maintained a consistently pro-American stance.

Kishi was not the only politician of prewar lineage who was saved by the cold war. Several of the Class A war criminals tried in the Tokyo Tribunal, such as Kaya Okinori (finance minister in the Tojo cabinet, governor general of the North China Development Co.), sentenced to imprisonment for life, and Shigemitsu Mamoru (foreign minister in the Tojo cabinet, Greater Asia minister in the Koiso cabinet), sentenced to seven years' imprisonment, were subsequently released and, after a respite, resumed political activities. Shigemitsu held the portfolio of foreign affairs again in the Hatoyama cabinet, and Kaya served as chairman of the political affairs research committee of the Liberal Party and justice minister in the Ikeda cabinet. (Needless to say, such appointments tended increasingly to blur Japan's accountability for the war.) For many years Kaya was also chairman of the Japan Association of the Bereaved Families of the War Dead, representing a large membership of families of soldiers and civilians killed in the war. Itagaki Tadashi (member of the House of Councilors at this writing), a son of Itagaki Seishiro, one of the unlucky convicted Class A war criminals who were hanged, is a former secretary general of the same Association. This cast of characters with prewar connections contributed to blurring the distinction between those responsible for starting the war and those who perished because of it. This lumping of perpetrator and victim together is presumably a major factor explaining the gradual transformation of the Association of Bereaved Families (ostensibly a peace organization at its inception) into a nationalistic lobby that opposed the fiftieth anniversary "apology" resolution of the Diet.

Of course, not every prewar politician who escaped indictment managed merely for that reason to keep his job and get off scot-free after the war: many who collaborated with the war regime in the national mobilization for the war effort were purged from public service and forbidden by SCAP to engage in political activities, at least for several years. But after the outbreak of hostilities in Korea, one after the other, purged politicians were rehabilitated in anticipation of Japan's independence, and many prewar political leaders reappeared on the political proscenium. The rationale for this leniency was substantially the same as for Kishi's acquittal: the United States sought to nurture and establish Japan in Asia as a stable bulwark in its fight against communism.

| # Yoshida Shigeru Before and After the War

THE OTHER SIDE OF THE "PRO-ANGLO-AMERICAN" STANCE

In the aftermath of the war, the office of prime minister in Japan changed hands several times in quick succession, and it was Yoshida Shigeru who stood at the helm of the administration when Japan regained its independence in 1952. It is well known that the man who set Japan's postwar political course had been "pro-Anglo-American" since prewar times, but who cared what his view of Asia was? I, for one, was not very much interested in this question until I stumbled across his archrival Ashida Hitoshi's appraisal of Yoshida.

A diplomat-turned-politician exactly like Yoshida, Ashida forged a coalition between his Democratic Party and the Socialist Party and succeeded Katayama Tetsu as prime minister in March 1948. As early as October of the same year, however, Ashida was forced to step down, implicated in the "Showa-Denko" bribery scandal. He was vindicated when the affair came to trial later, but even while a defendant, he was present in October 1951 at the Diet debate over the ratification of the San Francisco Peace Treaty where he cuttingly grilled Yoshida, who prevaricated on issues related to rearmament and the constitutional amendment he proposed. In the course of re-searching this celebrated debate for inclusion in my book *Wasurerarenai kokkai ronsen* (Unforgettable debates in the Diet),[1] I paid a visit to Shimokobe Motoharu, his grandson and editor of *Ashida Hitoshi nikki* (The Ashida Hitoshi diary)[2] toward the end of 1993.

Although Ashida's advocacy of rearmament and constitutional amendment tended more often than not to make him look like a reactionary in contrast to Yoshida, Ashida was a confirmed liberal and widely known as such. As a diplomat, he followed foreign minister Shidehara Kijuro's line of non-intervention in China, and was so incensed at the military's self-granted license in the Manchurian Incident that he quit the foreign service and turned to politics. As a freshman in the Diet taking the floor for the first time, he gained instant fame for daring army minister Araki Sadao to "cleanse the military of its self-righteousness." He was sympathetic with Saito Takao's famous speech that demanded "a purge of the army" (namely its high command), and was one of the few who adamantly opposed to Saito's subsequent expulsion from the Diet for his impassioned criticism of escalating hostilities between Japan and China.

Yoshida entered the foreign service six years ahead of Ashida; from the start, the two of them never got along well together, it seems. According to Shimokobe, Yoshida denigrated Ashida as "a monkey from Tamba"; Ashida consistently took Yoshida to task for supporting Japan's expansionist policy in Manchuria, even as consul general in Hoten (now Shenyang in Liaoning province), and for failing to stem the rampaging military.

I was much intrigued by the crossing reversals in the two veteran politicians' policies. The war over, Ashida played an important role in establishing a new constitution, only to do a turnabout when hostilities broke out in Korea and China turned communist, when he joined the pro-rearmament camp. Yoshida did not feel seriously threatened by the communist take-over in China, and held to a light armament policy.

If Kishi Nobusuke personified continuity in pre- and postwar politics, Yoshida was typical of the postwar period's politics and politicians. Son-in-law of the moderate senior statesman Makino Nobuaki, Yoshida was involved as an ambassador to Great Britain in Japan's withdrawal from the League of Nations, and in the formation of the triple alliance of Japan, Germany, and Italy. He was opposed to the declaration of war against the United States, and got himself thrown into jail in the closing days of the

© Asahi Shimbunsha

Prime Minister Yoshida Shigeru reading a statement aloud at San Francisco Airport when he visited the United States in October 1951 to sign the peace treaty officially ending World War II. By adopting a pro-American foreign policy, Yoshida set a new course for Japanese politics.

war for his collusion with Konoe Fumimaro and others who drew up a draft memorandum to the Throne anticipating the war's end. Such a track record stood him in good stead later in his relations with the occupation authorities, allowing him to steer his country through the difficult postwar period as Japan's prime minister both during the last few years of the occupation as well as in the tumultuous years immediately following it.

Yoshida's pro-Anglo-American stance thus came into full bloom after the war. His "pro-American, light armament, business comes first" approach shaped a mainstream conservative line that differed from Kishi's "autonomous constitution, rearmament, politics first" position. On the one hand, Yoshida was a product of the postwar political climate; on the other, he had not strongly resisted the aggressive moves by his country into Asia that culminated in the Pacific war. Quite the contrary, as Ashida pointed out: Yoshida had played an active role in Japan's expansion into continental China as consul general in Hoten and as vice-minister of foreign affairs.

Yoshida entered the foreign service in 1906; his first post overseas was consulate general in Hoten in Manchuria (then part of China under the Qing [or Ch'ing] dynasty) which Japan regarded as its "lifeline." He became consul general at Tientsin in 1922 and went to Manchuria again in October 1925 as consul general at Hoten under the Tanaka Giichi cabinet. In the meantime, Sun Yatsen (also known as Sun Wen) organized the Xinhai Geming (the 1911 revolution), established a provisional government in Nanjing, and through a compromise with Yuan Shikai put an end to the 290-year-old Qing dynasty. After the death of Yuan and the end of his despotic rule, however, confusion reigned as rival military cliques ran amok. By the time he retired as consul general in Hoten in March 1928, Yoshida had been in China for a total of 11 years.

Six months prior to Yoshida's assumption of office in Hoten in October 1925, the Kuomintang and the Communist Party forged the first "Kuo-Com Collaboration" to topple the government; its supreme commander, Sun Yatsen, had died in Beijing in March 1925, during the "northern expedition." It was not until July 1928 that Chiang Kaishek, who had taken over the command of Kuomintang troops, reported the "completion of the northern expedition" to Sun Yatsen (who was already in his tomb). Yoshida's stay in Hoten falls precisely within the span of these three years and four months of upheavals in China.

Taking advantage of China in disarray

In the sizable literature on Yoshida Shigeru, two works have been acclaimed as authoritative masterpieces, *Saisho Yoshida Shigeru* (Yoshida the Prime Minister)[3] by Kosaka Masataka and *Empire and Aftermath: Yoshida Shigeru and the Japanese Experience*[4] by John W. Dower—Kosaka's work for its sensible appraisal of Yoshida's status in postwar politics, and Dower's magnum opus for its detailed and richly documented exposition of Yoshida's track record before and after the war. Both books touch on Yoshida's hard-line stance on China as consul general in Hoten. Let us for a while trace his steps as described in these two tomes.

The tide of nationalism was running as strong in Manchuria as elsewhere. In the wake of its successful Bolshevik Revolution of

1917, the Soviet Communist Party based in Northern Manchuria stepped up its activity, supplying arms to the Kuomintang after the Kuo-Com Collaboration. Having expanded its vested interests in Manchuria, which it regarded as its "lifeline," Japan was quite wary of such developments, and in particular feared that Zhang Zuolin and his military clique, on which Japan depended heavily, might become involved in the civil war in mainland China and neglect Manchuria's management. The ministry of foreign affairs supported a wait-and-see policy; the military wanted to soften up Zhang and make a puppet of him. Yoshida's proposal was to present Zhang with a forthright demand that he concentrate on managing Manchuria while urging that Japan should simultaneously further expand its interests by increasing its financial aid.

Yoshida's approach came to be adopted by Tanaka Giichi's cabinet. Zhang was forced to yield to Japan's arrogant demands. Noting that the Kei–Ho railway siding that led to Zhang's ammunitions plant happened to cross the Manchurian Railway tracks in Japan's possession, Yoshida suggested that Japan block the crossing. Imposing a blockade on the ammunitions plant would have exerted marvelous leverage, putting pressure on the military regime, but in the end it did not work. Yoshida was nonetheless much more of a hard-liner on this score than the military. According to Kosaka:

> The military wanted to soften up Zhang and make a puppet of him; Yoshida's failure to engineer the plot thoroughly in advance exposed him to the military's objections that Yoshida's plan was either too rough or premature. He was forced to back off, using ill health as a pretext.[5]

Zhang Zuolin continued to be a tough customer for Yoshida to control. Zhang was killed by a bomb planted by Kanto Army soldiers in June 1928, three months after Yoshida's departure from Hoten. Yoshida's stance and conduct during this period have been summarized in a set of eight "broad observations" by Dower based on his analysis of the relevant foreign ministry archives: Herewith a selection:[6]

— [Yoshida] laid particular stress upon the legal framework of overseas expansion and control—the specific treaty rights Japan had wrested from China in the course of some two decades—and warned of the dangers of relying upon "vague notions of Sino–Japanese goodwill," or being taken in by one's own propaganda.

— To a greater extent than some of his colleagues, he recognized that Japan's actions on the continent required the support of the Anglo-American powers; this led him not merely to emphasize Japan's international image, but also to propose that cooperation with the Western imperialists be manifested in joint military intervention in China south of the Great Wall.

— His view of the empire was a dynamic one in that he endeavored to use economic linkages (as through loans) and legalistic devices (such as treaty rights) as a lever for the steady enlargement of Japan's position abroad; in addition, he advocated taking advantage of disorder, distress, and misfortune in China to extract further rights and concessions.

— Like the majority of his associates, his attitude toward the Chinese, both for private and public consumption, was condescending and shaped by a pervasive sense of moral righteousness and implicit racial superiority.

— To a greater extent than almost any other Japanese at that time, he endorsed the use of force, threats, and intimidation to gain compliance with Japanese demands, and proposed military or "police" intervention to suppress anti-Japanese disturbances and protect Japan's "special rights and interests." In fact, it can be argued that Yoshida implicitly advocated taking over northeast China by military force as early as April 1927, more than four years before the Manchurian Incident.

Yoshida's contempt for the Chinese apparently stemmed from China's seemingly endless corruption, civil wars, and internal strife in the wake of the British intervention in China during the Opium War. Having observed this chaos, he was convinced that the great powers had to step in to bring China under control if peace was ever to be restored. In June 1928, he sent an official telegram to prime minister Tanaka Giichi to emphasize that:

> It would be vain to hope to let them go their way to peace, order, and security. It is up to the world powers to take the initiative and step in to establish stability in China. . . .
>
> Internal strife in China will be not confined to China, but is bound to bring calamity upon the great world powers. Even in strictly economic terms alone, Japan cannot afford to let the current situation go unchecked.[7]

In March 1928, Yoshida was slated to be stationed in Sweden as resident minister, but he went to see Tanaka Giichi at his private residence and pleaded to be appointed vice minister of foreign affairs instead. His pleas were answered, and he was promoted to the coveted position in July. Yoshida's promotion meant that his aggressive stance on China had won Tanaka's approval. In the meantime, Yoshida drew up a memorandum on Japanese policy in Manchuria, in which he argued that the rising tide of nationalism in Asia ran counter to Japanese interests and should be checked:

> National self-determination and similar notions became widely known and popularized in the aftermath of the hostilities in Europe as a reaction to war, and we simply took them at face value. . . .
>
> We paid too much attention to empty phrases like Japan–China friendship, coexistence and co-prosperity, etc.[8]

The ministry of foreign affairs at that time espoused a policy of non-intervention in China's civil war, a position that could be traced back to Shidehara Kijuro and others who opted for expansion by means of trade. Ashida Hitoshi belonged to that school of thought; Yoshida rejected it as "sheer spinelessness." Together with Hirota Koki, his contemporary at the foreign ministry, Yoshida was thus close to Tanaka Giichi, a former army general. Zhang Zuolin was assassinated after Yoshida's departure from Hoten but before his appointment as vice-minister, at a time when the situation continued to deteriorate, culminating in the Manchurian Incident of 1931. Though Zhang's death was not directly linked to Yoshida, it was a consequence of the hard-line policy that Yoshida advocated. It was on these counts that Ashida was severely critical of Yoshida.

When Hirota Koki became prime minister, Yoshida recommended himself for the office of foreign minister and was on the verge of obtaining it. But the military objected to the appointment on the grounds that his father-in-law Makino Nobuaki had been a confirmed liberal, and Yoshida had to settle for an ambassadorship in Great Britain. It was about this time that Yoshida turned more antimilitary. Had he been appointed foreign minister of the Hirota cabinet, he might have shared the fate of Hirota, the only civilian to be hanged by the Tokyo Tribunal.

In Kosaka's view, Yoshida's hard-line stance differed from that of the military on three counts. Firstly, in terms of means, Yoshida was adamantly opposed to any conspiracy to engineer a puppet government. Instead, he urged that forthright demands be addressed to Zhang Zuolin. Secondly, he conceived of the notion of "national interests" differently. As Yoshida saw it, diplomacy was a game of furthering national interests by means of treaties and rights sanctioned by treaties. He did not care whether or not such rights were ethically justified, nor was he interested at all in the military's fabricated ideological justification that overthrowing Manchurian military cliques was in the interest of the Manchurian people as a whole. Thirdly, in relations with Great Britain and the United States, Yoshida envisaged cooperation, and had no intention of confronting them to preserve Japanese interests in Manchuria.

In other words, Yoshida thought it natural for Japan to rule over Asia, but it was to be a game on a par with Great Britain and the United States, and was different in nature from the concept of a "Greater East Asia Co-Prosperity Sphere," which would put Japan, once it established a foothold in Asia, on a collision course with the Western powers.

I am reminded in this context of *Datsu A ron* (Out of Asia into the West),[9] a book published in 1885 by Fukuzawa Yukichi. Disappointed by Asian nations' failure to ride the tide of modernization, Fukuzawa asserted that Japan should part company with Asia, join the Western powers, and deal with the rest of Asia without compunctions. Details aside, what Yoshida did was to put Fukuzawa's theory into practice. He must have thought that Japan invited its own downfall when it opted for confrontation rather than cooperation with Great Britain and the United States. Because Japan was defeated in a war that he did not support, he probably felt no sense of guilt for the colonization policy Japan had pursued in Korea and Taiwan since the Meiji years, or for the high-handed way he had sought to expand Japanese interests in China.

CONTEMPT FOR ASIA: ANOTHER WAR SURVIVOR

Yoshida's outlook on Asia comes sharply into focus in the first volume of his *Kaiso junen* (Ten years in retrospect),[10] written after he stepped down as prime minister.

In brief, he makes the following points:

— A distinction must be drawn between Japan, which has been an independent country for a long time, and other Asian countries, which acquired independence relatively recently.

— Japan's political, economic, and social conditions are Western rather than Asian.

— Asian and African countries are marked by low standards of living, and still underdeveloped and backward.

— For geographical and racial reasons, however, the Japanese people feel a greater affinity for Asia than Westerners do.

— It stands to reason to develop Asia through the combination of American money and Japanese technology.

— Japan should accelerate the economic advancement of Asia and Africa and help these regions to come to recognize the value of a free economy.

While garbed in more moderate clothing than his prewar advocacy of Asian rule, the leadership Yoshida envisages in Asia in cooperation with the West represents an extension of Fukuzawa's "Out of Asia" views.

According to Tanaka Hiroshi's *Zainichi gaikokujin* (Resident aliens in Japan),[11] Yoshida wrote to General Douglas MacArthur in 1949 to request the repatriation of South and North Korean residents in Japan. He cited three reasons:

(1) The food situation, now and in Future, of Japan does not permit the maintenance of the excess population. Through the generosity of U.S. we are importing large quantities of foodstuff, of which a part is used to feed the Korean residents. These imports will constitute a liability upon our people for generations to come. Of course, we are determined to pay back every penny of it, but it seems unfair to let our future generations to shoulder a part of the debt to U.S. which is being incurred on account of the Koreans.

(2) A great majority of the Koreans are not contributing at all to the economic reconstruction of Japan.

(3) Worse still, there is a large percentage of criminal elements among the Koreans. They are habitual violators of our economic laws and regulations. A great many are Communists and fellow-travellers, prone to commit political offenses of the most vicious kind. More than 7,000 are always in jail.[12]

Any reader of this letter today finds it shocking, replete with the basest prejudice and bias. (As might be expected, MacArthur turned down Yoshida's request.) Even taking into consideration that his letter was written soon after the war and that law and order was a critical problem at the time, nowhere in it is there any hint of a moral sense of responsibility for the plight of resident

Koreans as a social by-product of Japan's colonial rule, for which Yoshida presumably felt no sense of guilt at all.

Kim Dongjo, witness to "Kishi's message" described in Part II, related to me an episode demonstrating Yoshida's lack of guilty conscience about the rule of the Government-General of Korea. When Kim met Yoshida the year after the conclusion of the Japan–Korea Treaty of 1965, Yoshida said the following to him:

> When I was consul general of Hoten, I used to visit Korea frequently, and was pleased on each occasion to be informed by the governor-general how well the Government-General was ruling Korea. I do not understand why Koreans hate the Japanese so much and voice such strong anti-Japanese sentiments.

Kim rebutted by saying that a man of Yoshida's painful experience under the American occupation should really know better. Yoshida's benumbed sensitivity was not his alone, however. Such a distorted perception on the part of a prime minister was indicative of the generally predominant view of Asia among contemporary Japanese.

I do not intend in any way to make light of Yoshida's achievements in laying down the course of postwar politics in Japan. However, his view of Asia cast a dark shadow on postwar Japan, precisely because of the magnitude of his presence.

The patronizing Japanese view of Asia typified by Yoshida was well known to and exploited by the United States. On his visit to Japan in January 1951, John Foster Dulles, special envoy in charge of the prospective peace treaty with Japan (who subsequently became Secretary of State), had a conference with British Ambassador Alvary Douglas Frederick Gascoigne, and is said to have remarked as follows:

> The Japanese think that they have attained the same measure of mental superiority over the people of the Asian continent (as people of the West) and want to be accepted by the West and admitted to their circle. Anything that encourages their sentiment, I submit, will be an attractive factor in keeping them on friendly terms with us.[13]

Though Yoshida was almost constitutionally contemptuous of Asia and Asians, he had a sharp and observant eye and made a cool-headed appraisal of the Chinese and of China, where he stayed for over ten years. Though falling short of any sense of atonement for Japan's sins against China, Yoshida apparently felt inclined to give China high marks for its perseverance in not yielding to Japan to the end. This should explain his optimistic view that communism would fail to take root in China and that the honeymoon between China and the Soviet Union would be short-lived. Under US pressure intended to contain China, Yoshida opted for normalizing diplomatic relations with Taiwan rather than with China, to his chagrin in the years to come.

In his *Giingaiko yonjunen* (Forty years of parliamentary diplomacy),[14] Kosaka Zentaro reports an episode on his trip to Taiwan in Yoshida's entourage in 1959. At a conference with Chang Kaishek, Vice President Zhen Zheng loudly denounced the Chinese Communist Party's heavy debts to the Russians, which prevented China from moving at all and thus kept it a mere puppet; Yoshida chose to rebut his argument, saying:

> You are entitled to your opinion, but the Chinese are a great race, and anyone trying to subdue them is bound to fail. Great Britain and the United States failed, and Japan went so far as to dispatch its troops but had to learn its lesson the hard way. Any attempt by the Soviet Union to seize China is doomed.[14]

It is not at all clear what Yoshida really meant when he called the Chinese "a great race," but at least we can say that his expressing this view of China represented a significant departure from his pre-war contempt for the Chinese.

Yoshida's new view of China was inherited by and exerted influence on the Japanese conservative mainstream for many years to come, creating a school of thought contrasting with the excessively anti-communist pro-Taiwan faction.

Chapter 3

The Tangled Roots of
"Out-of-Asia" and
"Greater Asianism"

FUKUZAWA YUKICHI AND HIS TURNABOUT

My thesis so far has been that Kishi Nobusuke was inspired by
Okawa Shumei's "Greater Asianism," whereas Yoshida Shigeru inherited Fukuzawa Yukichi's "Out-of-Asia-into-the West" ideology.
As both left their mark on the course of postwar politics, it is help-
ful at this point to trace their roots.

The Japanese are an Asian nation not only in ethnic and geographical terms, but also in the sense that *kanji* ideographs,
Buddhism, Confucianism, and other major cultural traits of theirs
come from China, Korea, and other Asian countries. The Japanese
once felt a sense of respect bordering on awe for China as the cra-
dle of civilization and were also well aware of the important roles
that naturalized Japanese of Korean descent played in the influx of
culture from abroad. Apart from major exceptions such as *wako* [or
sporadic rampages of Japanese pirates along the coasts of the
Korean peninsula and mainland China in the 13th to 16th cen-
turies], *genko* [or the Mongolian Invasions of 1274 and 1281], and
Toyotomi Hideyoshi's invasion of Korea in 1592–1593, the history
of Japan's active and passive exchanges with Asia were generally
peaceful and friendly until modern times.

It was not until the Meiji era, in other words, when Japan opened
itself to the outside world and embarked on modernization, that, in
a complete reversal of values, the traditionally friendly view of Asia
became distorted and was replaced by contempt for Asia. Japan as

a modern nation-state in the making observed the terrible plight of China under the Qing (Ch'ing) dynasty in the wake of the Opium War and the state of other Asian countries being invaded by Western powers, and it came to regard them as so many object lessons of the penalty for failing to modernize in time.

It was in this chronological context that Fukuzawa Yukichi formulated his "out-of-Asia-into-the West" theory of Japan's modernization on the model of its predecessors in the West. In his view, Asia was a collection of stupid and stubborn *anciens regimes* that refused to modernize both at the social and the state levels.

To Fukuzawa's great credit, his widely acknowledged writings like *Bunmeiron no gairyaku* (An Outline of a Theory of Civilization)[1] and *Seiyo jijo* (An Introduction to the West and Its Conditions)[2] contributed significantly to the propagation of a modern Western value system in Japan. But Fukuzawa went over and beyond the confines of things Japanese to preach modern Western modes of thought—and there was the rub. It was not long before he became disgruntled by the situation in China and Korea and hardened his position, turning his back on these Asian neighbors to let Japan join the ranks of the Western powers and be ready if necessary to carry out schemes of domination and division. According to his line of reasoning, if Asia was inferior to the West and could not even begin to hope for autonomy on its own, then in order for Japan to prevent a Western imperialist invasion of the type witnessed elsewhere, Japan should, if necessary, sally out into Asia on its own and have no qualms about it. This change in his thinking was of course pregnant with political and diplomatic implications.

At the start, Fukuzawa had been a protagonist for Asia's defense against the West. In September 1881, in his "Remarks on Current Issues" he had this to say:

> Who but the Japanese can play the central role among the Eastern nations and be in the vanguard of engagements with the Western powers? We should be prepared to shoulder the burden of responsibility for protecting East Asia. . . . Western countries' domineering encroachments upon the East today are like a roaring fire

spreading beyond control, and Asian countries—nearby China and Korea in particular—are too slow to cope with them, doomed to be razed utterly to the ground like so many wooden shacks. We should realize that it is in its own interest for Japan to take up arms in their support and defense.[3]

As the first country in Asia to achieve modernization, argued Fukuzawa, it behooved Japan to promote its Asian neighbors' modernization and to protect them. The idea was to apply to the rest of Asia the Japanese model of modernizing and opening itself to the world.

But less than four years later, in March 1885, in what was to be a major turning point in Japanese attitudes (the "reversal" to which I alluded above), Fukuzawa published his "out-of-Asia" theory in *Jiji-Shimpo*, a newspaper that he had founded in 1882, and advocated a harsher approach to fellow Asians in the following terms:

Though our land is located on the eastern border of Asia, the spirit of the nation has disengaged itself from the narrow-minded obstinacy of Asia and turned to Western civilization. Unfortunately, there are in Japan's close proximity two neighboring countries, namely China and Korea. . . . I look at them and observe that the tide of eastward expansion of civilization is such that they simply have neither ways nor means to maintain their independence on their own. Japan should part company with them and join the ranks of the civilized nations of the West. In our relations with China and Korea, we should not feel obliged to make special allowances for these countries just because they happen to be our neighbors, but deal with them just the way Westerners deal with them. Bad company ruins good morals. I refuse to keep company with bad acquaintances in East Asia.[4]

Neither Korea nor China could even begin to hope for independence on their own. By branding them "bad acquaintances" whose fellowship was expendable, Fukuzawa performed a turnabout, adopting a divisionist Asian policy in the manner of his Western models. Having successfully westernized itself, so his argument goes, Japan should have no qualms about dealing with other parts of Asia as it saw fit, just as the Western powers were doing.

What made Fukuzawa change his mind? An aborted coup d'état by Kim Okkyoon and others in Korea in December of the previous year (also known in Japan as the Koshin Incident of 1884) has often been cited as a major cause of Fukuzawa's reversal. Since his first visit to Japan in 1881, Kim Okkyoon had put himself under Fukuzawa's tutelage and won the Japanese government's support for his radical enlightenment campaign. Japan had been attempting for several years to expand its interests in Korea: in 1875, only eight years after the Meiji Restoration began, Japan had sent a warship to force its way into Kanghwado and open Korea's doors to the world. But when Japan urged Korea to "civilize" and modernize itself, it was Qing dynasty China (historically Korea's suzerain) that stood in Japan's way. The pro-Chinese old guard remained influential in Korea under the Li dynasty, and it was a contingent of Chinese troops that immediately stepped in and put down the coup d'état by Kim Okkyoon that the Japanese had been supporting behind the scenes. While Ito Hirobumi and Li Hongzhang were conducting negotiations in Tientsin to sort things out in the aftermath, Fukuzawa wrote his "out-of-Asia" manifesto, evidently resentful and disappointed at China and Korea for their lack of will to modernize themselves in the Western manner.

Fukuzawa at that time was calling for arms expansion as part and parcel of Japan's "political strategy in Asia," and the October 16, 1894, issue of *Jiji-Shimpo* carried a map purporting to show the prospective "Divided Empire of China" to be controlled by Japan and the Western powers. Both his "out-of-Asia" writings and the map suggest that Fukuzawa is prone to be carried away by his feelings, but it was his call to desert Asia that was to become, so to speak, the root of Japan's nationalist ideology as a belated newcomer in imperialist circles. Having won the Sino–Japanese War of 1894–95, Japan yielded in 1895 to the Triple Intervention by Russia, France, and Germany and gave up the Liaodong peninsula, but it obtained Taiwan and joined the ranks of the imperialist colonial powers nevertheless. The Japanese view of China, which thus far had been marked by a sense of respect bordering on awe, changed dramatically, replaced by a sense of contempt when China was beaten too easily.

In the same year, the pro-Russian Li dynasty Queen Min (Min Bi) of Korea was assassinated through the machinations of a Japanese military figure and resident minister in Korea. The plot was counterproductive, in that Russia's influence on Korea became more powerful and the Japan–Russia confrontation more pronounced.

Japan won in the Russo–Japanese war that broke out in 1904, and proceeded to establish its rule over Korea with the United States' approval. In Part I above, I described how Ito Hirobumi in the same year exacted an agreement on the Japan–Korea Protection Treaty (Second Japan–Korea Agreement), which led to Japan's annexation of Korea in 1910. Emperor Kojong of the Empire of Greater Korea made a solitary appeal to the international community to oppose the Protection Treaty's validity and intensified royalist resistance, which was quashed militarily by Japan.

In Japan, Fukuzawa Yukichi is revered as a distinguished modern thinker and his face appears on the ¥10,000 bill. In Korea even now, he has a very poor reputation because of his 'out-of-Asia' theory. As I mentioned above, Ito Hirobumi's face appears on the ¥1,000 bill. That the two men's portraits could still adorn Japan's currency is symptomatic of the sheer gap in perceptions between Japan and Korea.

Permit me another short digression: in 1972, when the Korean anti-establishment politician Kim Daejung was staying in a Japanese hotel in Tokyo, he was kidnapped by the Korean secret police and taken back to Korea. Japanese public opinion howled at this "blatant violation of Japan's sovereignty." Yet it was Japan that had perpetrated an outrage far worse than a kidnapping when it assassinated a Korean queen in the Meiji era. Japan has yet to pay the price for this worst possible violation of a nation's sovereignty.

In his "Korea–Japan Conflicts and Gaps in Historical Perceptions" in *Ajia kara mita Nihon* (Japan as viewed from Asia,)[5] Kim Yangki researched the two contrasting cases and pointed out how the ringleaders of the Min Bi assassination, acquitted "for lack of sufficient evidence," were later commended for their devotion to the Japanese cause. Those were different times, to be sure, but Japan's contempt for Asia was a major factor in the difference then and the gap in perceptions now.

THE LAW OF THE JUNGLE: PREWAR DIPLOMACY'S CONVENTIONAL WISDOM?

Japan, China, and Korea comprised a triad in those years, and it was their respective varying degrees of success or failure in modernization, each on its own initiative, that crucially determined who was to rule over (or to be ruled by) whom. While the Sino–Japanese and Russo–Japanese Wars aggravated Japan's imperialistic stance, Japan's encroachments on Asia were already disguised as defensive acts of resistance against Western tentacles; Japan's most blatant offenses were perceived as being on a par with them. They were extrapolations, so to speak, of Fukuzawa's "out-of-Asia-into-the West" theory, which had been intended to encourage Japan to catch up with the Western powers.

The conservative historian Inoki Masamichi, who criticized what he termed the "Utopian pacifism" of the progressive elements in postwar Japan, had this to say about Japan's options in a climate of euphoric extremism:

> Once a respectable stage of modernization is reached, ideally, a nation ought not venture to invade or conquer its neighbors but proceed to improve its people's living conditions at home. Yet whether for a nation-state or an individual, it is no easy task to realize that there are limits to one's success.[6]

Given the state of affairs in the world in those years, Japan's expansionist moves in Asia were understandable, according to Inoki's rationale. At a time when imperialism was not regarded as evil, Japan's wars with China and Russia and its colonial rule over Korea did not flagrantly contravene the contemporary "international conventional wisdom," a version of the law of the jungle, namely victimization of the weak by the strong. Whereas today the Social Democratic Party holds that Japan's wars with China and Russia were part and parcel of Japanese aggression of Asia, conservative forces in general tend to use Inoki's rationale to defend these first steps in the march into Asia that almost destroyed Japan.

It is not absolutely certain that Yoshida Shigeru, born in 1878, read Fukuzawa's "out-of-Asia" writings. There should be no need, however, to point out that Yoshida's mode of thought overlapped Fukuzawa's: in his contempt for the Chinese people, whom he denigrated as being "incapable of governing themselves," Yoshida had no qualms about relentlessly expanding Japan's interests in China; he nevertheless tried stubbornly to maintain cooperative relations with the United States and Great Britain.

In contrast, from the Manchurian Incident of 1931 to the Marco Polo Bridge Incident of 1937, which triggered the opening of hostilities against China, the course of events had nothing to do with Japan defending itself against the West's tentacles, nor with cooperating with the United States and Great Britain. It was instead a course of sheer aggression and expansion. The Nine-Power Treaty on China concluded in Washington in 1922 had recognized China's independent sovereignty and territorial integrity; the Kellogg-Briand Pact was signed in Paris in 1928; the days of rampant imperialism were over: the internationally shared sense of regret in the aftermath of World War I had resulted in a new set of rules for the conduct of international affairs. Therefore, for Japan, a party to the emerging international framework, to have initiated aggression was a drastic departure even from the "out-of-Asia" theory.

One of the right wing's strenuous objections to the fiftieth anniversary resolution was that Japan's rule over Korea and aggression into China were defensible, of a kind with Britain's aggression in India in the 19th century, and therefore there was no need for Japan alone to apologize. The argument, however, was unacceptable even to Inoki Masamichi, who held, as we saw above, that Japan's initial imperialistic expansionism, in the Meiji era, was understandable. Pointing out how the international conventional wisdom had changed after World War I, he judged that

Japan was "as guilty" at least for the founding of Manchukuo and subsequent invasion into China as Great Britain was for its conduct in India.[7] The line he draws may well represent a line of demarcation in Japanese politics between right-wing and more moderate conservatives.

The tragedy of Sun Yatsen: the insult to his Greater Asian ideals

In its blatant expansionism and attempts to rival the United States and Great Britain, Japan committed the sin of allowing the military to overstep civilian control. There was a need for a loftier cause than the "out-of-Asia" theory to justify such an act of defiance, and the grand design for the Greater East Asia Co-Prosperity Sphere provided precisely the ideological cloak Japan's militarists needed. This visionary scheme would destine Japan to assume leadership in Asia and defend it, liberate Asian countries from Western imperialistic rule, and construct a zone of shared prosperity founded on uniquely Asian values. It was similar to Fukuzawa's initial "defense-of-Asia" theory, which he rejected several years later as an impossible scenario. It differed totally from his initial design, however, in its outright hostility to the West and its assertion of Asian superiority.

Of the abundant literature on the Greater East Asia Co-Prosperity Sphere, I find Irie Akira's analysis in his *Shin-Nihon no gaiko* (New Japanese diplomacy)[8] to be among the most readable and insightful. The opening chapter begins quite succinctly as follows:

> Japan on the eve of the Pacific War was a military giant but an economic midget. For such a nation to wage war against military and economic superpowers of the West, there was a need for an ideology to justify such a war. The appellation "Greater East Asia War" in itself expressed the idea of a war of defense of Asia against the West.

The Pacific War so conceived, however, wrought havoc upon Japan in military, economic, and ideological terms. Japan's military advantages in the first round dwindled to nothing in less than six months, the economic resources of the "Greater East Asia Co-Prosperity Sphere" could not be effectively exploited, and Japan's inferiority to the Allies (the United States in particular) in sheer productive capacity went from bad to worse with every passing day. The putative cause of a war on behalf of East Asia failed to win the support of the peoples of China and Southeast Asia, while anti-Japanese resistance movements were on the rise in the areas under occupation by the Japanese armed forces. Leaders in Japan, however, apparently clung to the last to the image of Japan as the "champion of Asian liberation," presumably because they had no other ideological support to fall back on. . . .[9]

The Greater East Asia Co-Prosperity plan was formulated on the "Greater Asianism" model, which in a very fundamental sense was antithetical to the "out-of-Asia-into-the West" theory, and advocated Asian solidarity to cope with the Western invasion in Asia. For instance, Okawa Shumei, one of Kishi Nobusuke's mentors (see Part III, Chapter 1), published a monograph in 1916 entitled *Indo ni okeru kokuminteki undo no genjo to sono yurai* (The origin and the present state of nationalist movements in India), in which he described the appalling suffering caused in India by Britain's draconian rule and persecution, and referring to the present state of resistance movements, he emphasized how the Indian movement for independence was inspired and encouraged by Japan's rapid rise after its victory in the Russo–Japanese War. Japan's victory in the Russo–Japanese War exerted considerable influence on Asian peoples, as we will see below, and the flush of victory undoubtedly buoyed up Japan's nationalistic fervor. Yet while Japan did win the war against the Russians, the postwar peace terms were settled quite realistically by the Meiji era's clairvoyant politicians, who were well aware of the overwhelming power that Russia held in reserve. Later, however, the Japanese allowed the euphoria of having beaten the "big Russian bear" to go to their head.

No discussion of Asianism or Greater Asianism can pass over in silence the Greater Asianism advocated by the Chinese revolutionary Sun Yatsen (also known as Sun Wen). In a China caught in the double bind of corruption within and deprivation imposed by the great powers from without, Sun Yatsen was a pioneering revolutionary who advocated San-Min Zhu-Yi, or the Three Principles of the People, namely democracy, civil rights, and the people's welfare. Sun visited Japan more than once, sojourning for longish periods both as an exile and otherwise, and had no small measure of influence in Japan. Of relevance here is that Sun Yatsen was not loath to admit that he for one had been inspired by Japan's victory in the Russo–Japanese War. On his visit to Japan in 1924, a year before his death in Beijing, he presented his version of Greater Asianism during a lecture in Kobe. The more salient features of his presentation are summarized in *Kakumeika Son Bun* (Sun Yatsen the revolutionary)[10] by Fujimura Hisao and are quoted here verbatim:

— Having the most ancient of all cultures in the world, but being in decline for several hundred years and eroded by European countries, the people of Asia have resurrected themselves in the past thirty years. Japan's success in abolishing unequal treaties, attaining independence, and winning the Russo–Japanese War have kindled hope in Asian nations that they may become independent.

— Western materialist civilization is a civilization of science and of military force brought to bear on Asia. In the terms of China's ancient wisdom, it represents the "rule of might" as distinct from the superior "rule of right" that prevails in Asia, whose culture is marked essentially by morality and righteousness.

— In order for Asia to resurrect itself, it behooves Asian peoples to be united on the basis of the rule of right under the banner of Greater Asianism.

— We advocate Greater Asianism based on the rule of right to stamp out injustice. The people of Asia are not the only ones suffering from oppression. Our Greater Asianism demands equality and liberation for all the peoples of the world.

Sun Yatsen concluded his lecture with an appeal to the Japanese people:

> You Japanese have adopted the Western culture of the rule of might, but yours is essentially an Asian culture of the rule of right. Whether Japan turns out to be a watchdog of the Occidental rule of might or a vanguard of the Oriental rule of right is a question of critical relevance to the future of world civilization. Much depends on what you decide to do after deep soul-searching.[11]

The audience is said to have been deeply impressed, giving Sun Yatsen a standing ovation. The Chinese revolutionary's thought, they say, was influenced by Okakura Tenshin's championing of Asian unity in *Toyo no riso* (The oriental ideal)[12] and by Fukuzawa Yukichi's writings on modernization. As expounded in this lecture, however, Sun Yatsen's Greater Asianism is sharply antithetical to Fukuzawa's "out-of-Asia" advocacy.

Instead of renouncing imperialism and awakening to the cause of genuine solidarity in Asia, as Sun Yatsen so devoutly wished, Japan grappled to conquer by the rule of might so brazenly as to shock even the West. Sun Yatsen's tragedy is that his version of Greater Asianism was distorted and exploited by the Japanese to justify their invasion of Asia: insult added to injury. He should be turning over in his grave still.

CHIANG KAISHEK'S CRITICISM OF "NEW ORDER IN EAST ASIA"

In 1927, three years after Sun Yatsen's lecture in Kobe, Okawa Shumei, a Greater Asianist in Japan, avowed in his *Nihon seishin kenkyu* (Studies in the spirit of Japan)[13] that Japan was charged with a "special mission to unify the world." This was to be accomplished first in Manchuria and Korea and then to "extend and expand to China and the rest of the world"—a preposterous flight of fantasy picturing Japan as establishing its hegemony not only in Asia but across the globe.

The notion of global hegemony was megalomanic; nevertheless, this distorted version of Greater Asianism calling first for hegemony in Asia motivated the founding of Manchukuo in 1931, was subsequently adopted as the guiding principle of military and political leaders' conduct in Japan, and culminated as Japan was about to launch itself into the Pacific War. Foreign minister Matsuoka Yosuke orchestrated Japan's secession from the League of Nations and envisaged the establishment of the Greater East Asia Co-Prosperity Sphere as the basis of Japan's foreign policy. The same slogan emboldened successive cabinets of Konoe Fumimaro and of Tojo Hideki. A reckless war was thus launched on the pretext of a most distorted version of Greater Asianism.

As Sun Yatsen admitted, Japan's victory in the Russo–Japanese war did encourage aspirations for independence from Western imperialism in many parts of Asia. There were Asian activists—such as Wang Zhaoming in China and Subhas Chandra Bose in India, who sympathized with the putative new order in East Asia under the leadership of Japan—but they were rather the exception, and by and large, Asian nationalists found Japan's Asianism unpalatable. In his *Shin-Nihon no gaiko* (New Japanese diplomacy), Irie Akira points out:

> Continental China was the natural testing ground for pitting the ideology of Japanese Asianism against that of the allied countries. Neither the Kuomintang nor the Communist Party showed the slightest interest in Japan's ideological manifesto, but joined the spheres of influence either of the United States or the Soviet Union.

> Even Chiang Kaishek and others who set greater store by traditional Chinese than by Western modes of thought took no account of a spiritual union with Japan and repeatedly voiced criticism that the notion of the "Greater East Asia Co-Prosperity Sphere" as propagated by the wartime Japanese was replete with hypocrisy.[14]

In the eyes of those born after the war, myself included, the most lasting image of Chiang Kaishek is that of a committed anticommunist generalissimo exiled to Taiwan who opposed communist China tenaciously. He had indeed been the successor to Sun Yatsen and the indomitable leader of the Chinese resistance to the Japanese invaders, but that earlier part of Chiang Kaishek's war record tended to be obscured or forgotten. Irie's book serves as a useful reminder in this respect. Hunting around in the reference library of the *Asahi Shimbun*, I dug up a jewel: a collection of Chiang Kaishek's wartime speeches and essays, published in 1947 and titled *Bo wo motte bo ni mukuyuru nakare* (Return not violence for violence).[15] The now well-known title of the booklet comes from the text of his speech in Chongqing on Japan's surrender on August 15th, 1945. The speech was broadcast on the radio all across China.

Extolling the victory of the Chinese people, his speech was at the same time an admonition to the Chinese not to wreak revenge on the Japanese:

> My fellow countrymen:
>
> We must bear in mind that, by tradition, the highest and noblest trait of the Chinese people has always been to let bygones be bygones and to do good to others, and that we have consistently stated, "We are fighting against the Japanese military clique, but we do not make an enemy of the Japanese people. . . ."
>
> If we should return violence for our enemy's violence, or insult for their mistaken pretense of superiority, grudge would breed grudge in a vicious circle forever, which would run flagrantly counter to the cause of righteousness that we espouse.

On this note and with other expressions of his credo in the same vein, Chiang Kaishek let the defeated Japanese troops go home peacefully.

What then was the nature of the violence committed by Japan? We can infer Chiang Kaishek's view of Japan during the war years from two pieces of evidence culled from the same booklet. One is an epistle written in Hankou and dated 7th July, 1938. Titled "A Proclamation to the Japanese People," it begins by addressing the Japanese people according to protocol and goes straight on to declare, "Today marks the first anniversary of the Republic of China's national mobilization for all-out defense and resistance against the brutal acts of aggression by the military of your nation," and goes on to describe the gory details as follows:

China and Japan are brothers by nature, closely related to each other ethnically and culturally. . . . The military clique of your country, however, is dominated by a mistaken ideology, returning violence for virtue, and its erroneous thinking has been allowed to go unchecked. . . . Your country's military has committed acts of aggression every year in succession and raged in villainous rampages continuously, intent on the total annihilation of the Chinese nation. . . .

Do you realize that your troops in active service at the front have by now become the most savage and destructive armed forces in the world? Do you realize that *yamatodamashii* (the soul of Japan) and *bushido* (the way of the samurai warrior), on which you have always prided yourselves, are now extinct? Poison gas and gas shells are being used openly. Opium and morphine are put on sale in broad daylight, and all international commitments and human justice have been trodden on completely by your troops invading China. In every sector of our land under military occupation by Japanese soldiers, plunder, assault, and arson are rampart, and carried away by the momentum of their sheer excess, your soldiers wreak wholesale slaughter upon vast numbers of Chinese—innocent people and wounded soldiers—who could not seek refuge in a far away place. Thousands have been bound together in public squares and machine-gunned, scores at a time have been packed into chambers, showered with oil, and burned to death. Your soldiers have even gone to the extreme of vying in excess and joking about the sheer numbers of murders they have committed.

The epistle also contains a detailed description of "violence perpetrated on Chinese women," and accuses:

> Scores of women have been herded together, stark naked, in rooms, raped first and then butchered, their breasts mutilated and their corpses disemboweled, as if to sate these insatiable beasts' inhumanity.

The other clue to Chiang Kaishek's feelings is provided in a speech he made in December 1938 in Chongqing, where he scathingly criticized the putative goal of "New Order in East Asia" professed by the Konoe cabinet. His criticism of the notion of "New Order in East Asia" goes into great detail, of which merely a small portion will suffice for the present:

> "The Establishment of New Order in East Asia" is a motto and a trick that Japan is most good at playing. . . .

> The idea is for Japan (i) to establish military control over China on the pretext of preventing Communism, (ii) to eliminate China's national culture on the pretext of defending Oriental civilization, (iii) to justify Japan's hegemony in the Pacific to the exclusion of Western powers on the pretext of removing economic barriers, and (iv) to control China's economic affairs on the pretext of serving the "Japan–Manchuria–China economic zone" or of establishing "economic blocs." Just consider what evil intentions are hidden under the disarmingly pithy motto "Establishment of New Order in East Asia." The language is global and unmasks Japan's ambition to overturn the international order in East Asia so as to make a slave of China, to achieve hegemony in the Pacific, and to conquer the entire world.

Irie's observation about the Greater East Asian Co-Prosperity Sphere, quoted at the outset of this section, thus proved to be right, and Chiang Kaishek had debunked its hypocrisy much more savagely than I had imagined. Around the year 1938, Mao Zedong and the Communist Party of China launched a war of attrition against Japan, but it was Chiang Kaishek and his Kuomintang army that opposed Japan frontally, while communist forces were expanding underground. As an analyst has put it:

By defeating Chiang Kaishek's Kuomintang army, Japan was, as if deliberately, paving the way for the Communist Party of China to establish control across China.[16]

When the normalization of diplomatic relations between Japan and China came up on the agenda (discussed in greater detail below), its opponents argued that Japan had fought the Kuomintang army in the Sino–Japanese War (1837–45), and that therefore the Japan–Republic of China Peace Treaty (1952) effectively put an end to the war: in other words, everything had been settled, once and for all, already. As I explained in Part I, however, it was precisely those who appealed to this rationale and emphasized their sense of indebtedness to Chiang Kaishek who asserted in the debate over the fiftieth anniversary Diet resolution that "it was a war of Asian liberation"—a veritable incongruity and contorted line of reasoning that Chiang Kaishek would have had a hard time fathoming!

The out-of-Asia-into-the-West and Greater East Asia threads of the militarist ideology arise from the same source and are in some respects difficult to separate. Yet the supposedly mutually antithetical notions that out-of-Asia and Greater East Asia imply were somehow harnessed together and amalgamated in the effort to justify Japan's invasion of Asia and its involvement in the Pacific War. Fukuzawa Yukichi could not have foreseen the twisted path that events would take after his death.

Chapter 4 | # The Tragedy of Ishibashi Tanzan

A UNIQUE "SMALL NIPPONIST"

The years 1994–1995 saw a seemingly inexplicable rush of publications on the life of Ishibashi Tanzan: Kyo Kokujitsu's (Jiang Keshi's) *Ishibashi Tanzan*,[1] Sataka Makoto's *Ryo-Nihonshugi no seijika—ima naze Ishibashi Tanzan ka?* (Statesman of sane Nipponism: Why Ishibashi Tanzan now?),[2] Masuda Hiroshi's *Ishibashi Tanzan*,[3] and Hando Kazutoshi's *Tatakau Ishibashi Tanzan* (Ishibashi Tanzan the fighter).[4] More than a score of years after his death, there must be more to this than mere coincidence.

A decade earlier, Matsuo Takayoshi edited and published *Ishibashi Tanzan hyoron shu* (Selected papers of Ishibashi Tanzan),[5] which set in motion a revival of interest in and a reappraisal of Tanzan's political career. The renewal of interest this time—half a century after the end of the war, and after the end of the cold war, for that matter—must, I believe, have been generated by the shining example of Ishibashi's life and thought.

Ishibashi succeeded Hatoyama Ichiro as prime minister in December 1956. In the final ballot of a three-way contest for the LDP leadership, the initial runner-up Ishibashi formed a coalition with the second runner-up Ishii Mitsujiro, successfully beating Kishi Nobusuke. The new prime minister was eager to achieve a breakthrough in Japan–China relations, but he was already 72 years old when he assumed office; a neglected cold soon confined him to bed and, a little more than two months later, in February 1957, he was forced to abdicate in favor of Kishi, who held the portfolio of foreign affairs in his cabinet.

Ishibashi's record tends to be overshadowed by his predecessors in postwar Japanese politics, Yoshida Shigeru, who restored Japan's independence, and Hatoyama Ichiro, who normalized Japan–USSR diplomatic relations, and by his successor Kishi Nobusuke, who amended the US–Japan Security Treaty. Yet Ishibashi was nonetheless great. Acknowledged to be a "genuine liberal" and a distinguished presence in the fourth estate before the war and in the world of politics after the war, Ishibashi had a remarkable worldview that deserves special mention. As editor-in-chief of the respected journal *Toyo Keizai Shimpo* (New Oriental Economic Review) before the war, Ishibashi advocated "Small Nipponism," a different view of Asia from Kishi's "Greater Asianism" and from Yoshida's "out-of-Asia-into-the West" aspirations. Ishibashi consistently made a powerful case against territorial expansion into China, the Korean peninsula, and other neighboring regions in Asia.

He was a tragic figure, beset by successive strokes of misfortune: the agonizing futility of wielding the pen against the sword before the war, followed by his unjustified purge from public service by the occupation authorities after the war, further compounded by the curse of ill health at the peak of his political career. Given the cold-war structure, neither the ideal world that he envisaged nor the kind of Asian policies he espoused was ever to become a reality in postwar Japan. It is in this sense that, several times over, Ishibashi's destiny as a statesman was tragic.

He was born in Tokyo in 1884. His father was a Buddhist priest of the Nichiren sect. At the age of ten, when the Sino–Japanese war broke out in 1894, he was put in the care of a Buddhist temple in Yamanashi prefecture. It was by the head priest there, Mochizuki Nichiken, a high priest who later became the prelate at Minobusan-Kuonji, the head temple of the Nichiren sect, that Ishibashi was inculcated in the virtues of independence and self-respect. Enrolled in the First Yamanashi prefectural junior high school, he had tutorials with the headmaster Oshima Masatake, a Christian educator who had been under the guidance of the legendary Dr. William

© Asahi Shimbunsha

At the Liberal Democratic Party's convention in December 1956, Ishibashi Tanzan (left) defeated Kishi Nobusuke (right) in the race for LDP president and became Japan's prime minister. Soon after, however, Ishibashi was forced to step down because of ill health. It is an irony of history that Kishi, who replaced him, had a diametrically opposed attitude toward Asia.

Clark at Sapporo Agrarian College. Ishibashi was deeply impressed and influenced by Oshima's American approach, which imbued him with liberalism and individualism.

Ishibashi entered the preparatory course of Waseda University in 1902, and moved up to the Department of Philosophy at Waseda in 1904. His supervisor was Tanaka Odo, the first academic to introduce John Dewey's philosophy of pragmatism in Japan and widely known for his critical writings based on liberalism and individualism. Ishibashi's student years were in striking contrast to those of Kishi, 12 years his junior, who was influenced at the Imperial University of Tokyo by an ultra-nationalist mentor, Uesugi Shinkichi. Though a Buddhist of the Nichiren sect by birth, Ishibashi did not hesitate at all from drawing on Christianity, pragmatism, liberalism, democracy, and individualism, as well as other influences, to nourish his intellectual development.[6]

Ishibashi began his career in 1908 as a reporter for the *Tokyo Mainichi Shimbun*, and then moved in 1911 to the *Toyo Keizai*

Shimpo (New Oriental Economic Review, which was issued every ten days), where his enthusiasm for writing redoubled. Its editor-in-chief Amano Tameyuki and his associates had established a liberal tradition and an editorial climate adverse to the military clique and the vestiges of feudal clan favoritism. From his post on the editorial staff of the monthly sister publication *Toyo Jihyo* (Oriental Critical Commentary), Ishibashi began a meteoric ascent, quickly becoming a star writer for the *Toyo Keizai Shimpo*, with which the *Toyo Jihyo* was merged in October 1912. The socialist Katayama Sen was on the same editorial staff.

It was in October 1911, the year Ishibashi joined the *Toyo Keizai Shimpo*, that Sun Yatsen and his associates launched the Xinhai Geming revolution in China. The *Shimpo* applauded their movement as a great turning point, comparable to the Meiji Restoration in Japan, and insisted on Japan's complete non-intervention and respect for the national self-determination of the Chinese.

The incumbent editor-in-chief Miura Tetsutaro initially articulated the journal's stand on "Small Nipponism." Though Ishibashi specialized initially in business and economic news, he gradually came to adopt Miura's line of thought on political and diplomatic affairs as well.

The next year (1912) Ishibashi penned and published a series of provocative editorials on "The Thoughtless Nation," "Greater Nipponism," "Renouncing Manchuria," and other topics in the same vein. In the first of these, Ishibashi sounded the alarm against Japan's headlong rush to build a Greater Nippon and expand militarily:

> I am chagrined that none at the time voiced their opposition to the Sino–Japanese War, and that likewise too few raised objections to the Russo–Japanese War.[7]

When World War I broke out in 1914, Ishibashi editorially remonstrated with both the government and the jingoistic national press on their belligerent attitude and insistence on Japan's entry into the war. That did not prevent Japan from making a quick foray against the German base in Qindao (Shandong Province) and capturing the German South Pacific islands north of the equator. As

public opinion grew increasingly in favor of seizing German interests in Shandong Province, Ishibashi again fulminated from the
editor's desk against taking possession of Qindao, following this
with an editorial titled "Why Qindao Should Never Be Possessed."
Vehemently opposed to any such move, he argued:

> We should not seek territorial expansion into the Asian continent;
> indeed, we should relinquish Manchuria as soon as possible. . . .
>
> Taking possession of Qindao will bring upon us many evils and
> dangers in its train, and should be avoided at all costs.[8]

It was Ishibashi's thesis that, because Japan was suspected of
entertaining territorial ambitions in China, if Japan should extend
its tentacles beyond Manchuria to Shandong, the United States
and Great Britain would be alarmed, regarding this as tantamount
to an invasion of China. What Japan should do instead was to ask
China to open its doors and to promote economic exchange based
on equality of opportunity. Seizing Qindao would be counterproductive.

His was a voice crying in the wilderness, however: the Okuma
cabinet imposed its "Twenty-One Demands" upon the Yuan Shikai
government, which was forced to agree, obtaining only minor concessions in the phrasing of Japan's demands. While in China anti-
Japanese sentiment ran high over this and negotiations were still in
progress, Ishibashi condemned the Japanese government for aiming
at "territorial annexation of Manchuria, as it had done with
Korea." Once the treaty was signed, he called it "a total fiasco"
that would undermine friendly relations between Japan and China
and be detrimental even to Japanese interests. To his mind, the prosperity and stability of its neighboring nations was most conducive
to a nation's own interests.

At the Versailles Conference of 1919 after the end of World War
I, China emphatically protested against Japan's usurpation of
German interests and possession of Shandong Province, and Japan
found itself under growing pressure from the major powers. It was
in the same year that students in Beijing organized protest rallies

demanding Qindao's return and revocation of the Twenty-One Demands. Protest rallies known as the May 4th movement spread from Beijing to other cities of China.

RENOUNCEMENT OF ALL TERRITORIAL AMBITIONS

Forming the core of "Small Nipponism" was a series of Ishibashi's papers on the renunciation of Manchuria, which in its turn was based on the simple proposition that Manchuria was part of China and that China was a sovereign country. He was alarmed by the danger of a precipitous landslide of pretensions if Japan, puffed with pride at its Sino–Japanese and Russo–Japanese war victories, should venture next to annex Manchuria, with the spurious rationale of Korea's annexation as a precedent. His far-ranging argumentation has been summarized by Masuda Hiroshi in his *Ishibashi Tanzan*[9] as follows:

(i) As long as Japan retains colonial territories and other special interests in South Manchuria and elsewhere in China, the Chinese people's anti-Japanese sentiment will never be quelled, and this will adversely affect Japan's political, diplomatic, economic, and trade relations with China;

(ii) As prospective depositories of natural resources and excess population, Manchuria and other colonial territories are not as potentially valuable as is generally assumed, nor is Japan blessed with enough domestic capital to afford overseas territories;

(iii) Colonial holdings require growing military spending, lower the quality of life of people at home in the long run, and run the risk of triggering unjustified wars;

(iv) Japan's possession of colonial territories generates conflict with the United States in particular and the other world powers in general, isolating Japan in the international community;

(v) Given the rising tide of nationalism, all colonies are destined eventually to become separate and independent.

As described earlier in this chapter, it was at about this time that Yoshida Shigeru was in Hoten, Manchuria, soon to become consul general there and to take coercive measures to consolidate Japan's interests. In Yoshida's view, expanding territorial and other interests was a legitimate move in the game of diplomacy; to him, the rise of nationalism in China was a cause for alarm, and he was adamantly opposed to "all empty talk of Japan–China friendship, co-existence, and co-prosperity." Yoshida and Ishibashi were thus in antipodal contrast, and in the contemporary climate of public opinion at the time, Ishibashi was decidedly in the minority.

It was shortly before and after the Washington Conference of November 1921 that Ishibashi's argument rang clearest and most resoundingly. As the nine countries concerned got together to seek a comprehensive solution to problems ranging from the arms race among the major powers to Japanese interests in Shandong Province, Manchuria, and Mongolia, Ishibashi pleaded vehemently for Japan to prepare itself to renounce territorial ambitions.[10]

His impassioned plea to "Renounce All Territorial Ambitions" and his analysis of the "Illusion of Greater Nipponism" (a sequel in three consecutive installments) have been lauded as "masterful tracts, landmarks in the modern history of Japan" by Ishida Hirohide (cabinet secretary in Ishibashi's short-lived cabinet) in his *Ishibashi seiken nanaju-ichi-nichi* (The seventy-one days of the Ishibashi cabinet).[11] Not only did he declare that:

> [I]t is natural and makes sense in terms of geography, history, and international relations for China and Japan to seek harmony, exchange, and solidarity, . . .

but went so far as to make a case for renouncing all territorial possessions on the ground that:

[I]t is up to Japan to adopt a policy of liberation for Taiwan, Korea, and China as soon as possible and to see that the peoples there do not dissociate themselves from Japan.

Once such a policy is firmly implemented, he concluded:

[T]hey will look up to Japan for leadership, and long maintain affinity and friendship, as if we all were one and the same nation in political and economic affairs.

The prospective "leadership" predicated on renouncing all territorial ambitions differed completely from the one envisaged by the proponents of the Greater East Asia Co-Prosperity Sphere.

It is particularly noteworthy that Ishibashi made abundant use of statistics and other relevant data in his analysis of the Illusion of Greater Nipponism to demonstrate how colonial holdings failed to generate economic returns. In 1920, for example, the aggregate volume of trade with Korea, Taiwan, and Manchuria registered a little over ¥900 million, compared to ¥1,438 million with the United States, ¥587 million with India, and ¥330 million with Great Britain. He also pointed out that Korea, Taiwan, and Manchuria had little to supply such industrially high-priority resources as iron, coal, oil, cotton, etc. Rejecting any need for territorial possession for the sake of national defense, he went on to stress that if Japan was prepared to renounce all territorial ambitions, there would be absolutely no threat of war.

He did not separately develop any specific line of argument on the colonial liberation of Korea, but in commenting in early 1919 on the rise of the "March 1st movement" that rallied the Korean people in support of independence, he expressed "Sympathy with the Rioting Koreans" and editorialized:

The Koreans are a nation in their own right. They have their own distinctive language. They have a long history of independence in the past. It would be surprising to find even a single Korean who is genuinely happy about being a vassal of Japan.

In sharp contrast again to Yoshida Shigeru's view of Korea and its people, he predicted that, given the advancing levels of knowledge and self-awareness among the Koreans, their opposition to colonial rule would grow stronger.

Far from being prepared to renounce all territorial ambitions at the Washington Conference, Japan soon engineered the Manchurian Incident, set up the puppet state of Manchukuo, and plunged headlong into a war with China. Ishibashi continued to sound the alarm, denounced Manchukuo's motto of "the Union of Five Races and a Realm of Peace and Prosperity" as "sheer farce," and urged that hostilities with China not be allowed to escalate. Despite increasingly severe restrictions on freedom of speech, he expressed deep skepticism about the Konoe cabinet's stated policy in 1938 of "no dealing with Chiang Kaishek."

Ishibashi considered the status quo in China (i.e. the revolution in progress) to be comparable to the Meiji Restoration in Japan, and he was sympathetic with the Communist Parties of Russia and later of China. Yet in his judgment, it was Chiang Kaishek and the Kuomintang that had been steadily building up the most popularity among intellectuals committed to restoring China's sovereignty. In a public lecture in April 1940, he asserted that "close solidarity between Japan and China" should be strengthened at any cost, and added:

> We should cooperate with China in good faith and deal with the European and American powers together. And by "dealing with" them, I do not necessarily mean to compete with them as rivals.[12]

His position thus differed totally and consistently from Greater Asianism, which called for solidarity with Asia against the West.

THE IDEALIST COLLIDES WITH POSTWAR REALITY

Japan's defeat in the Pacific theatre represented to Ishibashi "a new departure for Japan that the nation should commemorate to all eternity," and it was only natural for him to editorialize (in the

August 15, 1945, issue of *Shimpo*) that "it is no time for shedding vain tears of indignation." He asserted that a new Japan should be built through economic reconstruction and democratization, and declared that Article 9 of the new constitution was "quite marvelously satisfying." He even dreamed at this time of constructing a cosmopolitan nation around the nation's new constitutional principles. Subsequently, when tensions grew high in the Asian situation, he revised his position, for a time supporting constitutional amendment, only to revert some years later to his original pro-constitutional position.

He chose for the first time to run in the general election of April 1946 on the Liberal rather than Socialist ticket, causing no small surprise to those around him. A man consistently committed to liberalism, Ishibashi believed he would be able to assert himself better in the Liberal Party. His campaign was not very well prepared and he failed in his first bid for elected office, but Hatoyama Ichiro's unexpected purge from public service then allowed Yoshida Shigeru to step in to fill the vacuum. Yoshida asked Ishibashi to serve as finance minister in the new cabinet, though it is doubtful that Yoshida was fully aware of the views Ishibashi had expounded over the years in the pages of the *Shimpo*. Yoshida made the offer on the recommendation of those close to him, who persuaded him of Ishibashi's solid reputation as an economist of liberal convictions.

But Yoshida and Ishibashi had quite different chemistries. While Yoshida was a realist who tried to be obedient to SCAP dictates and at the same time to use its power and authority to his own ends, Ishibashi was a man of principle, an idealist committed to national self-determination for Japan. As Ishibashi's attempts to energize the national economy and utilize rather than dismantle the zaibatsu (financial combines) soon ran afoul of occupation authorities, Yoshida began to distance himself from Ishibashi, whose adamant objection to the SCAP decision to "discontinue war-time reparations" precipitated a confrontation that ended in his purge from public service in May 1947. The stated reason for his purge— that as Editor-in-Chief and President of *Toyo Keizai Shimpo* he supported military and economic imperialism in Asia and promoted Japan's subservience to the Axis powers—was of course sheer nonsense.

As he struggled with the sheer absurdity of this accusation, he grew understandably distrustful of the United States. Yoshida Shigeru doggedly went along with US dictates. Kishi Nobusuke, for all his inherent anti-American feelings, compromised with the United States to ensure his political rehabilitation. Each one differed from the others in their stance towards the United States. But Ishibashi Tanzan, the most liberal of the three, became gradually more anti-American as time went by.

Years later, when Hatoyama was prime minister, Ishibashi and Kishi teamed up for a while in opposition to Yoshida, but they were patently as incompatible with each other as oil and water. Kishi is the founding father of the LDP's right-wing faction. Ishibashi founded the left-wing minority. It was Yoshida's middle-of-the-road course that was to develop into the conservative mainstream in the years ahead.

The increasingly chilly winds of the cold war effectively increased the difficulty of relations between China and Japan in the postwar years, as will be described later in detail. It was nonetheless only natural that Ishibashi should have been eager to normalize diplomatic relations with China. As soon as he returned to the world of politics from his purge from public service, Ishibashi made every effort to achieve a breakthrough in the reestablishment of Japan and China's severed ties. After illness forced him to step down as prime minister, he feared that his successor Kishi's anti-communist hard-line would jeopardize Japan's precarious ties with China. As soon as he was well again, therefore, he visited China, for the first time in September 1959 and repeatedly thereafter, consistently striving to restore bilateral relations. His basic position was that it would be unfortunate for the two nations to be opposed to each other on ideological grounds, that Japan and China were ultimately destined to become allies in the future, and that politics and economic interests were inseparable. His insistence on the "inseparableness of political and economic affairs" was regarded to be so controversial as to put him at the risk of expulsion from the party.

His visits to China had the effect of estranging Ishibashi from Kishi irrevocably.

Interestingly, Ishibashi was proposing a "Japan–China–USA–USSR peace alliance" at the time, a cherished idea of his which he broached at his meeting with premier Zhou Enlai and for which he continued to solicit support at home and abroad. In the cold war climate, his grand design tended to be dismissed as a pipe dream, but Ishibashi planned to visit Moscow to promote his pet theory and never gave up trying. His calls for a quadrilateral peace alliance, like his prewar Small Nipponism, fell mostly on deaf ears, but the course of events since the end of cold war has vindicated his foresightedness.

ISHIBASHI'S LOFTY "SYMPATHY FOR ASIA"

The renowned Japanese Sinologist Takeuchi Yoshimi had never even heard of Ishibashi Tanzan before the war; he came across *Ishibashi Tanzan zenshu* (The collected works of Ishibashi Tanzan) after the war and was profoundly impressed, at last finding in him "a liberalist and Asianist, the combination that for years I had sought in vain and was about to abandon hope of ever encountering."[13]

The author of an outstanding book on Ishibashi Tanzan, Masuda Hiroshi goes a step farther and says Ishibashi was a cosmopolitan rather than Asianist. Ishibashi looked up to Fukuzawa Yukichi as his ideological mentor, and watched Asia more soberly than did Matsumura Kenzo and others (who will be discussed below). His eyes were turned, says Masuda, not just to Asia but to the entire world:

> Tanzan's spiritual basis was an out-of-Asia orientation like Fukuzawa Yukichi's, and the goal he pursued therefrom was solidarity between Japan and China and other Asian nations, in coexistence and co-prosperity, based on the principles of equality, reciprocity, and peaceful coexistence.[14]

While Fukuzawa's despair at the Asian situation led his out-of-Asia theory to evolve into a philosophy of parting company with Asia, Ishibashi's thought was much more decidedly sympathetic with Asia. As in his admonition "to be prepared to renounce all territorial ambitions," his proposed scenario would have had Japan give up its territorial possessions in Asia, setting the good example of Asian solidarity and taking the moral high ground to counter the threat of western imperialism. Inconceivable to Fukuzawa, his vision had much in common with Sun Yatsen's Greater Asianism. Once quibbles over definitions have been set aside, Ishibashi's view of Asia is refreshingly persuasive. This, in the final analysis, accounts for the spate of publications on his life and work fifty years after the end of World War II.

Chapter 5 | Scant Awareness of Having Been Defeated by Asia

DEFIANT IN DEFEAT, JAPAN REFUSES TO ACKNOWLEDGE THE
VICTOR

Japan was soundly defeated in Asia and the Pacific during the
Second World War. The cause for which Japan ostensibly fought,
"Asian liberation," has been refuted and denied by the "liberated"
Asians themselves. How is it then that the Asian liberation view of
the war is still held by postwar Japanese politicians, even to this
day?

Japan's erstwhile dream of hegemony in Asia was shattered when
World War II ended. Nothing since has implanted or nurtured in
postwar Japanese conservative politicians a sense of guilt or in-
debtedness toward Asia. How is it then that, far from guilt,
Japanese leaders persist in expressing contempt for their fellow
Asians, even to this day?

A politician of Ishibashi Tanzan's stature and foresightedness
counseled Japan to renounce all territorial ambitions. How could he
have failed to gain due recognition for so many years—until the belated reappraisal in the last few years, decades after his death? (He
died in 1973.)

Takeuchi Yoshimi and others have suggested that any act of soul-
searching about Japan's defeat should reexamine also the superfi-
ciality of Japan's westernization since Meiji, beginning with an impartial reappraisal of China. Why has this way of thinking failed to
win a majority following?

101

In his *Shin Nihon no gaiko* (New Japanese diplomacy),[1] Irie Akira addresses these questions, pointing out that:

The Japanese people with their own particular conception of Asianism may not have been consciously aware of any defeat.

He goes on to explain as follows:

It is presumably because, basically, the Japanese have doggedly clung to their rationale (as they persuaded themselves to see it) for the Pacific War. They were uncomfortable thinking of the war as an act of aggression designed solely to boost exclusively Japanese interests and Japan's plans for territorial aggrandizement. If a plausible case could be made, even fictitiously, for their having launched the whole venture for Asia's sake, Japan's "noble cause" could be regarded as intact, even in defeat. . . . Japan's leaders tried to persuade themselves that they had "lost the battle but won the war" and, having achieved their "ultimate" goal, sued the Allies for peace.[2]

If Irie's account is right, it is arguable that Japan's cause was vindicated because many European and American colonies in Asia did achieve independence, one after another, in the wake of the war.

Rhetoric of justification apart, the lack of awareness of having been defeated by Asia is mainly attributable to the way many Japanese felt that they had been humiliated by the sheer material advantage and scientific superiority of Europe and the United States. The presumed cause of defeat was most succinctly presented by prime minister Higashikuni-no-miya (Prince) Naruhiko in his speech on administrative policies to the Imperial Diet on September 4, 1945. Quite candidly, he pointed out that Japan's defeat was caused by the wide gap in war potential between Japan and the United States, which he enumerated in great detail. It was Japan's eroded potential to wage war and its exhausted national resources that had brought about its ruin.

At a press conference earlier, on August 28th, Prince Higashikuni stated that "the first step in the rebuilding of our country is for the entire nation to show penitence." His suggestion, labeled "repentance by one hundred million Japanese for their sins" in effect diffused the question of war accountability and encouraged subsequent equivocation. In addition, as Awaya Kentaro points out in his "Postwar Settlements at the Tokyo Trials" in *Senso sekinin sengo sekinin* (Responsibility for war and its aftermath),[3] Prince Higashikuni's emphatic and exclusive attribution of the cause of defeat to the sheer material advantage and scientific superiority of the United States may also have helped to limit or contain whatever awareness the Japanese had of having been beaten by fellow Asians.

Even today, the Japanese for the most part do not seem to be consciously aware (or refuse to accept the idea) that they were beaten by Asia. When, in a special Japan Broadcasting Corporation TV program on the fiftieth anniversary of the end of the war in early January 1995, the writer Ishikawa Yoshimi made a statement to the effect that "Japan was beaten by Asia," viewers called in to chastise him for "taking such a subservient attitude during the festive New Year week."

I was intrigued and had a chance to ask former prime minister Miyazawa Kiichi for his comments on the episode. He said to me:

> I find it rather strange. The Manchurian Incident apart, beginning with the outbreak of hostilities with China in 1937, Japan ventured headlong into such a vast and populous expanse of territory that it stood no chance, from the very outset, of winning at all. There was talk then of engagements limited to "points and lines," but, given the sheer size of the continental theatre of war, nothing could possibly have been accomplished by way of "points and lines." I was a college student at that time and I felt, and I do so even now, that Japan had got itself involved in a war that it had no chance at all of winning.[4]

As a student, Miyazawa found himself in sympathy with Ishibashi Tanzan's Small Nipponism, and there was no doubt in his mind that Japan had been defeated by China. The Japanese nation as a whole, however, and the political community in particular, have shown little awareness over the years since the immediate aftermath of their defeat of having been defeated by Asia. In a public lecture titled "Hoho to shite no Ajia" (Asia as a method), Takeuchi Yoshimi, responding to a question from the floor, said:

> I think it's undeniable that the Japanese never had any real sense of having been beaten by China. The question is why this is so.
>
> Japan surrendered unconditionally to the Allies, mainly the UK, the USA, the USSR, and China. Yet the feeling is particularly strong that Japan went down on its knees to the USA. The Japanese had hardly any real sense of having been beaten by the USSR, let alone by China.
>
> Such gaps in perception stem from complicated circumstances. For one thing, the troops that occupied Japan were mainly American. And there was then, and still is, a vicious feeling of contempt for China. The Japanese thought, "We can't possibly lose to them." And this made sense militarily, perhaps: Japan's war-making capacity at the time was far superior to China's. But by the same token, the USA was militarily so overwhelmingly superior to Japan that it made sense to accept that Japan had to lose to the US only.[5]

If the Japanese people in general were hardly ever consciously aware of having been defeated by China, they had no sense at all of having been defeated by Korea. As demonstrated by its tenacious struggle for independence during the years of Japanese colonial rule, Korea never succumbed spiritually to Japan, and yet because Japan's colonial rule was not actually overturned by Korea's indigenous nationalistic movement, Korea's liberation was won not by the Korean people's struggle, but as a consequence of Japan's defeat in the Pacific war and "thanks to" the United States, which forced Japan to desist. That is what the Japanese tend to think, at any rate. Soon after the Japanese left Taiwan, it was taken over by Chinese mainlanders, and this change of occupiers similarly clouded the picture, helping the Japanese to avoid blame for their colonialism. Having others they could point their finger at, the postwar Japanese were never made to confront the right accusers at the right time and thus they failed to develop any noticeable sense of guilt for having colonized their neighbors.

The deplorable lack of any sense of having been beaten by Asia allowed the Japanese people to continue to carry their prewar attitudes toward Asia into the postwar years. Their wartime hatred of the "Anglo-American fiends and brutes" metamorphosed virtually overnight into a kind of pro-American team spirit, but their contempt for Asia has remained unchanged.

The Tokyo Trials leave crimes unpunished

The International Military Tribunal for the Far East was convened under dominantly Western leadership and failed to expose the warped self-image of the Japanese people and of their politicians in particular. Twenty-eight defendants were indicted as "serious (Class A) war criminals" and all except three (two who died during their trial and one who was ruled mentally incompetent) were found guilty and sentenced, seven to death and the rest to lesser penalties. Yet the main charges against them had to do with their responsibility for starting a war against the United States; their involvement in acts of aggression in Asia was in the main not examined.

To be precise, acts of aggression in China after the Manchurian Incident were included in the charges, but those political leaders who were known to have positively promoted or at least condoned such acts were not even prosecuted, provided that they were judged to have been subsequently opposed to or cautious about beginning hostilities against the United States. The responsibility for acts of aggression in Asia was thus exclusively laid on those in favor of war against the US, most military officers. Most of the "moderate" leaders who collaborated with the trial proceedings managed to be exonerated, and their responsibility for acts of aggression in Asia remained shrouded in ambiguity as a result. The whole process has been vividly exposed by Yoshida Yutaka in his *Showa Tenno no shusen-shi* (The postwar history of Emperor Showa's reign).[6]

Not a few of the senior statesmen close to the Emperor belonged to this category. The Lord Keeper of the Privy Seal and father-in-law of Yoshida Shigeru, Makino Nobuaki, for instance, had been a typical "moderate" critical of beginning a war with the US and the UK. After combing *Makino Nobuaki nikki* (The diary of Makino Nobuaki), however, Yoshida Yutaka concludes that Makino was:

> . . . very cautious about escalating or prolonging the Pacific war, but, when it came to China, tended to justify warring with China, either as a way to improve Japan's chances of survival under difficult conditions of excess population and food shortages, or as a counteroffensive against the anti-Japanese movement organized by China.[7]

It was presumably for similar reasons that Yoshida favored controlling China by force. The Allied powers apparently judged that because they would have to use pro-Anglo-American politicians to rehabilitate Japan after the war, they should bring war crimes charges almost exclusively against the military (only one civilian was hanged, Hirota Koki) and those in favor of fighting a war against the United States (Hirota was one of those). (And similar political considerations seemingly motivated their decision also to pass over Emperor Showa's responsibility for the war.) As Yoshida Yutaka has demonstrated in detail in his book, Emperor Showa did set great store on cooperating with the UK and the USA, but in the end gave his approval to the declaration of war against the United States. Much less contestable is the Emperor's belief that expansion of Japan's interests in China was a matter of national policy. A book of his soliloquies records him as ruminating: "An incident or two in rural Manchuria will not have grave consequences." Had the responsibility for aggression in China been examined, the Allied powers could not have guaranteed him against possible prosecution, let alone have granted him exoneration without controversy.

It is public knowledge by now that those involved in the war crimes committed by Imperial Japanese Army "Unit 731," which conducted extensive and cruel biological experiments on living human beings in Manchuria and R&D work on bacteriological warfare in violation of international law, were exonerated in a *nolo contendere* deal with prosecutors on condition that they supply the US with whatever sordid data they had obtained. Despite all the talk about the possibility of prosecution in the name of humanity, the prosecutors' approach was the same connivance with perpetrators of atrocities and acts of suppression against Korean independence activists. To the extent that not a few of those sitting on the bench at the Tokyo Trials represented suzerain powers, they were reluctant (to say the least) to conduct an open and across the board examination of practices of imperialistic colonial rule. Having condoned Japan's annexation of Korea in a *quid pro quo* deal designed decades ago to establish its own share of other countries' territories, the United States had no right to pass judgment on Japan's colonial rule over Korea.

The composition of the bench was also problematical. The judges represented eleven countries, only three of them Asian: China, India, and the Philippines. Neither Korea nor Taiwan, though liberated from long years of Japanese colonial rule, were represented.

In short, soon after the end of the war, the curtain went down on the history of Japan's pursuit of hegemony in Asia before it could be properly examined and its authors could be put on trial.

This said, the US undeniably sought during the early postwar years to reeducate Japan ideologically and to root out its Greater Asianism. By purging offending politicians from public service and strictly controlling freedom of speech, it purely and simply suppressed Japanese nationalism and Greater Asianism, nurturing Western liberalism and moderate socialism at the same time. The whole process has naturally caused Greater Asianism generally to ebb over the years, and it has encouraged a tendency for Japan to follow in the United States' footsteps. It has not, however, helped generate a genuine feeling of respect for Asia and solidarity with the rest of Asia in Japan.

Chapter 6

The Context of Post-War Diplomacy: Options Under Cold War Conditions

THE IMPACT OF THE KOREAN WAR

The dominant view of Asia in the political community did not significantly change over the years spanning the Pacific war, nor has Japan's defeat proved since the war to have boosted minority views like Ishibashi Tanzan's. In addition to the immediate postwar's state of affairs described in the preceding chapter, another obvious factor—the cold war in progress—operated tenaciously behind the scenes. The protracted cold war between the US and the USSR spawned one communist state after another in Asia and intensified tensions across the region.

Kishi Nobusuke's release, as discussed above, symbolized a substantial change in US policy toward Japan as the cold war set in. In October 1949, Mao Zedong's Communist Party defeated Chiang Kaishek's Kuomintang and established the People's Republic of China. The Korean War broke out the next year. With Soviet backing, Kim Ilsung announced the founding of the Democratic People's Republic of Korea (North Korea) in September 1948, and in June 1950, his troops crossed the border along the 38th North parallel and opened hostilities against the US-backed Republic of Korea (South Korea). Sometime later, the Chinese People's Liberation Army intervened in support of North Korea.

The outbreak of a hot war on the Korean peninsula, unlike the defeat in World War II, did have an immeasurable influence on the Japanese view of Asia. First, it weakened the minority position, since this new factor was a setback to Ishibashi's consistent urging that Japan consolidate friendly relations between Japan and China. Not long after its liberation from Japan's colonial rule, the Korean peninsula was now the theatre, not of a cold war but of a veritable hot war, with its northern half an enemy of Japan. Engaging the advancing enemy on behalf of the southern half were forces nominally of the United Nations, in fact American troops based in Japan. Prohibited by its constitution from remilitarizing, Japan managed to avoid direct military involvement, but had to meet growing US expectations that Japan would play the role of base and factory for Western forces. Indeed, this was the only practical way to guarantee Japan's road back to economic development and membership in the international community.

Given the unforeseen turn of events, Ishibashi, too, was bewildered. In his *Ishibashi Tanzan*, Masuda Hiroshi summarizes the recently discovered essay titled "The Inevitability of World War III and the Cosmopolitan State,"[1] which Ishibashi wrote immediately after the outbreak of the Korean War. Herewith Ishibashi's line of reasoning in a nutshell (my summary):

> Neither the US nor the USSR can afford to opt out now, and the current situation is likely sooner or later to escalate into a face-to-face confrontation. The USSR will not involve itself in the Korean War directly, but may choose instead to use Communist China as its proxy. China's capacity to make war is now much greater than it was during the Sino–Japanese War (1937–45), and the USSR today has superior global military might. In order to fortify its war potential and cope with such a formidable combination, the US must turn Japan and West Germany into completely dependable allies, and to do this, the US will have to learn to stop looking down disparagingly on all its friends.

> With regard specifically to Japan, the US should (i) grant Japan complete independence, (ii) rebuild Japan's army, navy, and air force (by placing the Constitution's Article 9 in abeyance), (iii) lift sanctions against Japan, and (iv) lift the purge from public service

immediately. The US will emerge victorious, Ishibashi predicted, once these drastic shifts in policy toward Japan are in place.

Ishibashi's argument goes further. I continue my summary:

The presumed US victory will not spell the end of all wars. Nationalism breeds hostility, and the best strategy to contain it is to establish a global cosmopolitan state. It must be a federal republic, in which different countries today will continue to exist as local autonomies. The US—the strongest, *primus inter pares*—should be the first to abolish its borders and usher in the prospective cosmopolitan state. Unless it does, World War III will have been waged in vain.

The spirit (if not the substance) of Ishibashi's vision, which must have appeared to be an unrealistic flight of fantasy in the early 1950s when he penned it, gains a measure of plausibility in the post cold-war world of the late 1990s.

Although Ishibashi's fear of the "inevitable" World War III has turned out to be groundless, his prediction that China would get itself involved in the Korean War proved to be right on the mark. It is intriguing to note how he abandoned his earlier, immediate postwar period, position and came to call for Japan's rearmament and constitutional amendment in preparedness for the next, "inevitable" world war. Though his reassessment was motivated by the vagaries of the international situation, typified by the Communists' seizing power in China and war's breaking out in Korea, Ishibashi must have been chagrined to think how long a way he still had to go (as he was forced painfully to admit) before his cherished dream of Japan–China friendship would be realized.

Nevertheless, Ishibashi was committed to the cosmopolitan worldview and did not mean deliberately to exclude communist nations from the global federal republic that he envisaged. Thus while Ishibashi continued to strive to improve Japan–China relations, regardless of intervening developments, Ashida Hitoshi—who had been extremely critical of Yoshida Shigeru's high-handed policy toward prewar China—being also a very committed anticommunist, was now seized with a fit of Sinophobia, and when the Korean War broke out, Ashida began to urge that Japan amend its constitution and rearm. With even the once-moderate Ashida doing such a turnabout, it is scarcely conceivable that lesser politicians with an only marginal interest in Asian affairs over the years would ever be stricken by contrition and guilt, however much they should have realized what they owed to Asia and their fellow Asians. In short, the Korean war might have provided a golden opportunity for genuine soul-searching and a sounder awareness of Asia. Sadly, it did not.

The upshot of all this was the San Francisco Peace Treaty, signed in September 1951, a separate peace concluded by the Western powers and Japan: the USSR and the Eastern bloc were not party to it. Communist China and Taiwan, and South and North Korea, two pairs of divided nations each contending for its own legitimacy over the other, did not participate in the proceedings, either. The postwar settlement in Japan was thus set in motion by bypassing Japan's next-door neighbors who had been most seriously affected by Japan's conduct in the war. This, too, was a contributing factor to the widespread feeling that Japan had been beaten not by the Asians, but by the Anglo-Americans.

Japan–China ties: severed by force

America's Asian policy of forcible containment of communism was directly projected onto Japan after the peace treaty as well. For all his anticommunist convictions and respect for the Kuomintang regime in Taiwan (Republic of China), Yoshida Shigeru, who negotiated the peace treaty, believed he could not simply ignore Mao Zedong's government in the People's Republic of China, because it controlled virtually all of mainland China. One way or another, the fifteen-year-long war with China had to be formally brought to an end. As pointed out toward the end of Part III, Chapter 2, Yoshida's view of China changed after the end of the war. He was careful not to overestimate Chinese communism, and predicted that the China–USSR honeymoon would not last long.

In negotiating the treaty, Yoshida tried to sound out his American counterpart about the suggestion that Japan be allowed to use its own discretion in choosing either Taiwan or China as the party to the prospective bilateral settlement. As mentioned above, he came to reassess his own view of the Chinese nation after the war, but continued to be convinced that China, with its vast territory and huge population, represented a potentially un-limited market and source of natural resources. His mind was set on trade with China.

It turned out to be a case of wishful thinking, however. The US at that time could simply not afford to see Japan teaming up with communist China while its own troops were engaged directly in combat with China's People's Army in Korea and the Red purge raged at home. Shocked at Yoshida's suggestion, the US team of ne-gotiators insinuated that the US Congress would not ratify the peace treaty if Japan intended to cozy up to communist China, and oth-erwise put heavy pressure on Japan to accommodate Chiang Kaishek and his government of the Republic of China.

Yoshida had no choice. While "the government of Japan hopes to ultimately establish comprehensive relations of political peace and commercial trade with China, our next-door neighbor," Yoshida whimpered lamely in an epistle to State Secretary J. F. Dulles in December 1951, the best and most practical step for the present would be to foster relations with the government of the Republic of China; he concluded by pledging that the government of Japan had no intention of concluding any bilateral agreement with the communist regime of China. Negotiations with the Republic of China began in February 1952, and the Japan–Republic of China Peace Treaty was signed on April 28th, the day the San Francisco Peace Treaty and the US–Japan Security Treaty came into effect. Now a *fait accompli*, Japan's complicity in the policy of con-taining and isolating Communist China was to continue for the next twenty years.

The US and the UK dissented over the extent of discretion to be left to Japan. Having itself already recognized the People's Republic of China, the UK held that Japan should be given leeway to make its own decisions and criticized the US for pressuring Japan to accept the other alternative. Years later in his *Kaiso junen* (Ten years in retrospect), Yoshida wrote the following:

> With years of hard-earned experience in Chinese affairs, it is the British and the Japanese who best understand the Chinese psyche. To be candid, the Americans have yet to come to know China for what it is. Practically all American postwar policies toward China have failed.[2]

Incidentally, the differences between the US and the UK over Japan's policy toward China seem to have stemmed in part from divergent economic interests. The UK feared that if Japan, denied access to China, came to play an important role in the Asian anticommunist version of the "co-prosperity sphere" envisaged by the US scenario, its own trade interests in Southeast Asia would be jeopardized. This fear, in the end, was not so misplaced. For a period of time thereafter, the Japanese worked very hard to establish and consolidate robust economic ties in Southeast Asia, compensating, as it were, for its exclusion from the Chinese market by brandishing the banner of democracy and free trade in Asia.

In stark contrast to the severance of relations with China and the contretemps in relation to both South and North Korea, Japan's economic aid to Southeast Asia, in tandem with war reparations, rapidly expanded in a series of reparations agreements and peace treaties concluded by successive cabinets—Yoshida, Hatoyama, and Kishi—with Burma (1954), the Philippines (1956), Indonesia (1958), and South Vietnam (1959), helping to restore and consolidate bilateral relations.

Yoshida in his *Kaiso junen* maintained that Japan should contribute its share of economic aid to Asia and promulgate liberalism's values across the region, and that Japanese technology should be harnessed to American financing to develop Southeast

Asia. His scenario came to be played out in actual policy. Prompted by SCAP, Japan sent its first economic mission to Southeast Asia as early as in the summer of 1951, just before it regained independence, and began to build up a regional framework of economic cooperation. As it regained its independence, Japan swung into action full-scale to build up a "triad of union" predicated on economic cooperation between the US, Japan, and Southeast Asia.

What the US expected of Japan was (i) production of goods of direct relevance to economic stability in Southeast Asia, (ii) local development of raw materials, and (iii) mass production of inexpensive war materiel for use in Japan and Southeast Asia. Yoshida was well aware of these expectations. In May 1952, Finance Minister Ikeda Hayato spoke of "developing Southeast Asia in cooperation with the US," and Yoshida in a speech on his administrative policies in October stressed "mutual understanding with Asian democracies" and "strengthening economic relations with Southeast Asia."

Virtually isolated from its neighbors China, North Korea, and even the Republic of Korea, which belonged to the Western bloc, Japan in those years had very strong motives to cultivate economic relations with Southeast Asia, and its interest in this region had multiple implications. In the process of its own economic reconstruction and growth, Japan entertained great expectations for the region in terms of supplying resources and developing markets. In order for Japan to present and consolidate its image as an "Asian nation," Southeast Asia was the only accessible testing ground: elsewhere, closer geographically to Japan, the vestiges of the past were still very much in evidence. The development of free economies in Asia furthered US policy of containing China, to which Japan's contribution was politically significant, both in boosting Japan's image and in eliciting US appreciation for its positive role. Yoshida's policy line would subsequently be faithfully followed and implemented by Kishi Nobusuke.

MAKING EYES AT CHINA AND THE USSR: THE HATOYAMA AND ISHIBASHI YEARS

When Yoshida was finally forced to step down, it was the conservative coalition of Hatoyama and Ishibashi that rose to power before Kishi took over. Hatoyama, like Yoshida, had been an advocate of liberalism in the prewar days and wary of starting a war against the US. Nevertheless, when interrogated by the occupiers after the war, Hatoyama stated:

> Though Japan and China badly needed to promote economic collaboration, there was in China a hard-liners' faction resolutely opposed to any collaboration with Japan, and that meant war. The Japanese also had a feeling that they needed to create a buffer state like Manchukuo in China to stem the infiltration of communism.[3]

Yoshida Yutaka, in his *Showa Tenno no shusen-shi* (The postwar history of Emperor Showa's reign), from which the above citation is taken, takes Hatoyama's lame attempt to justify Japan's invasion of China as an indication of the "vast limitations of Hatoyama's 'liberalism'."

Upon fulfilling his long-cherished desire to topple the Yoshida cabinet, Hatoyama launched a retrogressive platform for autonomous constitutional amendment and rearmament and tried to revise the out-and-out pro-American stance of the Yoshida cabinet. He staked his political life on restoring diplomatic relations with China and with the USSR. Without resolving the questions of the reversion of the USSR-occupied Northern Islands, which was regrettably shelved, Japan–USSR relations were normalized by the Joint Declaration of October 1956. Japan then regained its membership in the international community in December upon its admission to the UN.

Hatoyama's diplomatic course correction was, in part, motivated by spitefulness toward Yoshida. Hatoyama had been within a hairbreadth of coming to power when he was purged from public service by order of the occupation authorities. Yoshida, who was charged with the task of taking up the slack, won the office of prime

minister as if by a windfall and thereafter maintained an undis-
guisedly pro-American platform, clinging to power tenaciously and
showing no sign of wanting ever to yield the office to Hatoyama,
who naturally harbored a personal grudge against him.

Given their inherently different persuasions, it would not have
made any sense for Ishibashi and Kishi to join hands in support of
Hatoyama had it not been for their sense of strange-bed-fellowship
from having been detained and purged by the occupiers. Yoshida
had not had to face any such harassment. Hatoyama and all of his
supporters had mixed feelings about the United States, and their
perspectives on diplomatic policies towards Asia naturally differed
from Yoshida's. So it was that the Hatoyama cabinet, over the
fierce opposition of the Yoshida group, took the plunge and restored diplomatic relations with the USSR, putting an end to the
state of war.

For Kishi on the rightmost end of the conservative spectrum and
Ishibashi on the leftmost end to join hands in the 1950s, says Sataka
Makoto in his *Ryo Nihon-shugi no seijika* (Statesman of sane
Nipponism),[4] was "like Ozawa Ichiro and Takemura Masayoshi
supporting the Hosokawa cabinet just because they both happened
to be "anti-LDP" [in 1993]. Politics makes strange bedfellows."
Sataka's comparison of Kishi and Ishibashi to Ozawa and
Takemura respectively, is doubly apt, because Ozawa thought to
turn Japan into a "normal" country (through constitutional amendment to relax restrictions on the role of the military) and Takemura
to maintain the peace constitution and have Japan set the good example by playing a "small but exemplary" role in international
affairs.

Hatoyama's departure from Yoshida's diplomatic stance is illustrated by the fact that, one and a half years before restoring diplomatic relations with the USSR, the Hatoyama cabinet sent Takasaki
Tatsunosuke as its official representative to the Asian and African
Nations' Conference held in Bandung, Indonesia, in April 1955.
With the US and USSR in open confrontation, it was third world
countries like India, Egypt, Indonesia, and most notably China, that
asserted themselves in promoting the Bandung Conference and its

set of ten principles including peaceful coexistence, non-intervention in the internal affairs of other countries, and arms reduction. For all its alliance with USSR, China adopted a very flexible stance, collaborating actively with non-aligned promoters of the conference like India. As the Indonesian President Sukarno put it, it was "the first meeting in the history of mankind of colored races spanning the two continents," and was symptomatic of the rising tide of nationalism in Asia and Africa in the wake of World War II.

While Yoshida Shigeru and his associates feigned an air of indifference, twenty-nine countries of Asia and Africa were represented at the Bandung Conference, and Takasaki and his counselor Fujiyama Aiichiro (president of the Japan Chamber of Commerce and Industry) had a chance to confer with China's Zhou Enlai during the Conference, in which as many as twenty-nine countries of Asia and Africa were represented. Had the Bandung Conference scenario been acted out on firmer ground in the follow-up, Japan's foreign policy in Asia might have been different. As it was, both the USA and USSR cold-shouldered the whole event, and the third world countries that rallied to Bandung failed to act in concert subsequently. With China adopting a vehemently anti-American posture soon afterwards, and Japan under the Kishi cabinet committing itself to a strong alliance with the USA, another rare opportunity for Japan to formulate a sound and viable version of "Asianism" vanished into thin air again.

Ishibashi Tanzan had been eager to make a breakthrough in Japan–China relations long before he received the portfolio of international trade and industry in the Hatoyama cabinet in late 1954. Even as the flow of bilateral trade dwindled after the outbreak of the Korean war and China's decision to send troops, in January 1952 Ishibashi put together a nonpartisan group dubbed the International Economic Affairs Forum with Murata Shozo (President of Osaka Merchant Shipping Co.), Hiratsuka Tsunejiro (President of Nichiro Fishing Industries, later elected to the House of Representatives), and Kazami Akira (Japan Socialist Party). Dedicated to the promotion of Japan's trade with the USSR and China, the Forum sent Hoashi Kei, a member of the House of

Councilors and others on a secret mission to Moscow in April. On their way home, they visited Beijing for the first time since the Revolution and concluded the first Japan–China Private Trade Agreement. Ishibashi fully supported this entire process.

With the Japan–Republic of China Peace Treaty due to be concluded just three months later in April 1952, Ishibashi's move at that particular point in time represented a bold departure from Yoshida's exclusively pro-American diplomatic stance. Given Yoshida's lasting assessment of China's potential importance to Japan, it is not hard to imagine Yoshida's mixed feelings about Ishibashi's daring performance. His commitment to a breakthrough in Japan–China ties unabated, Ishibashi managed, with Hiratsuka, Murata, and others, to launch the International Trade Promotion Association of Japan in September 1954. Before the year was out, Yoshida was forced to step down and Hatoyama took over.

The Bandung Conference of April 1955 roughly coincided with a visit to Japan of a Chinese trade mission, and Ishibashi, who happened then to be the minister of international trade and industry and to attend the welcome luncheon meeting for the leader of the Chinese delegation, got to be the first cabinet minister in postwar Japan to establish formal contacts with Chinese VIPs. In May, the third "Japan–China Private Trade Agreement" marked a dramatic step forward in bilateral trade relations by including provisions for the establishment of an Office of Trade Representative. Anxious to loosen the COCOM (Coordinating Committee for Export to Communist Areas) restrictions on trade with the communist bloc, Ishibashi argued for promoting Japan–China trade in a paper he contributed to the *Nippon Keizai Shimbun* (June 25, 1956), in which he stressed the importance of China both as a source of raw materials for Japan and as a market for manufactured goods from Japan, expressed his regret that the cold war hampered economic exchange, and stressed (i) that trading with China was different from politically and ideologically sympathizing with communism, (ii) that economic relations between Japan and China were of vital importance, and (iii) that Southeast Asia, for example, did not offer an adequate alternative to China.

When Ishibashi finally assumed office as Prime Minister in December 1956, China had high hopes, as shown by the editorial welcoming his rise to power in the *People's Daily*, China's Communist Party organ. The Ishibashi cabinet's basic approach was "to actively expand Japan–China trade and to begin to work for normalizing diplomatic relations once adjustments have been made with the United Nations and with free-world countries." Ishida Hirohide, then cabinet secretary, recalls how he was instructed to visit Yoshida and persuade him to back the policy.[5] Yoshida is said to have responded that the proposition was acceptable, but added that he wanted Ishida to convey a message to Ishibashi to the effect that "China and Russia say their alliance is as tight as a knot, but they are bound sooner or later to split up." Upon receiving the message, Ishibashi admitted it was "a good piece of advice, an insight becoming a diplomat of Yoshida's maturity." That Yoshida gave this advice to Ishibashi is an interesting clue to what Yoshida was really thinking in his heart of hearts.

The United States was naturally wary of Ishibashi. The *Yomiuri Shimbun* published an interesting story in this connection on February 3, 1995. Then British Minister to the US de la Mare had a conference with Howard Parsons, Director of the Northeast Asia Bureau at the US Department of State, and sent a classified report to his home office.

As de la Mare saw it, the United States was apprehensive about Japan and China getting too close to each other and was undoubtedly flustered at Ishibashi's assumption of office as Prime Minister. Having "invested in Kishi" for so many years, the Americans were now wishfully hoping that Kishi as Foreign Minister in the Ishibashi cabinet would put a brake on Ishibashi, and that Kishi would succeed to Ishibashi. Parsons himself told de la Mare, "If we are lucky, Ishibashi may not last very long." Strangely enough, this wishful thinking came true before long: ill health forced Ishibashi to step down, and his foreign minister, the man whom the Americans had "invested in" for so long, took over. As the irony of history would have it, Kishi then proceeded to do everything he could to help "contain" China and to chill

Japan–China relations, as if he wanted to curry favor with his transpacific patrons.

Ishida speculates, "If the Ishibashi cabinet had lasted longer, the subsequent evolution of Japan–China relations would have been completely different."[6] Given the cold war structure, even Ishibashi, hemmed in as it were by the constraints of the times, could not have departed significantly from the basic course of Japan–US relations. As Tominomori Eiji points out in his *Sengo hoshutoshi* (The post-war history of Japan's conservative parties):

> If Ishibashi's health had allowed him to remain in office long enough, Japan–China relations would have been improved substantially, even if not necessarily to the point of Japan's granting diplomatic recognition to mainland China immediately. In any event, had Ishibashi remained in power, Japan–China diplomatic relations would have been normalized much sooner than they were, and Japan would have been able, if necessary, to stir up noticeably the international situation in the Far East in ways affecting the Russian–Chinese conflict, US–China relations, and other key parameters. . . . The Kishi cabinet might not have been born after all, the doves in the LDP might have become slightly more powerful, and the course of conservative politics would naturally have been different from what it turned out to be in reality.[7]

All of the tragedies that befell Ishibashi Tanzan—his ineffective prewar attempts to sway public opinion, his postwar purge, and his ill health—were tragedies for Japan as well.

The Fringes of the Free World

In May 1957, Kishi made a round of visits to India, Pakistan, Sri Lanka, Thailand, and Taiwan. Apart from Tojo Hideki's tour of inspection of southern Asia during the war, Kishi's was the first Asian tour of an incumbent Japanese premier.

He chose this move deliberately. Not entirely cleansed of the vestiges of his prewar nationalism and fervently committed to giving

Japan a constitution that had not been imposed by the United States, Kishi had staked his political survival on revising the US–Japan Security Treaty, changing it from a unilateral agreement that covered virtually nothing but the stationing of American troops in Japan to a bilateral collective defense pact. His visit to the United States was scheduled for the next month, June, when revision negotiations would, he hoped, get under way. Recounting in his memoirs the purpose of his Asian junket on the eve of his visit to the United States, Kishi reasoned that his negotiating position on the proposed revision of the US–Japan Security Treaty would be strengthened by "putting into bold relief the fact that Asia is centered round Japan."[8]

During his round of visits to Asian countries, Kishi cultivated a close friendship with Chiang Kaishek in Taiwan and supported Chiang's plan to mount a "counteroffensive against the mainland," which naturally infuriated Beijing. At a press conference on his return, Kishi stated:

> Free-world countries would be seriously concerned, and the United States in particular would be in trouble, if [Asia] were to be thrown into turmoil by communism. I intend to talk candidly [with the Americans] about what Japan should do to cope with the prevailing realities in Southeast Asia and what the United States is trying to do there.[9]

He then met with the US Ambassador Douglas MacArthur, Jr., and broached his plan for the Southeast Asia Development Fund. The idea was for Japan and the United States jointly to "liberate Asia from poverty," such that:

> Putting such a scheme in place will firmly establish Japan's leadership in Southeast Asia, which will then remain outside the sphere of influence of Communist China and the USSR, significantly strengthening the position of the free-world countries. Japanese industry will benefit of course, but even more importantly, the scheme will be identified as Japan's global policy.[10]

Kishi's characteristic strategy-mindedness is eloquently in evidence here. He had no qualms about trying as best he could to turn the cold war situation to what he believed to be Japan's own advantage. His was definitely different from Ishibashi's orientation.

After his visit to the United States, Kishi made another round of visits to the Asian and Pacific countries he had not yet visited in November 1957—Vietnam, Cambodia, Laos, Malaysia, Singapore, Indonesia, Australia, New Zealand, and the Philippines. Eager to effect a reconciliation with Southeast Asia and to build an anti-communist alliance, Kishi was naturally keenly interested in the Republic of Korea, the indisputable frontier of anticommunism. In his attempt to win Rhee Syngman's favor, Kishi even went so far as to specifically refer to "the wrongs committed by Ito Hirobumi," as discussed in Part II of this volume. In hindsight, this gesture on strategically minded Kishi's part did indeed make perfectly good sense.

Thereafter, the course of Japan's diplomacy as charted by Yoshida and Kishi was not substantially modified until Japan–China diplomatic relations were normalized in 1972. The crucial breakthrough in Japan–China relations came as a result of a breakdown in China–Russia relations as well as of the Vietnam fiasco, which caused the United States to do a turnabout and seek a reconciliation with China. The result was a dramatic change in the cold war power structure. Since Yoshida, the Japanese had long nursed strong aspirations for an accommodation with China, knowing its great potential importance to Japan. Now there was nothing to stop them.

| # The Pro-Taiwan Faction and "Repaying Violence with Virtue"

IN CHIANG'S DEBT ON FOUR COUNTS

The conservative coalition that gave birth to the Liberal Democratic Party did not resolve all policy line conflicts among its strange bed-fellows. Apart from the constitutional controversy, it was the China problem that turned out by degrees to be a particularly conspicu-ous and serious bone of contention. The tension peaked in 1972 when the government of Tanaka Kakuei went ahead and normal-ized diplomatic relations with China.

After regaining its independence, Japan was obliged to choose either China or Taiwan for its new partner, and the Yoshida cabi-net under US pressure had no alternative but to seek accommoda-tion with Taiwan, as described in Part II of this volume. With Japan–mainland China ties still severed, however, the problem fes-tered, and when awareness began to spread that mainland China's international status was outstripping Taiwan's, it was no longer possible to bypass indefinitely the question of normalizing diplo-matic relations between Japan and China. What brought matters to a head was the bombshell announcement in July 1971, towards the end of Sato Eisaku's premiership, that US President Nixon planned to visit China in February the next year and seek a rapprochement with China, virtually "leapfrogging over Tokyo's head to Beijing" as the Japanese press put it at that time.

That October, the long-pending question of China's admission to the United Nations was settled at last, and Taiwan was expelled.

Both Washington and Tokyo, however, stood firm in defense of Taiwan throughout the process. Counter to the majority-backed Albanian proposal for "inviting China and ousting Taiwan," Japan and the United States came up with an eclectic proposal of "dual representation," whereby "China's membership in the UN is to be recognized, while Taiwan is to retain its seat in the UN and its status as permanent member of the Security Council." Japan went ahead and moved that both China's admission to the UN and Taiwan's expulsion be separately designated as "an important item on the agenda" (requiring a two-thirds majority vote). The motion failed to carry. Back at home in the Japanese Diet, opposition parties moved a vote of no confidence in foreign minister Fukuda Takeo, the inheritor of Kishi Nobusuke's faction. Twelve pro-China members of the ruling Liberal Democratic Party, including the influential Fujiyama Aiichiro, in effect supported the no-confidence motion by absenting themselves from the plenary session of the House of Representatives. Yet a majority of LDP members accepted the government's pro-Taiwan maneuvering at the UN as "understandable" or "unavoidable."

They could not stem the tide for long. Once Tanaka Kakuei, who took office as Prime Minister in July 1972, decided to normalize relations with China, bilateral negotiations, until then stalemated, began to proceed apace. It was the pro-Taiwan faction of the LDP that protested in chorus this time. They claimed they were not opposed to Japan–China diplomatic relations as such, but they would never agree to breaking off relations with Taiwan in exchange for the proposed normalization. Inasmuch as China was adamant about the "one China" principle, the idea of maintaining relations with both China and Taiwan was unrealistic, but the pro-Taiwan faction raised this battlecry nonetheless.

The pro-Taiwan faction's leading spokesman, Kaya Okinori, published an essay in August 1972 titled *Taiwan kirisute no bokyo o imashimeru* (Remonstrance against the recklessness of abandoning Taiwan), in which he contended on jurisprudential grounds that, in terms of international law, China's recognition should not necessarily mean Taiwan's ouster. He then listed six reasons why Japan should not abandon Taiwan: (i) the long years of friendly relations until now, (ii) Taiwan's track record of collaboration with fellow members of the free-world camp, (iii) the sheer injustice of normalizing relations with a communist country and de-normalizing them with a free country, (iv) the blatant discourtesy and immorality of unilaterally abandoning Taiwan, a country that had done nothing either unjust or unlawful to Japan, (v) Japan's four-fold deep indebtedness to Taiwan, and (vi) the absence of any contingent crisis that might provide an excuse for not acknowledging Japan's serious debts of gratitude to Taiwan.[1]

It is on his point (v), Japan's serious indebtedness on four counts, that Kaya elaborated most extensively, and those "four counts" came to serve as the rationale and battle cry of the pro-Taiwan position. He argues:

(a) Given the antagonism of the Chinese toward Japan for its long years of invasion and given the many difficulties caused by the sheer chaos in the systems of transportation and other domestic infrastructure in the Republic of China in the immediate aftermath of the war, it would normally be simply inconceivable to rapidly and safely repatriate the 2.2 million Japanese soldiers and residents stranded in mainland China at that time; any number of tragedies and atrocities might have been triggered, reported, and accepted as inevitable and unavoidable, but as it turned out, Generalissimo Chiang Kaishek's famous motto of "Repaying Violence with Virtue" was translated into action literally and thoroughly. Despite all the obstacles encountered and requirements involved, Japanese residents and soldiers were sent home swiftly and safely, for which Japan is deeply indebted to him and to the Republic of China.

(b) In order to ensure political stability under the postwar conditions prevailing in Japan and to preserve the continuity of the nation-state and its perpetual regime, it was absolutely necessary to preserve the Emperor system in Japan. Again, it was Generalissimo Chiang Kaishek who blocked USSR-led machinations to abolish it. It should be up to the Japanese people themselves to decide whether to retain or to scrap the centuries-old institution, he insisted, and the monarchy survived the crisis that threatened its very existence thanks in no small measure to his principled insistence.

(c)   Thirdly, it was also Generalissimo Chiang Kaishek who saved Japan from being divided and occupied by multiple powers after the war. Having accepted the Potsdam Declaration, Japan was in no position to protest against its occupation by the Allied Powers, which as a matter of common sense meant that Japan had no further right to complain if, say, the Russians had occupied Hokkaido, the Americans Honshu, and the Chinese Kyushu. Had this actually taken place, divided Japan would have been penalized much more painfully than it was in fact, and defeated Japan could not have been rehabilitated as swiftly as it was in fact. Suffice to observe what happened to those countries that had the misfortune to be both divided and occupied.

(d)   In the matter of reparations, China was entitled to the largest share of rights and claims. Had China insisted on obtaining them, Japan would have been obliged to pay crippling reparations amidst the misery and squalor of its postwar economic conditions, and, needless to say, whatever prospects Japan had for economic reconstruction and development would have been severely compromised.[2]

Kaya, quondam Class A war criminal at the Tokyo Trials and president of the Japan Association of the Bereaved Families of War Dead, interestingly appears in paragraph (a) above to accept Japan's "invasion" as an incontrovertible premise. Be that as it may, it is obvious that all four counts of indebtedness were indeed owed by Japan to Chiang Kaishek, who ran the Kuomintang regime, which controlled China at that time. Inasmuch as he was subsequently defeated by the Chinese Communist Party and expelled to Taiwan, the pro-Taiwan elements in Japan felt some squeamishness about betraying their benefactor in distress. In the same essay Kaya declared, "Japan has yet to officially and gratefully acknowledge its indebtedness. . . . Far from repaying this obligation, Japan is disregarding reason and breaking faith by severing its diplomatic relations with Taiwan—the very height of immorality." In this he was invoking compassion rather than the emotionless logic of international diplomacy.

"Repaying Violence with Virtue": A motto with an anti-communist motive

The four counts of indebtedness require some explaining. Chiang Kaishek's motto of "repaying violence with virtue" in paragraph (a) above was used in his radio appeal to the nation broadcast from Chongqing on August 15th, 1945, the day of Japan's unconditional surrender. He in effect exhorted the Chinese "not to repay violence with violence." His appeal was heeded, the motto was translated into action, and apart from those detained as war criminals, over two million Japanese soldiers, paramilitaries, and civilian residents were allowed to come home in safety by June 1946, without being subjected to retaliatory measures like forced labor. This benevolent treatment was in stark contrast to the way the Russian army hauled Japanese soldiers to Siberian forced labor camps.

The question of whether the Emperor system should be preserved, mentioned in paragraph (b) above, dates back to November 1943. At the triumviri conference with American president Roosevelt and British prime minister Churchill on what to do with Japan after the war, Chiang opined that "the Japanese people should decide whether to keep the Emperor system," but added that, in his personal opinion, he believed that "Japan needs the Emperor system." On learning about this statement some years later in Japan, nationalist elements in particular found it gratifying, even titillating.

The reference in paragraph (c) above to "blocking the Russian occupation" refers to the five-nation (the US, the UK, France, China, and the USSR) foreign ministers' conference held in

London in September 1945. Anxious to prevent the exclusively American occupation of Japan and to have a Russian contingent included in the occupation forces, Russian foreign minister Molotov unexpectedly moved to demand a joint occupation of Japan, to which foreign minister Wang Shijie of the Republic of China, in consultation with US Secretary of State Burns, strenuously objected and managed to shelve the Molotov proposal. While the USSR persistently and vehemently repeated its demand, Chiang Kaishek in January 1946 declined at the last moment the US invitation to dispatch and station a Chinese contingent in Japan, his reason being that "for the Republic of China to send troops to Japan would afford a convenient excuse for the Russians to insist on their demand."

I find this rationale intriguing. Having been directly victimized by fifteen years of invasion by the Japanese military, China could indisputably have claimed the right to occupy Japan. If China had acted on its right, the Japanese people's lopsided sense of having been beaten by the Americans (as discussed earlier, in Part III, Chapter 5) might have been attenuated and at least some awareness of having been beaten by Asia might have developed instead. There is more to it than this, however. If the Republic of China had actually sent troops to Japan, the USSR would most likely have acted on its demand. A most problematic "what if . . ." of history!

The final item, "renouncing the right to war reparations," mentioned in paragraph (d) above, was indeed an important factor in Japan's economic reconstruction. The fifteen-year war had caused immeasurable damage to China. Casualties exceeded ten million, and economic losses had reached astronomical proportions. While the San Francisco Peace Treaty provided for war reparations, the Republic of China in its peace treaty with Japan renounced all such claims except for those on its overseas assets. Reminiscing about those days, Chiang Kaishek spoke as follows:

> This is how we thought about it. The damages that the Republic of China had suffered indeed reached astronomical proportions, and the sadness of those bereaved of their own flesh and blood

could not be assuaged by monetary compensations. But exacting from Japan huge sums of money in reparation at this point in time would be tantamount to depriving it of its sustenance. With the Red imperialist forces now intent on grabbing Japan, anything in our policy likely to enfeeble Japan would be counterproductive. It is in the interest of stability in Asia that Japan remain a fortified bastion of anti-communism.[3]

The "four counts of indebtedness" in Kaya's tract were thus not simply a matter of repaying kindness in general, but were all closely tied up with the cause of anti-communism.

Kaya's rationale for not rashly normalizing diplomatic relations between Japan and China, widely shared by the pro-Taiwan elements in Japan, included these facts among others:

(i)   The state of war between Japan and China ceased as of August 1945.

(ii) The Republic of China that Japan had fought against was represented by Chiang Kaishek's regime, not by the communist government that seized power in 1949.

(iii) The so-called "Five Principles of Peace" touted by China, including "mutual non-aggression" etc., are largely bogus—witness China's involvement in support of North Korea in the Korean War, its support of North Vietnam in the Vietnam War, and its backing of leftist revolutionary elements in Japan.

THE GENEALOGY OF THE PRO-TAIWAN FACTION AND THE FOREIGN MINISTRY'S ULTERIOR MOTIVE

In the final analysis, Kishi Nobusuke appears to be the founder-father of the pro-Taiwan faction, or the Taiwan lobby, in Japan. On his tour of Asian countries in 1957, Kishi established a close friendship with Chiang Kaishek, avowing that Japan would not espouse pro-communist positions and that the special relations between Japan and the Republic of China should dictate closer ties of association between them than with the rest of Southeast Asia. He went on to say, "The Chinese continent is now under communist rule, and I am very sympathetic about the difficult plight in which the Republic of China currently finds itself. All the deeper, however, is our sense that the two countries should collaborate more than ever."[4]

Chiang emphasized the need to "restore the Chinese people's freedom," and Kishi agreed with him, saying: "In sharp contrast to the way the Japanese people in general have had hostile, cold, or even irate feelings toward the USSR, they have affection for the Chinese people. This has nothing to do with whether they espouse communism. So in a sense, communist infiltration into Japan by way of China rather than of Russia would be more ominous and harder to bring under control. If the Chinese continent is restored to freedom, therefore, I shall be very, very happy."[5]

When Kishi conveyed his deepest sense of gratitude to Chiang for the "four counts of indebtedness"—as he reminisces about the meeting years later in his *Reminiscences*—Chiang replied, "'The idea of repaying violence with virtue' was really an application of the spirit of *bushido* [the code of the samurai warrior] that had been inculcated in me by practice as a young student in Japan under the tutelage of Messrs Tooyama, Inukai, and others. It represented the very foundation of Oriental philosophy and at the same time, quite impressively, of the Japanese spirit. It is not to me but to your own Japanese seniors and the spirit they embodied that you should be thankful."[6]

The reference here to Tooyama and Inukai means the nationalist Tooyama Mitsuru, who headed the right-wing Genyosha fraternity, and Inukai Tsuyoshi, who later became prime minister and was assassinated in the May 15th Incident. Both Tooyama and Inukai had given shelter to Sun Yatsen and other exiles and had also been to China at one time or another in support of the Xinhai Geming (the revolution of 1911 that toppled the Qing dynasty). That Chiang mentioned their names at all may have been designed to indirectly express his displeasure at Japan and the Japanese for having forgotten that same spirit and chosen instead to commit acts of aggression in Asia. Impervious to such implications, however, Kishi was simply "impressed" by Chiang's words. Influenced as he had been by ultra-nationalist mentors, Kishi may even have felt quite flattered.

On his visit to the United States after his first Asian tour, Kishi repeatedly mentioned the Chinese peril. For example, in his address to the US Senate, he warned, "International communism is scheming to sweep over the whole of Asia by exploiting the nationalistic fever of Asian peoples and their anxiety to overcome poverty and scarcity."[7] Kishi's warning was in sharp contrast to Yoshida Shigeru's attitude: Yoshida, though no less anti-communist, did not regard Chinese communism as a major threat but calculated pragmatically that associating with China rather than with Taiwan would bring more benefits.

When Kishi met Chiang Kaishek sometime later, according to Kishi Nobusuke's *Reminiscences*, Kishi once admonished him against discriminatory treatment of the indigenous population in Taiwan. To which Chiang replied, "The Taiwanese have been here all the time and have their roots firmly put down so they have no difficulty living the way they do. Those who have followed me and came over here with me have left everything behind on the continent. I am aware of the inequalities you mean, but I do not intend to stay here very long anyway."[8] When Kishi suggested that it would be impossible to conquer the continent by military means and that it would be better to build a "realm of peace and prosperity" in Taiwan and demonstrate the superiority of freedom, Chiang is said to have replied, "I will take your very moderate proposal into consideration, but I am afraid that a solution will have to be found in military terms."[9]

At the time when Tanaka Kakuei made up his mind to normalize diplomatic relations between Japan and China, the Taiwan lobby was centered round Kaya and senior politicians of his ilk like Shiina Etsusaburo, Funada Naka, Nadao Hirokichi, and young turks like Fujio Masayuki, Watanabe Michio, Nakagawa Ichiro, Ishihara Shintaro, Nakayama Masaaki, and Hamada Koichi. The Council on Normalizing Japan–China Relations that was set up during the Tanaka cabinet turned out to be an arena for a clash between the pro-China and pro-Taiwan factions. At a session held on August 15, 1972, in which Ohira Masayoshi, the foreign minister proposing to sever relations with Taiwan, was called to witness, Kaya, Watanabe, Nakagawa, and Fujio treated him like an accused in a kangaroo court trial, stressing the importance of Japan's long-standing and special relations with Taiwan.

It is worth noting that the pro-Taiwan faction's logic coincided with the ulterior motive of the foreign ministry officials. Having been almost exclusively concerned over the years just with collaboration with the United States, an overwhelming majority of them were reluctant to see Japan acting on its own and standing out when the United States, even after the Washington–Beijing summitry, had some qualms, because of its relations with Taiwan, about going ahead and normalizing diplomatic relations with China. In their bureaucratic frame of mind, they also probably hated to jeopardize or undermine their long-standing claim that "the state of war with China ceased with the Japan–Republic of China Peace Treaty." It appeared at that point in time that Hashimoto Hiroshi, then chief of the China section and later ambassador to China, was the solitary proponent in the entire ministry for establishing diplomatic relations with China. Such a climate of opinion at the foreign ministry was encouraging to the pro-Taiwan faction in the LDP. The younger members—Watanabe, Nakagawa, and Ishihara—would later organize a clique named Seiran-kai (meaning literally "refreshing mountain air meeting") to rally the party's hawks.

Sato Eisaku, Kishi's younger brother, was the last of the postwar prime ministers in Japan to stay loyal to Taiwan. Like his predecessor Ikeda Hayato, Sato was a disciple of Yoshida Shigeru and belonged to Yoshida's circle of personal connections. Probably for that reason, he was well aware of the unfinished business of improving Japan–China relations, and for a time before he assumed power, was eager to do something about it. With utmost secrecy in 1964, for instance, he had a meeting with the Chinese business tycoon Nan Hanchen on his visit to Japan (for which the stage had been set by Kuno Chuji, one of the few pro-China members in the

Sato faction). Furthermore, Sato even had a scheme to arrange a conference with Zhou Enlai.[10] Once in power, however, Sato managed to conclude the Japan–Republic of Korea Treaty but dragged his feet about breaking the deadlock in Japan–China relations. Soon after he assumed office as prime minister, the war in Vietnam escalated as the United States began bombing the North, and the onset of the Great Proletarian Cultural Revolution threw the whole of China into a state of utter confusion, so that Sato, *nolens volens*, drifted into an increasingly pro-Taiwan and anti-China position.

Having staked his political career on bringing off the reversion of Okinawa, Sato presumably had every reason to comply as much as possible with US intentions. It was at the Nixon–Sato summitry of November 1969 that the prospective reversion of Okinawa in 1972 was finalized, the agreement being that Okinawa would be nuclear-free and that US troops stationed in Okinawa would be subject to the same Status of Forces Treaty as those on the mainland. The joint declaration issued on that occasion specifically contained the so-called "ROK and Taiwan" clauses that recognized the vital importance of Korea's security to Japan's security and the great importance also to Japan's security of the maintenance of peace and security in the Taiwan area. China naturally found these provisos quite provocative, but Sato presumably was prepared to take that particular risk for the time being in order to consolidate the Japan–US axis and to bring off the coveted reversion of Okinawa.

There were some signs in the Sato cabinet of gropings toward a breakthrough in Japan–China relations. When Governor Minobe Ryokichi of Tokyo visited China, for example, Sato's cabinet secretary, Hori Shigeru, asked him to convey a written message to Beijing. The basic anti-China stance of the Sato cabinet remained unchanged to the end. Though under Yoshida's tutelage, Sato himself felt indebted to Chiang Kaishek, and was in addition fettered by the need of his own cabinet to secure the support of his brother Kishi and pro-Taiwan elders like Ishii Mitsujiro, Kaya, Funada, and Nadao. Sato Shinji, his second son, is now a Dietman and a prominent member of the Diet Round-Table of Japan–Republic of China

Relations set up by the pro-Taiwan faction and chaired by Fujio Masayuki.

THE DELICATE BALANCE BETWEEN CHINA AND THE USSR

Fukuda Takeo expected that Sato would abdicate and that he would be next, but Tanaka Kakuei beat him to it. The Kishi faction's heir apparent and the foreign minister in the Sato cabinet who voiced opposition to China's admission to the United Nations, Fukuda had natural links with the Taiwan lobby. In his autobiography, *Kaiko kyujunen* (Ninety years in retrospect),[11] published just before his death in July 1995, Fukuda admits that "If there seemed to be a general feeling at that time that Japan's diplomatic measures vis-à-vis China lacked initiative and were largely belated reactions after the event, it was because the party failed to achieve a consensus and because we had to take President Chiang Kaishek of Taiwan into consideration. . . . At a time when Taiwan under his leadership found itself in a very difficult position in the international community, I thought it was reasonable for us keep in mind our indebtedness to him and to conduct ourselves accordingly."

Having been a member of the finance ministry elite in prewar times, Fukuda did not have a grandiose sense like Kishi of "Greater Asianism," but, like Kishi, he did have his formative experience in China. During his seven years of service as a paymaster in charge of the Army Ministry, he made frequent trips of inspection in Manchuria and elsewhere in China, and later for two years beginning in 1941 at the height of the Sino–Japanese War, served as fiscal adviser to the pro-Japanese puppet government of Wang Zhaoming in Nanjing. It was in Nanjing that he learned about the declaration of war against the United States.

Fukuda had gained the full confidence of Wang Zhaoming by the time he turned to Japan in June 1943. As he put it in his autobiography:

Chairman Wang Zhaoming appeared to be very sorry about my departure. More than anyone else in the group of advisers, he had taken me into his confidence, and consulted me on not just fiscal but other matters as well. He joked to those around him, "Chinese clothing becomes Adviser Fukuda very well. He looks just like one of us and we feel at ease talking to him. . . ." Shortly before the day of my departure, the Chairman gave a farewell party for me, wrote a poem in calligraphy that read, "The ume (Japanese apricot) blossom is pure in spirit," had it mounted on a hanging scroll, and handed it to me as a farewell present.[12]

Once a follower and protégé of Sun Yatsen in the Xinhai Geming (revolution of 1911 that toppled the Qing dynasty), Wang Zhaoming rose to the highest position in the Kuomintang next only to Chiang Kaishek after Sun Yatsen's death, but soon parted company with Chiang: while Chiang's scenario for saving the nation called for resistance against Japan, Wang advocated peace with Japan. So it was with Japan's backing that Wang established a nationalist government in Nanjing in 1940.

Fukuda's formative experience as fiscal advisor in the puppet regime was analogous in a way to Kishi's as a high-echelon official in Manchukuo. Though Fukuda recognized that the current of the times dictated the normalization of relations with China, he hesitated to go ahead and be done with it, because on the one hand, he had to take Taiwan into consideration, and on the other, he needed to strike a delicate balance between China and the Soviet Union. As he later attested in his autobiography:

> Given that China and the Soviet Union are locked in a deadly family feud with each other, Japan as their common neighbor finds itself in a dilemma. Make friends with China, and Russia will get sore; go along with Russia, and our relations with China will be jeopardized.[13]

Even after the normalization of Japan–China relations, the hawkish Seiran-kai was adamantly opposed to bilateral airline negotiations, and it was an open secret in the political community that Fukuda was pulling the strings. The Fukuda faction included many pro-Taiwan members for one thing, and Fukuda undoubtedly wanted to make a nuisance of himself to the Tanaka cabinet over the controversial issue.

Fukuda eventually became prime minister and managed to conclude the Treaty of Peace and Friendship between Japan and the People's Republic of China, but the hardest knot to untangle in the process of negotiations had to do with the question of balancing China and Russia. The Taiwan Lobby put up a strong resistance and caused him great distress, but Fukuda reminisces:

> Central in the so-called "cautious" school were not a few close friends of mine like Nadao Hirokichi, Machimura Kingo, Fujio Masayuki, and others. We had been through a lot together, in both good times and bad, and I was sure that in the end they would accept whatever decision I was going to make. As it turned out, I was right. But I did have to work damn hard to put together a package acceptable to them all. As a matter of fact, I flattered myself that nobody but me could bring off this deal.[14]

Miki Takeo, Tanaka's successor and Fukuda's predecessor in office and a leader of the pro-China faction, had failed to achieve unanimity in the LDP for a peace treaty with China. Fukuda had reasons for gloating over his achievement.

Chapter 8 | The Pro-China Faction and Nostalgia for the Continent

THE PRO-CHINA FACTION ON THE OFFENSIVE: TOWARD NOR-MALIZATION

THE PRO-CHINA FACTION ON THE OFFENSIVE: TOWARD NOR-MALIZATION

Once the Tanaka cabinet decided to go ahead and normalize diplomatic relations with China, pro-China members of the LDP rallied to overpower the resistance of the pro-Taiwan faction. Earlier in December 1970, the nonpartisan Parliamentarians' Union for the Normalization of Relations with China was organized, with Fujiyama Aiichiro as Chairman. A majority of both the Houses of Representatives and of Councilors, and of both the ruling and opposition parties, including nearly a hundred members of the LDP, joined the bipartisan group. Participating in the World Ping Pong Championship held in Nagoya in March 1971, China exercised "ping pong diplomacy" a few months ahead of the announcement in July of US President Nixon's visit to China. In an attempt to pave the way for the prospective normalization, the Parliamentarians' Union sent to China a delegation headed by Fujiyama in September.

As related in Chapter 7, however, the Japanese government kept up its vain opposition to United Nations recognition for mainland China to the bitter end. When the opposition parties moved a vote of no-confidence in then foreign minister Fukuda Takeo, Fujiyama and eleven other members of the LDP went along with it by absenting themselves from the plenary session of the House of Representatives. Fujiyama's rebels included Utsunomiya Tokuma, Kawasaki Hideji, Furui Yoshimi, Kujiraoka Hyosuke, Tagawa

139

Seiichi, Kono Yohei, Nishioka Takeo, Yamaguchi Toshio, Sakamoto Misoji, Shionoya Kazuo, and Suganami Shigeru. Kono at that time was still a two-term fledgling but already a vocal member of the party's Council on Normalizing Japan–China Relations who braved the ire of the pro-Taiwan faction by openly calling for "decisively severing relations with Taiwan."

Kono's father Ichiro was a dyed-in-the-wool LDP politician who had supported Hatoyama Ichiro and headed his own faction, with his mind set on seizing power, when Ikeda Hayato stepped down. When Sun Pinghua and Wang Xiaoyun of the China–Japan Friendship Association came to Japan in 1963 as "Representatives of the Orchid-Lovers Association of China," he had a meal together with them—in utmost secrecy because he was an LDP cabinet minister—and according to Tagawa Seiichi, told them with abundant self-confidence:

> Bureaucrats-turned-politicians like Ikeda and Sato are just not up to the job of restoring relations with China. Leave it to me and I will do it when the time is ripe.[1]

If Kono Ichiro, and not Sato Eisaku, had succeeded to Ikeda Hayato, Japan–China relations would have turned out somewhat differently, to say the least. Kono Ichiro's untimely death prevented him from making it to the top, but his son Yohei's youthful commitment to the restoration of ties with China presumably was more genuinely motivated than his father's and had much less to do with any rivalry with political peers with bureaucrat backgrounds.

In sharp contrast to the way hawkish young Turks set up the Seiran-kai fraternity within the LDP, Kono, Tagawa, Nishioka, and Yamaguchi would later make a foursome, secede from the LDP and form the Shinjiyu (or New Liberal) Club. As the new political group was launched in the wake of the Lockheed scandal, it was often regarded as a splinter party with anti-Tanaka motives, but there was more to it than that. Kono and other supporters of the pro-China line had originally been pro-Tanaka in diplomatic policy, and rather strongly anti-Fukuda in sentiment. In the "Forty-Day Contest" for power between Fukuda and Ohira Masayoshi in 1979, the New

Liberal Club voted for the incumbent Ohira largely because of a sense of affinity cultivated since the days leading up to the controversial establishment of Japan–China relations.

As for the rebellious dozen who went along with the vote of nonconfidence in Fukuda, it is noteworthy that more than half of them, including Utsunomiya, belonged to the Miki faction. Miki Takeo, who shared a political destiny with Matsumura Kenzo, was favorable to the normalization of relations between Japan and China, and often asked Tagawa Seiichi to act as his intermediary with any visiting VIP from China. Miki was as certain as Kono Ichiro that "no bureaucrat could restore diplomatic relations between Japan and China."

As it turned out, it was Tanaka Kakuei campaigning on a normalization platform who carried off the palm in the post-Sato contest for power. Of the four candidates for the Presidency in the 1972 LDP election—Tanaka, Fukuda Takeo, Miki Takeo, and Ohira Masayoshi—it was Tanaka and Fukuda who survived the first ballot and were placed in the run-off. The matter was settled when Miki and Ohira decided to support Tanaka because he pledged a breakthrough in Japan–China relations. Years before, in 1954, Hatoyama Ichiro had come to power on a platform of normalizing diplomatic relations between Japan and the USSR; now history repeated itself as diplomatic relations between Japan and China became a crucial bone of contention in another change of regime.

If the Taiwan Lobby had its own logic and sentiment, what then of the pro-China faction? The mainstay indisputably of the proChina school had been Matsumura Kenzo, whose direct political descendents included Tagawa Seiichi, who made a foursome with Kono Yohei and others, bolted from the LDP, and formed the New Liberal Club. In June 1972, just before the Tanaka cabinet got started, Tagawa published a collection of essays titled *Matsumura Kenzo to Chugoku* (Matsumura Kenzo and China) in memory of his mentor who had died the summer before. The last essay in the volume, "Essentials of the Japan–China Problem," presents a easy-to-understand exegesis of the logic of Sino–Japanese diplomatic relations, as summarized in the following:[2]

— The state of war with China has not ceased in terms of international law: the Japan–Republic of China Peace Treaty, which some argue put an end to the said state of war, was concluded with Chiang Kaishek's government in exile in Taiwan two and a half years after China's government in Beijing was established, and could in no way be taken as a legitimate treaty with China.

— It was under strong pressure from the United States that Japan, after the San Francisco Peace Treaty, opted for Taiwan as its partner and concluded the Japan–Republic of China Peace Treaty. The government of Japan did not thereby recognize the Taiwan regime as the lawful government representing the whole of China: witness the limited range of the text of the said Treaty. Chiang Kaishek had no say in the disposal of the territory and people in China that he had lost.

— The statement regarding "repaying violence with virtue" in the immediate aftermath of the war spoke not for Chiang personally but for the people of China as a whole. Acts of mercy extended to the Japanese soldiers in defeat represented China's moral principles. Chiang no doubt was magnanimous, but it is to the people of China, not to Chiang personally, that we should bear debts of gratitude.

— The enemy that Japan fought in its war with China was, some would theorize, Chiang Kaishek's regime. Have they forgotten how the Japanese government issued a statement during the war that it would "have nothing to do with Chiang Kaishek" and set up a puppet regime instead? The Chinese government has indicated it will renounce its reparation claims, so that Japan need not fear new claims.

Scathing in his criticism of the pro-Taiwan elements, Tagawa writes in the same essay:

> They emotionally detest China, do not care to know anything about China, and object purely and simply to the normalization of any relations with China. They don't want to have anything to do with

China, merely because China maintains socialistic institutions and because, fanatic believers in anti-communism, they fear that any exchange with China would only precipitate the spread of communism in Japan. Those who hold to such a position are often precisely those who not only measure China with the same yardstick and prejudice as in the prewar years but also cultivate an indulgent sense of their own superiority over Chinese and other Asians while suffering at the same time from an inferiority complex vis-à-vis Europeans and Americans.[3]

MATSUMURA KENZO AND HIS SENSE OF "ATONEMENT"

There was a robust pro-China strain in Japan that survived the long years of ruptured diplomatic relations and a prolonged state of hostility between Japan and China, and ran through the postwar conservative community. Apart from Ishibashi Tanzan, whose relevance was discussed above in Part III, Chapter 4, it was Matsumura Kenzo who was the mainstay of the pro-China line. Special mention should be given to his role in steering the course of events leading to the normalization of diplomatic relations with China.

Matsumura's career was somewhat different from Ishibashi's, whose out-and-out resistance to Japan's invasion into China dated back to the prewar years. Born in 1883 into an old apothecary family in Toyama Prefecture, Matsumura graduated from Waseda University, served on the staff of the *Hochi Shimbun* newspaper, was elected to the Toyama prefectural assembly, joined the Democratic Party and won a seat in the House of Representatives in 1928. The climate of the times was against political parties: they were being disbanded as war loomed ever more ominously on the horizon. Matsumura sensed "a national crisis" and joined the national mobilization machinery, serving as Chairman of the Political Affairs Research Committee of the Imperial Rule Assistance Party, and then as Secretary General of the Greater Japan Political Association. He complied with a government request to supervise a program to increase food production in Manchuria and was stalked by a US submarine when crossing the Strait of Korea.

Matsumura later came to repent of the way he had conducted himself in the prewar years. As he admitted in private, "I had no choice but to act the way I did, but the fact that I failed to resist the military even single-handedly and to hold fast to my convictions has left an indelible stain on my career."[4] His postwar commitment to friendly relations between Japan and China stemmed, in other words, from self-critique. He embodied, as it were, a sense of atonement, and he differed in this respect from Ishibashi.

When his purge from public service after the war was lifted, Matsumura worked closely with Miki Takeo and others, and became secretary general of the Progressive Party, a minor conservative group. After the grand conservative coalition, he headed the "Miki–Matsumura" faction, and achieved renown as a politician of impeccable integrity. In the 1959 LDP election in which Kishi Nobusuke was re-elected President, Matsumura ran as the representative of the anti-Kishi camp, heedless of his small chances of victory. In all probability, he wanted to stand for a view of China that was antipodal to Kishi's.

His encounter with China dated back to 1904 when he visited China for the first time as a Waseda University student. In those closing years of the Qing dynasty, China's territory had been overrun by Western powers and was in a state of utter chaos. Later, as a newspaperman, he visited Manchuria as a special correspondent and interviewed Zhang Zuolin. In 1922 he went to China in the suite of Nagai Ryutaro, a House Democrat and a Waseda graduate like him. Soon after he himself won a seat in the House of Representatives in 1928, he made another visit to China with a team of investigators of the Jinan Incident, and happened to be on the scene when Zhang Zuolin was killed by a bomb. It is these repeated experiences in China while he was relatively young that account for the intensity of feeling and concern for China that he would manifest years later. In short, Matsumura differed from Ishibashi also in terms of formative experience.

Matsumura's postwar reencounter with China occurred at his meeting with Guo Moruo and Liao Chengzhi, two Japanologists who visited Japan in 1955 and 1957 one on the heels of the other. He was deeply impressed with the writer-politician Guo Moruo's likening the revolution in the New China to the Meiji Restoration in Japan, and the meeting soon afterwards with Liao Chengzhi cemented his sense of affinity.

Guo Moruo's reference to the Meiji Restoration was repeated in a round-table talk with Tanizaki Junichiro and others as reported in the *Asahi Shimbun* (December 7, 1955):

> Everything has changed. The Chinese used to be all lazy, but now it is all different. And they have done a lot of work in the last six years. How did it happen? The way I interpret it, nothing is unprecedented: the Meiji Restoration was definitely a precedent, and the Reformation of the Taika era, a still earlier example. . . . Western historians regard the Meiji Restoration as an "Oriental miracle." It is in precisely the same sense that we may regard the changes in the new China as a "second Oriental miracle."

According to Furukawa Mantaro's *Nitchu sengo kankei-shi* (A history of postwar Japan–China relations), Matsumura met Guo Moruo the day before the round-table talk above. When Matsumura asked what had been the key to the success of the Chinese Revolution in achieving national unification and in winning popular support, Guo answered: "Compare the Meiji Restoration or the Reformation of the Taika era in Japan with the recent liberation of China, and you will find a lot of similarities." As Furukawa put it, "The dialogue with Guo Moruo seems to have aroused in Matsumura a feeling, not for 'socialistic China,' but for 'nationalistic China' fired with high hopes for national unity and development, which left a deep impression on him." His reaction contrasts sharply with Kishi's description in 1957 (see Chapter 7) of "China exploiting nationalistic fever in Asia."

Be that as it may, Guo Moruo's reference to the Meiji Restoration and his description of the Chinese Revolution as a "second Oriental miracle" appear linked to the notion since Sun

Yatsen of solidarity in the New Asia. As described above, Kishi was moved by Chiang Kaishek's revelation that he had learned the spirit of "repaying violence with virtue" from his Japanese mentors like Tooyama Mitsuru and Inukai Tsuyoshi. Sun Yatsen from an Asian point of view admired Japan for its victory in the Russo–Japanese war. As will be discussed below, Kishi on his visit to India was congratulated by prime minister Nehru on "Japan's accomplishment in the Russo–Japanese war"; Ikeda Hayato was told in Burma (now Myanmar) of that country's desire for "nation building on the model of the Meiji Revolution." Different though they were in political outlook, these political leaders of Meiji generation Japan had their vanity tickled by such praise from Asian leaders.

Matsumura's first visit to China after the war was in the fall of 1959, shortly after Ishibashi Tanzan's long-hoped-for visit to China the previous summer. Kishi was in power then and the US–Japan Security Treaty was due for revision the next year. There had been a deplorable incident at the Chinese Philatelic Exhibition held in Nagasaki, in which some right-wingers dragged down the Five-Golden-Stars-in-the-Red-Sky Flag of China, and Japan–China trade was suspended, which also reflected China's objections to Kishi's political stance: China was extremely nervous about pro-Taiwan Kishi negotiating a revision of the US–Japan Security Treaty.

Matsumura had forty days to visit the back regions and elsewhere across China's vast territory, and his visit successfully paved the way for the "Liao-Takasaki (L-T) trade" agreement to be later signed and put into effect by Liao Chengshi and Takasaki Tatsunosuke, for a journalists' exchange program, and for ashes-gathering tours by the war-bereaved. Yet by far the biggest fruit of the visit was his meeting and frank exchange with Zhou Enlai on four occasions as well as with other Chinese leaders.

In contradistinction to Asanuma Inejiro, Secretary General of the Japan Socialist Party, who aroused criticism by declaring, on his visit to China earlier in the spring of the same year, that "American imperialism is the common enemy of the peoples of Japan and China," Matsumura was conservative enough to be prepared to defend the Kishi cabinet and its political orientation. Bitter words were exchanged, therefore, at his meetings with Zhou Enlai, but they managed nonetheless to establish a relationship of mutual trust. And while he did not live long enough to see diplomatic relations normalized between Japan and China, Matsumura did contribute immeasurably to the process.

The right-wingers hated him, branded him as public enemy, and threatened him with "death by the hand of God for the treacherous attempt via Japan–China negotiations to turn Japan into a communist state." An extremist armed with a gun did once force his way into his home, but Matsumura laughed him off by saying, "The Japanese people are knowledgeable enough to not to be easily brainwashed by any ideological warfare from abroad"[6]—another sign, it might be said, of the nationalistic disposition typical of Meiji generation leaders.

After his second visit to China after the war in 1962, Matsumura contributed an essay titled *Watashi no Ajia-kan* (My view of Asia) to the January 1963 issue of the prestigious monthly *Shiso* (Thoughts and ideas).[7] Impressed during a previous recent visit to Europe with the way the European Economic Community was being geared for political integration, he wrote: "Once the political integration of the EEC is complete, it may be too late for us to begin cudgeling our brains about problems in Asia." He then went on to present his view of China, which clearly reflected his feeling of affinity with other Asian races. The Chinese people, or the Han race, had their own tradition distinct from the Soviet version of communism, he pointed out, as reflected for example in the survival in China of love of their country and in their religion, and in such magnificent architectural monuments as the Renmin Dahuitang (Great Hall of the People) "which was reminiscent of palaces built by Emperor Shihuangdi of the Qin Dynasty."

His expertise in agronomy made him worry about China's stalled agriculture. "The planted acreage of paddy fields in particular is in bad shape," Matsumura noted, "as a result, I suspect, of having listened to Russian farming experts with no experience in wet-rice cultivation. I believe it is only Japan that can be of help in remedying the situation in terms of human resources, fertilizers, and other agricultural requirements." He concluded this section of the essay by noting, "I keenly feel that negotiations for these and other matters are facilitated and mutual perceptions improved by historical associations between the Chinese and the Japanese—particularly those bonds of affinity based on 'the same script and the same race.'" Moreover, he said:

> It will be necessary for us to stake our future on working with the rest of Asia, to extend willing hands to China in a spirit of mutual helpfulness. Pundits in the USA and elsewhere, and mind you, in some quarters in Japan as well, suggest that we should just turn a cold shoulder to China for some more time and a crippling shortage of food will put a natural end to it. Nothing could be more dangerous than their presumption that they could, in the meantime, rely on the USA to stay in the background while Japan, the ROK, and Taiwan consolidate their systems of joint defense. It is only natural for Japan as a member of the free nations to be friendly with the USA, but the very idea of turning a cold shoulder to China is as anachronistic as Napoleon's notion two hundred years ago of a continental blockade.

Matsumura was worried about the possible perpetuation of antagonism between the USA and China, once enemies in the Korean war, and entertained dreams of seeing Japan play the role of go-between bringing the USA "as a fellow member of the Free World" closer to China as a nation sharing "the same script and the same race" as Japan.

A PRO-CHINA MEMBER WHO DID A TURNABOUT

The first group of people to try to cultivate friendly relations with China after the war included some unconventional politicians. Hoashi Kei and others who visited the USSR and China in secret in June 1952 (and who signed into effect the first Japan–China Private Trade Agreement, as mentioned above in Part III, Chapter

6) were not of conservative lineage. Ikeda Masanosuke, who headed the parliamentary delegation to finalize the second Japan–China Private Trade Agreement, was a Liberal Party member of the House of Representatives, a close associate of Miki Bukichi and a self-appointed "shock trooper" of the Hatoyama faction. Affectionately nicknamed *Ike-Sho* (*Sho* being another reading of *Masa* of *Masa-no-suke*), he involved himself actively in negotiating the second through fourth rounds of the Japan–China Private Trade Agreement, and thus played a substantial role in the incipient phase of post-war Japan–China relations.

On his prewar visit to China in 1927 as a special correspondent for the *Yamato-Shimbun*, Ikeda availed himself of reference library resources at the South Manchuria Railway Company and familiarized himself with Chinese affairs, which later prompted him to fancy himself as a "China hand." He thus had motivation enough in the postwar situation to aim for a breakthrough in the deadlocked Japan–China talks. Subsequently, however, as Japan–China relations were put on the back burner during the Kishi cabinet, Ikeda turned anti-Chinese. This turnabout was presumably triggered by the acrimonious negotiations he conducted on his visit to China in 1957 in connection with the Agreement's fourth round. He found himself torn between the conflicting demands of the two governments concerning the proposed establishment of trade representatives and presumably got utterly sick of the whole business.

During these arduous negotiations, Ikeda was, as he himself put it, "confined in a cramped little hotel for over forty days, and as spent mentally and physically as if I had been placed under house arrest."[8] The negotiations hit a snag when the Kishi cabinet balked at a provision in the joint Note on the Establishment of Trade Representatives granting semi-governmental status to the proposed agencies, including the right to hoist the national colors. After the death of Miki Bukichi, his mentor, Ikeda had joined the Kishi faction, which included a number of pro-Taiwan members, so that his turnabout was said to have been partly motivated by factional considerations as well. Ikeda subsequently published two books in succession—*Nazo no kuni—Chugoku tairiku no jittai* (The realities of a mysterious country: communist continental China)[9] and *Shina minzoku no kaimei* (Explorations into the ethnicity of the Chinese)[10]—and distanced himself from China by his opposition to the normalization of diplomatic relations as being "premature." Matsumura and other pro-Chinese conservatives shared Ikeda's experience of being torn between conflicting demands of the two governments, so that Ikeda's turnabout bespoke the subtly shifting view of China inside the conservative camp.

The *Asahi Shimbun* once sponsored and published a dialogue (on 2 May 1968) between Ikeda and Utsunomiya Tokuma, an acknowledged leader of the pro-China camp, on the pros and cons of normalizing diplomatic relations between Japan and China. His conception of the Chinese Peril rested on a different dimension, one unrelated to fear of Chinese communism. As Ikeda put it to Utsunomiya:

> The Chinese historically have not been a peace-loving nation. Since the time of Emperor Shihuangdi of the Qin Imperial Reign, it was only during the Sui, Tang, and Song dynasties that they did not sally out on aggressive adventures abroad. There is no other country like that. In their attitude toward foreigners, they are quite ethnocentric, seeing themselves surrounded by "savages and barbarians on the east and the south, and aliens and primitives on the west and the north." There is no other nation like that in the whole world.

This sense of alarm at China may represent the other side of the coin to the sense of awe at China discussed below.

An active leader of the pro-Taiwan camp, Kishi of course was not on good terms with Matsumura and other members of the pro-China camp, nor was he enthusiastic about trade relations with China. In his *Reminiscences*, Kishi Nobusuke recalled how trade with China:

> . . . was not very attractive. The alleged principle of separating economic from political affairs purported to consolidate economic relations, but aimed in the long run at opening diplomatic relations with Communist China, for which economic and trade relations were

necessary trimmings. Trading with Communist China was not discussed in terms of its possible impact on Japan's industrial structure.

Kishi was savagely critical of:

> . . . a great majority of the LDP members in favor of promoting trade with communist China, who in fact make up the so-called pro-Chicom faction, and are ready to swallow whatever the Chicoms say, hook, line and sinker. Ikeda Masanosuke, I hasten to add, is an honorable exception.[11]

Regardless of Ikeda's turnabout, which presumably earned him the above-quoted flattering mention in Kishi's book, talks on establishing Japan–China ties continued to move forward. According to the principle of separating economic from political affairs, "Liao–Takasaki Trade" got under way in 1961, which provided, among other things, for Japanese exports to China on a deferred payment basis and for the export of a chemical plant to China. "Liao" was Liao Chengshi and Takasaki was Takasaki Tatsunosuke, who put together and signed the trade agreement. Takasaki was a businessman-turned-politician who had once served as president of Manchurian Heavy Industries. During the Kishi cabinet, he tried in vain to make a breakthrough in Japan–China trade, and had to wait until Matsumura's visit to China during the Ikeda cabinet to see his dream come true. Pragmatic in economic affairs, he was somewhat different from Matsumura in outlook, but his past record at Manchurian Heavy Industries apparently amplified his aspirations vis-à-vis China. He, too, had been touched by continental nostalgia. The political implications of the Liao–Takasaki trade agreement were naturally as significant as the economic ones.

THE OUTLOOK OF A PREWAR BUSINESSMAN: FUJIYAMA AIICHIRO

There was yet another businessman-turned-politician of influence, Fujiyama Aiichiro, who had had a formative experience in prewar

China. While still a student at Keio University he acted on his father's suggestion and traveled by ship from Nagasaki to Shanghai in 1917. He spent two months on a tour of China, and, as he put it in his *Seiji wagamichi* (My way in politics), he was:

> . . . in a word, awed by the country's sheer immensity . . . and by the vast number of people toiling for their livelihood in abject poverty.[12]

As fate would have it, he caught pleurisy while mountaineering in the rain on one occasion, which forced him to remain under medical care for the next seven years.

Even as a young man, Fujiyama was interested in China. His father owned and ran Dai-Nippon Sugar Manufacturing Company there. On the eve of the outbreak of war between Japan and China, he visited China again, in March 1937, as a member of the economic mission sent by the business community. He had a meeting with Chiang Kaishek, who pointedly reminded them of how "Viscount Shibusawa Eiichi, your senior by many years, admired the Analects of Confucius, in which it is said, 'Do not do unto others what you do not want to be done unto you.' Japan–China relations should be founded on this maxim." Meeting in Shanghai with university presidents, young entrepreneurs, fledging Kuomintang politicians, and others, Fujiyama expressed what he keenly felt:

> China is undergoing a momentous change. The Chinese are brimming with aspirations, more enthusiastic than I was given to understand, hoping to rebuff interference and oppression from abroad and to build a new China. It is absolutely necessary for Japan and China to do all they can to deepen mutual understanding.[13]

But he was swimming against the current of the times, and the two nations went to war. Fujiyama found himself caught up in the war regime and was named a standing member of the political division of the Imperial Rule Assistance Association. He tried to keep himself informed of events in China by collecting Chinese newspapers and magazines. He opened a flour milling joint venture in

Hangzhou, and a ship building company in Hongkong, and often went to China during the war.

Fujiyama's zeal for restoring diplomatic relations between Japan and China after the war must have been motivated by his prewar experiences. Having run a sugar manufacturing operation in Taiwan and known Chiang Kaishek personally, he wondered why the Kuomintang with its clever leaders, some of whom had even been educated abroad, should have been defeated by the Communist Party. He eventually came to believe that:

> ... it was because the Kuomintang was not loved by the people. The Communist troops waging a battle requisitioned provisions from the community, but returned goods once the battle was over, and they didn't move on to another front until the aftermath had been dealt with. They acted on the people's side. The Kuomintang soldiers, in contrast, were armed with state-of-the-art weapons but failed to have such consideration for the people. I keenly realized that the Kuomintang, being alienated from the people, failed to win their hearts, and got beaten as they should.[14]

REASONS OF THE HEART TRANSCENDING REASON

It is the cultural closeness between Japan and China that undoubtedly generates a deep sense of affinity on the part of Japanese politicians and ordinary Japanese as well. Take Kosaka Zentaro, for instance. He headed the LDP's Council on Normalizing Japan–China Relations and had a very hard time smoothing out intra-party disputes over the proposed normalization. Kosaka visited China in September 1992, during the 20th anniversary year of the restoration of diplomatic ties. Atop the Belvedere of the Yellow Crane in Wuhan, he complied with a request for a specimen of his handwriting by writing a couplet by his favorite poet Cui Hao, dating back to the 8th century. Based on an ancient Chinese legend, it went like this:

> Once the yellow crane has flown away, it will never return,
> And the sky is empty but for white clouds,
> Which hover there for a thousand years.

Miyazawa Kiichi, widely known as a devotee of Western rationalism, has also been familiar with the Chinese classics since childhood, and his erudition often proves a trial to political reporters who cover him. On stepping down from the office of prime minister in August 1993, he was asked at the press conference to speak his mind; tersely, he recited the following couplet in the original:

> If my close friend in Luoyang asks you how I am getting along these days,
>
> Tell him that my mind is as serene as a piece of ice floating in a jade urn.

Few reporters on that occasion could have recognized immediately it as a quotation from the poet Wang Changling dating back to the Tang dynasty.

The former Speaker of the Korean Parliament Kim Jaesun remembered reading a newspaper article on this particular feat of Miyazawa's upon his resignation, and, when he happened to meet Miyazawa during his visit to Japan in 1994, he commended Miyazawa for this act "befitting a great man." I happened to be there and heard the exchange, and I felt overwhelmed by their shared erudition. This cultural commonality is peculiar to Asia, or to be more exact, to the sphere of influence of the Chinese ideographic system of writing. This should also be true, *mutatis mutandis*, in Europe and the United States. Yet it is uncertain whether politicians in Japan and Korea will be able to keep alive this sort of sophisticated discourse in the years ahead. It is certain, in any event, that cultural commonalities have generated not only a deep sense of affinity to, but also a sense of awe of China.

As illustrated by Tagawa Seiichi's essay on Matsumura and Japan's Sinophobes at the outset of this chapter, the pro-China school clearly had a legitimate case in international geopolitical terms. But those early members who did their pioneering work during the years when the pro-Taiwan camp held undisputed sway seem to have been galvanized into action by reasons of the heart transcending reason. Their formative prewar experiences in China, the vastitude of the continent, the immensity of its population, the depth of its culture and history may have overlapped with their fond memories of the Meiji Restoration and combined to lead them, as it were, to fall in love with China.

Chapter 9 | # Yoshida's Disciples' Cool and Calm View on China: From Ikeda Hayato to Miyazawa Kiichi and Tanaka Kakuei

A DOUBLE STANDARD FOR CHINA AND THE USSR

Let us begin by tracing the political "family trees" of Ishibashi Tanzan and Matsumura Kenzo in the "Yoshida school" (the ideological family that grew up almost spontaneously around the political patriarch Yoshida Shigeru). Ishibashi Tanzan had such pro-China successors as Utsunomiya Tokuma. Matsumura Kenzo had such pro-China successors as Furui Yoshimi and Tagawa Seiichi. Yet although members of the LDP, none of these men was ever in the mainstream or about to be short-listed to become prime minister. Still, it is interesting how these pro-China successors of Ishibashi and Matsumura received both overt and covert support, not only from influential non-mainstream conservatives like Kono Ichiro and Miki Takeo, but also from mainstream conservatives like Ikeda Hayato.

Earlier I mentioned that postwar ties between Japan and China had been severed under strong pressure from the United States. China had fought the United States fiercely in the Korean War, and the United States saw in China a very serious threat. The Cuban missile crisis led (once it was over) to a climate of increasing US–Soviet dialogue, while China began to lambaste the Soviet Union for its "revisionism." American leaders came increasingly to think that the Chinese Communist Party, parading its militant Marxist fundamentalism and opposing the United States openly in the hot Korean War, was a more dangerous and unfathomable foe than the revisionist Soviet Union. The United States feared the un-known opponent more.

Japan's stance differed somewhat from the US stance towards China. Before the war, Yoshida Shigeru had instinctively looked down on China. But even he felt much closer to China than to the Soviet Union, whose sudden declaration of war against Japan just before its capitulation to the Allies had resulted in Soviet troops' pouring into Manchuria and finally in their occupation of the Northern territories. China had bitterly resisted Japan's military in-vasion, yet a deep-seated sense of closeness to China led Yoshida in the end to a favorable reassessment. The above-mentioned writings of Matsumura Kenzo also contain a similar sympathy for and affin-ity with China at the expense of the USSR.[1]

Indeed, these sentiments seem not to have been limited to the pro-mainland group. Kishi Nobusuke was noted for his pro-Taiwan stance and felt great sympathy towards Chiang Kaishek, his erst-while enemy. Fukuda Takeo felt an affinity for China, as he says in his *Kaiko kyujunen* (Ninety years in retrospect): "China is located much closer to Japan than the USSR. Throughout the Sino–Japanese War, the Japanese people came, as a general trend, to be very inter-ested in China and strongly attached to the Chinese people."[2] The conservatives' defining the improvement of Sino–Japanese ties as a high priority is in part due to the emotional, rather than rational, argument that normalization of diplomatic relations with China had fallen behind by comparison with normalization of ties with the USSR, for which Japan's postwar conservatives (particularly Yoshida Shigeru and Ikeda Hayato, who strongly opposed the Japan–USSR joint communiqué), felt no fondness at all.

The reason why the Japanese showed more concern for China than the Americans did is probably the result of both the historical depth of Sino–Japanese ties and geographical proximity. Japan has had a long history of exchange with China and has been an im-porter of Chinese culture for centuries; the fact that the establish-ment of Manchuria and the Sino–Japanese War had caused severe harm and hardship to the Chinese people also weighed heavily on the minds of some Japanese. Moreover, it was evident that China

© Asahi Shimbunsha

In January 1964, Prime Minister Ikeda Hayato (right) received Indonesian President Sukarno (left) at the entrance to his official residence. At the time, Ikeda was drawing up a plan for an Asian version of the European Economic Community.

would become a major power and that friendly Sino–Japanese relations were the key to peace in Asia. Japan's leaders judged that Japan could not begin to play a new leadership role in Asia without first establishing close ties with China. Finally, a latent awe of China and respect for the Chinese was the other side of the coin, in a sense, to modern Japan's contemptuous attitude and perception of Communist China as a threat.

Ikeda Hayato, successor to Yoshida with the latter's blessing, saw international relations in economic terms. According to *Ikeda Hayato to sono jidai* (Ikeda Hayato and his age) by Ito Masaya, secretary to Ikeda at the time, Ikeda was very frank about China when he received an important visitor from Taiwan: "The economic situation in mainland China under the Kuomintang was so miserable," he said, "that, in contrast, the improvement achieved by the Chinese Communist Party has been considerable. That's why its political power has been so stable. The best anti-Communist defense policy for Taiwan is therefore to outperform Communist China."[3]

During his visit to Europe, Ikeda's remarks were the same, every time he was asked about Sino–Japanese relations: "Relations between Japan and mainland China have been historically and traditionally particular," he would say, adding: "Many Japanese feel very close to the Chinese people. Even in the LDP, there are those who urge that diplomatic relations between the two countries should be restored." Ties between Japan and Taiwan and other Southeast Asian countries did not permit Japan to move at once to restore diplomatic relations with China, he said, but it was Japan's intention, whatever should happen, to continue Sino–Japanese trade, "keeping politics and economics separate," as before. He also spoke plainly during a visit to Japan of a VIP from France in 1964: "Before long, an opportunity will definitely present itself for France, Britain, and Japan to persuade the United States to change its mind about China." During his US visit in June 1961, Ikeda stressed to President Kennedy the importance of the historical ties between Japan and China and sought Kennedy's understanding that Japan had just as much right to trade with China as Europe did.

According to Tagawa Seiichi's *Nitchu koryu to Jiminto ryoshutachi* (Sino–Japanese contacts and leading members of the LDP), prime minister Ikeda used to encourage Tagawa on every occasion, saying: "My political position obliges me to conduct a consistently US-oriented foreign policy, which forces me to move slowly to normalize Sino–Japanese diplomatic relations, but China's certain to be important for Japan in the future. I count on you younger politicians to dismantle the hurdles that have blocked me and carry this normalization through." When Tagawa asked, "Won't there be a storm from Oiso?" (where Yoshida Shigeru was living in retirement), Ikeda calmly replied, "Don't worry: Yoshida gets the picture."[4]

In November 1962, deliberately ignoring the displeasure of Taiwan and the USA, Ikeda gave Matsumura Kenzo the go-ahead to visit China and allowed the Liao–Takasaki trade agreement (named after Liao Chengshi and Takasaki Tatsunosuke, who negotiated it) to go into effect.

In *Sengo hoshuto-shi* (The postwar history of Japan's conservative parties) Tominomori Eiji writes that only while Ikeda was prime minister could the pro-China group in the LDP have achieved full acceptance.[5] While on the one hand Ikeda was Yoshida's disciple, Ishibashi Tanzan's influence is also discernible. Ikeda, who had been appointed by finance minister Ishibashi to be his deputy finance minister, sometimes opposed Ishibashi politically because he was one of Yoshida's aides, but he adored Ishibashi personally and as a politician carried out his Keynesian economic policies most faithfully. As a reward for his cooperation, Ishibashi picked Ikeda to be his finance minister in the Ishibashi cabinet.

Ohira Masayoshi, who served under Tanaka Kakuei as foreign minister and worked hard with him to restore Sino–Japanese diplomatic ties, was Ikeda's official secretary when Ikeda was finance minister; he is therefore a disciple of Yoshida's, albeit indirectly. And having worked closely with Ikeda, it is likely that Ohira was deeply marked by Ikeda's attitudes toward China.

Ohira himself had lived in prewar China: in 1939, he was seconded by the Ministry of Finance to the Koain (Asia Promotion Board) in charge of administration in the Japanese-occupied part of China. He spent more than one year in Zhangjiakou, in Inner Mongolia, and he often reminisced fondly about those times. That is where he met his colleague and lifelong friend, Ito Masayoshi, who was also working at the Asia Promotion Board; like Ohira, Ito had been seconded to China, but by the Ministry of Agriculture. (Ito was later to be foreign minister and president of the Federation of Parliamentarians for China–Japan Friendship.) So he, too, like the pro-mainland group, might well have felt nostalgia for old China. Indeed, whenever Ohira visited the United States as minister of foreign affairs under Ikeda, he stressed the necessity of reopening Sino–Japanese trade.

In March 1971, toward the end of the Sato premiership, the World Ping Pong Championship was being held in Nagoya. China sent a team of players with Wang Xiaoyun as deputy team-leader to Japan, where he launched what the world quickly came to call "ping-pong diplomacy," a series of contacts with leaders of Japanese business and finance. Taking advantage through Furui Yoshimi of this opportunity, Ohira dined with Wang in complete secrecy. This was precisely the time when the Great Proletarian Cultural Revolution was winding down in China and Sato was expected to step down from his premiership in the course of the following year. Ohira had just withdrawn his faction from Maeo Shigesaburo's; he was clearly aware of the importance of settling the Taiwan question as a crucial step toward progress on the China issue, and he was willing to push ahead with it, having no personal sentimental attachment to Taiwan. Furui, who foresaw that Tanaka would succeed the retiring Sato, had been asking Ohira to back Tanaka by accepting the post of minister of foreign affairs. Having agreed to this, Ohira told Wang, he was "willing to make every effort to settle the Taiwan question and later to restore Sino–Japanese diplomatic relations and recognize the People's Republic as the sole legitimate government of China."[6]

MIYAZAWA KIICHI'S PROPHESY

Miyazawa Kiichi is another of Ikeda's political disciples, but he showed far more perspicuity in his perceptions of postwar China than did Ikeda. In 1965, while Sato was prime minister, Miyazawa wrote a book titled *Shakaito tono taiwa* (Dialogues with the Socialist Party), in which he reported what US Secretary of State Dean Rusk had told him in a conversation comparing the USSR and China: "Communist China has been belligerent since the Korean War, a kind of unruly child as it were, and we must discipline it." Miyazawa, in his book, reflects:

> This judgmental attitude seems to stem from the overly emotional aspect of US education since Dulles. This doesn't coincide with the traditional Japanese view of China. Moreoever, even if Communist

China were as belligerent as the United States thinks it is, would it be wise of us to leave it in prolonged isolation?[7]

It was Yoshida who had prophesized that the honeymoon between China and the USSR would not last. In his book, Miyazawa adopted the same view as Yoshida, mincing no words:

> I really doubt that a people as smart as the Chinese can truly believe in an ideology as stupid as Marxism. In thirty to fifty years, history will clearly prove that I'm right.[8]

Developing this line of reasoning, Miyazawa presents the following conversation with a certain key Chinese figure in his book:

> I don't believe that a people as clever as the Chinese can seriously believe in Marxism forever. As soon as the Chinese people's standard of living reaches a certain level of affluence, they'll abandon Marxist ideology.
>
> *That will never happen: in this world, exploitation, inequality, and class divisions are realities. To eliminate them is the target of the Revolution. It's a fact that, for now, someone who works more than another is paid more than the other, but this is a just temporary expedient.*
>
> That it's a 'temporary expedient' as you say is questionable: look at the USSR. What they expected to be "temporary expedients" still exist and are taken for granted. No economic prosperity can be expected without resorting to such means.
>
> *That's why I insist that the Soviet Union's revisionism is wrong!*[9]

Today, thirty years after this book was published, Miyazawa holds firmly to his beliefs, while China continues to uphold Marxism politically. But at least from the economic point of view, it can fairly be said that Miyazawa's prophecy proved right.

A tendency to confound the Chinese Revolution with nationalism is a trait common to every conservative Japanese politician. But Yoshida and his pupils regarded the Chinese Revolution coolly and calmly, as a transient stage in the evolution of Chinese nationalism, compared with Matsumura, who took a more emotional view of the Chinese Revolution, likening it to the Meiji Restoration, and with Kishi, who was afraid that China would take advantage of nationalism to overwhelm the Asian region. The view of China's future espoused by Miyazawa in his book is optimistic, tempered with the observation that most of China's leaders know very little about Western Europe and tend to indulge in self-righteousness. Sighing, he expresses his concern: "It reminds one of the bygone days of the Imperial Japanese Army."

THE "ASIAN VILLAGE" CONCEPT: TANAKA KAKUEI'S SYMPATHY FOR CHINA

Though Tanaka Kakuei was not a pupil of Yoshida in direct line of descent, he played the leading role in normalizing Sino–Japanese relations, and his view of China belongs basically in the Yoshida Shigeru family tree. Indeed, as the ultimate pragmatic politician, Tanaka typically held views that left ideology by the wayside.

No sooner had Tanaka Kakuei won the LDP presidential election than he announced, full of enthusiasm, to Hayasaka Shigezo, the prime minister elect's secretary: "The tide is high: I'll do the Japan–China thing in one fell swoop." Hayasaka says he will never forget the words that followed: "Mao and Zhou (Mao Zedong and Zhou Enlai) are Commies. But those guys built everything from the ground up: they're founders and owners. They've seen death face-to-face dozens of times, and they've seen bloodshed hundreds of times and survived. The way they were able to bring together and unify such a huge country and its people is something absolutely out of the ordinary. It stands to reason that they're able to calculate and take into account what their nation needs to get from Japan in order to get by. They've sent a message to us saying that when we begin to talk about restoring ties, the US–Japan Security Treaty can stand as is, but we have to break off diplomatic relations with Taiwan; they won't demand reparations. I'll take their word and get it all done in a jiffy."

Tanaka also said at about this time that Japan ought to give generous aid to China, on a grant basis, since it was China that had proposed to relinquish reparations claims. He told Hayasaka, half in jest and half serious: "Let's first send, say, 10 million TV sets to Beijing, and set up antennas throughout the city. Then we'll make powerful broadcasts from Japan to China, showing our highways, Toyota's factories, and girls wearing mini-skirts. Communism? It'll collapse!"

When Deng Xiaoping came to Japan to commemorate the conclusion of the Treaty of Peace and Friendship between Japan and the People's Republic of China initiated by the Fukuda cabinet, he paid a visit to Tanaka, then an accused criminal, at his residence. According to Hayasaka, Tanaka said to Deng: "Pardon me for saying this, but if you say everyone in your country follows communism, I say it's a communism of convenience. To govern your enormous country, you're writing 'Communism' in big letters and underlining it on billboards, to win the people's hearts, right? It must be a tough job: I have great sympathy for you." Hayasaka says that Deng clapped his hands in delight at Tanaka's words.

This was when Tanaka gave Deng the following advice: "You need credits terribly, but you'd better not borrow from Japan or foreign countries, because interest rates overseas are so high. But think of the homing instinct of overseas Chinese all over the world: every Chinese migrant would like eventually to return home to China in glory: it's as instinctive as the salmon returning to the river where they were spawned. So it'd be a good idea to set up a mainland free port, like Hong Kong, to encourage overseas Chinese to come home willingly and repatriate their money." This was eight months before China established a special economic zone in Shenzhen Province.

How he expressed these ideas is uniquely Tanaka's, but he had no monopoly on similar suggestions: witness Miyazawa's statements above, for instance. Before Japan–China ties were restored, Ishida Hirohide, a pupil of Ishibashi Tanzan, used to say: "Once ties have been restored, it's China that will be in trouble, not Japan, because the Chinese will be more attracted to Japan's freedom and affluence than the Japanese are to anything in China. It's absurd to be too much afraid of Communism. If we can, let's have Chinese come to Japan and travel by sightseeing bus throughout Japan." (He was quoted by Tanaka Shusei, then secretary to Ishida [later New Party Sakigake member of the House of Representatives], in an explanatory note to Ishida's memoirs, *Myogonichi eno michishirube* (Signpost to the day after tomorrow.)[10]

Another characteristic of Tanaka Kakuei's view of China is an underlying "Asian village" type of community consciousness. Tanaka was notoriously a country boy from Echigo (Niigata Prefecture), a poor region of heavy snowfalls; while in the seat of power in Tokyo, the Pacific "front" of Japan, he strove tirelessly to bring some prosperity to his less-developed "backside" coast of the Sea of Japan. And in a way, he viewed the rest of Asia as a backwater in a situation similar to his home on the Sea of Japan coast. Hayasaka says Tanaka often compared Asia to a village community. One day he said, for example, "Where there's only one rich family [i.e., Japan] living in a palace on the top of a hill, wallowing in luxury, while the rest of the people down in the village are barely eking out an existence, there'll be no peace or stability."

While Tanaka never doubted that the US–Japanese alliance had been the most fundamental pillar of Japanese policy since Yoshida Shigeru, it is no wonder that he identified the West with the 'front' on the one hand and tended to confound Asia to a greater or lesser extent with his backwater hometown on the other. Before Japan–China ties were officially restored, Tanaka, making no secret of his sympathies with the poor, admonished a person who had been running a little business between Japan and China: "Don't be greedy when you deal with China. The Chinese are poor. Over there, people toil with all their might, just to earn enough for their evening supper. Make your profits from richer nations."

The utilitarian Tanaka obviously kept in mind Japan's interests and an eye on the oil fields then under development in China, hoping to secure resources that would make Japan less dependent on the major US oil companies. Tanaka directed his 'resource diplo-macy' efforts primarily at the Arab nations (without advance notice to or permission from the United States) after the 1973 oil shock, but his resource diplomacy was foreshadowed by this early stage of Sino–Japanese rapprochement.

The other side of the coin was Tanaka's awareness that the framework of the cold war in Asia was changing remarkably with the US–Chinese rapprochement and Soviet–Chinese rift. Hayasaka wrote later on this transition in his book *Seijika Tanaka Kakuei* (Tanaka Kakuei, politician):

> The conditions were ripe for Japan to recover some relative freedom of maneuver and to initiate a strategy for living in peace and har-mony with others. The establishment of a peaceful order, interregional economic cooperation, the resolution of conflicts through negotiations—these now became the new tide of events in Asia. Tanaka acutely and correctly perceived these needs, and in due course set diplomatic relations with China on a new course and aggressively deployed his own independent "resource diplomacy" from a standpoint of resource nationalism. The tide of the times made Tanaka's diplomacy possible.[11]

Some believe that Tanaka's arrest and imprisonment in the Lockheed affair was a surreptitious retaliation by the United States for having "stepped on the tiger's tail" with his independent re-source diplomacy. Tahara Soichiro, in "Amerika no tora-no-o o funda Tanaka Kakuei (Tanaka Kakuei, who stepped on the tail of the US tiger)" in the July 1976 issue of *Chuo Koron* and "Pekin no harebutai de Tanaka Kakuei wa nani o mitaka (What Tanaka Kakuei saw on the ceremonial stage in Beijing)" in the August issue of the same, quotes Tanaka's words to Morozumi Yoshihiko, then administrative vice-minister for international trade and industry, several years before the normalization of Sino–Japanese relations. When Tanaka said, "Let's propose to China to develop the deep–sea oilfield on the continental shelf of the Senkaku Islands together," Morozumi replied with surprise: "Sir, it will be very difficult before restoring diplomatic relations." Tanaka answered: "We'd better ask

France to work this out, because the French are friendly with Beijing. But first, we have to do France a favor." Tanaka began immediately to examine specific projects involving France. (Vintage Tanaka!)

Incidentally, as the normalization of Sino–Japanese diplomatic relations began to take shape, Japanese business was becoming increasingly eager to do business with China. "Business could no longer ignore the existence of the enormous Chinese market, nor its potential as an outlet for Japanese exports of manufactured goods," writes Hayasaka. "Such resources as crude oil, coal for steelmaking and so on were very attractive to resource-poor Japan. Nor could Japan ignore the 16 million overseas Chinese and their economic clout in developing economic relations with Southeast Asia. Political coordination between Japan and China was needed to settle these issues and to thoroughly globalize the Japanese economy. The logic of capital and of economics motivated Japanese business people to put pressure on Japan's politicians to get moving. . . . But the smiles of merchants and bankers and the logic of accountants could not, alone, overcome the political barriers."[12] At last, the time was ripe to settle an issue kept on the back burner since Yoshida.

Chapter 10

Nakasone Yasuhiro's Worshipful Visit to Yasukuni Shrine

TRUE TO HIS NATIONALIST NATURE

It was a sweltering summer. On August 12, 1985, a JAL jumbo jet lost contact with air traffic controllers, crashed, and before long was found on top of Osutaka Mountain in Gunma Prefecture. In the middle of the summer vacation, this accident of unprecedented proportions (over 500 passengers were killed) was an abrupt shock. My newspaper colleagues, especially those working for the local edition, were in pandemonium.

I was a front-line reporter assigned to the Cabinet at the time. As if it were yesterday, I remember that time of extraordinary tension in the prime minister's residence. We reporters in charge of political news also had a hectic, sweltering summer, but it was for another reason. On August 15, three days after the accident, prime minister Nakasone, accompanied by his cabinet ministers, assumed a determined mien and went officially to worship at Yasukuni Shrine. That in particular was what made it a hot summer for me. Yasukuni Shrine, dedicated to the memory of those killed in the war, was and is a symbol of national Shintoism as well as a presence that lent an aura of religious devotion to Japan's prewar policy of militaristic expansion. Ishibashi Tanzan had even advocated its demolition after the war.

Miki Takeo was the first postwar prime minister to visit and worship at Yasukuni Shrine, on August 15, 1975, the 30th anniversary of the end of the war. Yielding to strong entreaties from the right wing, including the Japan Association of the Bereaved Families of the War Dead, a group that supported the LDP, Miki made his visit, but he did it ostensibly as a private citizen, in order to respect the constitutional separation of politics from religion. Yet even "as a private citizen," he went there in his official car, was accompanied by guards as a government employee, and put his signature on the shrine's guest list followed by his title, Prime Minister. Under the circumstances, it is difficult to say how one could distinguish this visit "as a private citizen" from a visit in his official capacity. Yet every prime minister from Miki onward continued to worship at Yasukuni Shrine ostensibly as a private person, observing the rule forbidding disbursement of public monies for offerings to the shrine.

It wasn't until 1978 that executed Class A war criminals, including Tojo Hideki, were enshrined together at Yasukuni. No one had objected to enshrining the ordinary war dead there, but to enshrine Class A war criminals there together with the rest predictably increased public resistance to cabinet ministers' visits. Yet even so, successive prime ministers continued to worship there on the anniversary of the war's end. The right wing was dissatisfied with so-called worship as private citizens. Almost every year, they continued to put pressure on the government to make their visits official, alleging that worship as private citizens was shameful.

Then along came Nakasone, who chose the fortieth anniversary of the war's end to yield to the right wing's calls for official devotional visits.

Nakasone, who had "declared postwar politics over" and espoused neo-nationalism as his campaign slogan, was clearly determined to take this step. Together with a move announced at almost the same time to abolish the ceiling on annual defense expenditures (capped at 1% of GNP since the Miki cabinet), the visit made the already hot summer in the prime minister's official residence markedly hotter.

Before his worshipful visit to Yasukuni, Nakasone had addressed a remarkable speech to the LDP's summer seminar in Karuizawa on July 27. After triumphantly trumpeting the success of his efforts to carry out administrative reforms, he announced his intention to

On August 15, 1985, the year marking the 40th anniversary of the end of the Pacific War, Prime Minister Nakasone Yasuhiro (second from the right), escorted by a Shinto priest, entered the sanctuary of Yasukuni Shrine to pay an official visit and worship.

"go the royal road" on the question of defense expenditures. He continued, as follows:

> Before the war, there was the imperial view of history. After Japan's defeat in the war, the Pacific War view (i.e., the International Military Tribunal for the Far East view) of history came into existence. The Allied powers accused and tried Japan by their law, in the name of civilization, peace, and humanity. History will render the ultimate verdict on that trial. But at the time, there spread throughout Japan a self-torturing belief that our country was to blame for everything. This thinking persists even today. It was fashionable to blame Japan alone and condemn everything prewar. I'm against this. Whatever happens, the state must continue to exist. It is the people who inevitably either bask in glory or are exposed to disgrace, because they are the people. Casting disgrace aside, advancing forward in the pursuit of glory—this is the essence of the nation and of the people. We must look critically

at Japan's actions in the past and establish our country's identity from this point of view.[1]

This type of rhetoric is the trademark of Nakasone the nationalist. From this day on, I could not contain my nervousness on my assignments, feeling that a critical turning point had been reached and breached at last. Nakasone marched off at the head of his cabinet ministers to worship at Yasukuni Shrine in this mood of exaltation.

To dilute the event's religious coloring, the cabinet members refrained from carrying out fully such Shintoistic gestures as bowing twice deeply, clapping hands twice, and bowing once, but to prove that this was an official visit, they disbursed public funds "to pay for flowers" instead of the customary offerings.

The cabinet ministers had been hesitant. Minister of finance Takeshita Noboru, who was eyeing the succession and impatient to see Nakasone step down, flaunted his disinclination for official worship at the press conference held before their visit by saying "praying with all one's heart is enough." Takeshita, who had gone together with members of the Group of All Worshippers at Yasukuni Shrine in his capacity as their ex-president and worshipped early in the morning August 15, learned later that all the other cabinet ministers were going to visit the shrine as a group in the afternoon. Not wanting to be the only one left out, he paid a second visit there the same day. "Twice in the same day" said the next day's *Asahi Shimbun*, to which Takeshita protested: "I've been ridiculed." Kato Koichi, then Director General of the Defense Agency but nonetheless a dovish Dietman of the postwar generation, resisted plans for the visit, but after much wavering finally aligned himself with Nakasone to avoid jeopardizing his post. But immediately after leaving Yasukuni Shrine, he went and worshipped across the street at the War Memorial Park at Chidorigafuchi, and in this way attempted to dilute the previous visit's militant coloring.

The fallout from Asian countries, particularly China, after Nakasone's resolute official visit to Yasukuni Shrine was much heavier than expected. The *People's Daily* (the Chinese Communist

Party organ) pointed out that Yasukuni Shrine was dedicated to Japanese military personnel killed in all wars since the Meiji Reformation, and that the executed Class A war criminals, including Tojo Hideki, were "enshrined there as martyrs" in 1978. After the cabinet's official visit, stinging criticism of how Japan had "hurt Asians' feelings" sprung up everywhere in China. Nakasone had tried with ingenious rhetoric to overcome the critical constitutional issue at home, which he was prepared for; the intensity of this storm of protest abroad took him by surprise. In the end, it forced him to cancel further official visits to Yasukuni Shrine.

Of Nakasone's successors in the prime minister's office, only Hashimoto Ryutaro openly dared to make a visit to Yasukuni Shrine. Half a year after he assumed office, Hashimoto ventured to do so on his birthday in July 1996, eleven years after Nakasone's last act of homage. That he did not do so on the August 15th anniversary of the end of the war was meant to underscore the more private nature of his visit, but this pretence helped little to alleviate the irate reaction by China. Having taken a nonchalant attitude to the Yasukuni problem up until then, Hashimoto had to learn the hard way not to repeat the visit while he was in office.

WHY NAKASONE CANCELLED FURTHER OFFICIAL VISITS TO YASUKUNI SHRINE

Nakasone Yasuhiro's Asian diplomacy is a mystery, on the surface. Despite his strong anti-Communist and nationalistic sentiments and the nationalist undertone of his decision to worship at Yasukuni Shrine officially, he was very quick to jettison this baggage. Furthermore, he showed great political agility in his efforts to promote friendship with Korea and China (including by cancelling his visits to Yasukuni Shrine) and worked very actively thereafter to ease frictions.

Yokoyama Hiroaki reports a November 1991 interview with Nakasone in his work *Nitchu no shoheki* (Barriers Between Japan and China)[2] and describes Nakasone's perceptions of China in great detail. I will now examine Nakasone's views on Asia, referring to interesting passages found here and there in Yokoyama's interview.

Nakasone made a tour of the USSR and China together with Matsumae Shigeyoshi of the Socialist Party and Kuroda Hisao of the Labor-Farmer Party in 1953, shortly after the San Francisco Peace Treaty restored Japan's independence. The first semi-official visit by a Japanese to postwar revolutionary China was made by a group led by Hoashi Kei in 1952; Nakasone's visit in 1953 is therefore one of the earliest and a sign of his keen interest. Later, though Nakasone persisted in adopting an anti-Soviet stance in his speeches and actions, he quickly concluded that China and Japan should be friendly to each other, declaring: "Japan's relations with a neighbor and the greatest superpower in Eurasia should not be in this irregular state. President Chiang Kaishek's regime in Taiwan is a problem, but I have held and still affirm a clear position: that Taiwan is China's internal affair and Japan should not adopt the 'Two Chinas' view. I presume that China is aware of our actions. I have kept very close company with Messrs Matsumura and Takasaki."

The influence of the two figures he mentions is certainly discernible, since Nakasone had been a favorite with Takasaki Tatsunosuke and Matsumura Kenzo and remained politically close to them. When Tanaka formed his government, Nakasone declared that "he supported Tanaka on condition that Tanaka restore diplomatic relations between China and Japan." Rumors abounded that this pose was too high-sounding and that in fact he had received a suspiciously large donation from Tanaka to cement the alliance. When Nakasone was summoned to appear as a witness to the Diet in the Lockheed affair, he denied this charge and cited the following reason why he had supported Tanaka at that time: "It was to show my gratitude to my mentor Mr. Matsumura that I was determined to make zealous efforts to normalize China–Japan relations."

According to Tagawa Seiichi, who was a direct political descendent of Matsumura and quondam member of the Nakasone faction, the real facts are slightly different from Nakasone's testimony in the Diet. Immediately after Nakasone became prime minister,

Tagawa, speaking for the Shinjiyu (New Liberal) Club, let fly harsh criticisms of Nakasone from the dais, singling out Nakasone's statement that he wanted to show his "gratitude to my mentor Mr. Matsumura." "There was no talk at all [inside the Nakasone faction] of supporting Tanaka to normalize China–Japan relations or to show gratitude to Mr. Matsumura," testified Tagawa. He added, "At that time in the Nakasone faction, there were quite a few Taiwan supporters and an argument over the China issue would have meant the faction's disintegration. These concerns made it taboo to argue about this whole issue."

Nakasone was astonished at this attack. He refuted it by noting that he was a favorite with Matsumura, that he saw how Matsumura had dedicated his whole life, even into advanced old age, to achieving a breakthrough on the China–Japan issue, and that he had the highest regard for Matsumura. Nakasone also emphasized the following point to corroborate his close relationship with Matsumura: "Mr. Matsumura wanted to considerably reinforce the Nakasone faction in order to use the power of this group, when the time was ripe, for the normalization of China–Japan relations."

Whatever the case may be, Nakasone as minister of international trade and industry in the Tanaka cabinet promoted friendship with China through, *inter alia*, a deliberate exchange of views with Zhou Enlai during his visit to China. According to Nakasone, he learned later that Zhou had said to his wife: "That man Nakasone will definitely become premier." Nakasone used to refer to this episode with pride and self-congratulation for China's opinion of him, saying: "I think that quite a few people in China found in me not an enemy but someone comparatively useful for their country."

On a later visit to China, he was introduced to Hu Yaopang and Zhao Ziyang by Deng Xiaoping, who mentioned to Nakasone: "These two shoulder responsibility for the next generation." When Nakasone was prime minister, his counterpart in China was Hu at the pinnacle of his career as Party General Secretary. Nakasone, who attaches great importance to friendship between top-level people, cultivated in succession the personal friendship and confidence of Chun Doohwan of Korea, Ronald Reagan of the United States, and Hu Yaopang of China: "First of all, to thaw our chilled relations with Korea, next to cement our ties with the USA, and then to establish friendly and amicable relations with China: we have to do our best in this order."

Yet why, despite Nakasone's evident determination to worship officially at Yasukuni Shrine and the extensive fanfare this visit received, did he submit so easily to pressure from China, heedless of the reaction from the domestic right wing? This is the central question in Yokoyama's interview with Nakasone, who revealed that criticism of Nakasone would probably have been used by forces in China seeking to dislodge Hu from his post. He mentioned that Chinese Communist Party conservatives had already begun to attack Hu for going too far in his drastic liberalization and pro-Japan posture.

Yet when Inayama Yoshihiro, then president of the Federation of Economic Organizations, visited China the following summer, Nakasone had him sound out Hu to find out whether Nakasone might somehow continue to visit the shrine. According to Inayama, early in the morning before he left Beijing for Tokyo, a person close to Hu came to the hotel to tell him with deadly seriousness, "Resuming the visits will have an undesirable effect, so make sure that Nakasone does not." Nakasone says: "From about that time, reports began to reach us that Hu was in a precarious situation. . . . That person came to see Inayama out of concern that my continuing to worship at Yasukuni Shrine regardless of these warnings would be risky for Hu and people close to him because of relations with conservatives. . . . Under the circumstances, it was better to give up, so I decided to stop worshipping at Yasukuni."

Nakasone's explanation betrays no trace of regret for failing to anticipate the foreseeable reaction of Asian countries, including China, to his official visits to Yasukuni Shrine. He made the visit officially because of his exaltation at being prime minister during the fortieth anniversary of the end of the war and his preoccupation with appeasing the war-bereaved lobby and the spirits of the war-dead. One gets the unmistakable impression that, by drawing attention to the power struggle in China, Nakasone was above all shirking personal responsibility.

In the following year, Nakasone simply put off the question of worshipping at Yasukuni Shrine. Why did he do this, despite the reaction of the right wing of the LDP? He says, "Of course it was to prevent relations with China from deteriorating by all means. . . . We had made the visits taking the opinions of the LDP into account," he explains, "But I said clearly that the spirits of the war dead would not be happy about worshippers undermining the national interest."

Even the nationalist Nakasone realized full well that relations with China were an important factor in Japan's rise to prominence in the international arena. He said, "The rightists ridiculed me, wrote letters to me, and protested." He tried every possible means, he recollects, to soothe the feelings of the influential diehard right-wing group Daitojuku.

Internationalism on the Horns of a Dilemma

The year Nakasone postponed official visits to Yasukuni Shrine (1986) coincided with the publication of "New Edition: Japanese History," a school textbook edited by the National Congress to Defend Japan, a lobby headed by Mayuzumi Toshiro and whose agenda included, *inter alia*, amendment of the Japanese Constitution. The textbook sparked a controversy ('the second textbook incident'). It had been edited to play down as much as possible Japan's responsibility for misdeeds during the war. It described the Imperial Rescript on Education, for instance, as "precepts of national morality that integrate human morals and the concept of nation passed down from ancient times"; the rescript is "well-known overseas, where it is viewed with high regard." In this and other ways, the editorial tone of this textbook was consistently different from other Japanese history textbooks.

When reports that a textbook of this kind would be published began to appear in the news, cries of protest went up in Korea,

China, and Southeast Asia, alleging that Japan was "beautifying its war of aggression." In this textbook, the Rape of Nanking, for example, is referred to as "the Nanking Incident"; Japan's robbing Korea of its rights of diplomatic representation through the Japan–Korean Protectorate Treaty is alluded to simply as the fact that Japan's "confiscation [of Korea's diplomatic rights] turned Korea into Japan's protectorate." China and Korea could not overlook this. Finally Nakasone intervened, instructing the ministry of education to take Asia's complaints "sufficiently into consideration"—acceding, in other words, to the Chinese and Korean requests to have the textbook rewritten.

Asked about his decision, Nakasone replied in the interview as follows: "I was of the opinion that it was an aggressive war, so I thought it was right that the facts should be so described, as facts, in the textbook; therefore I would say I reined in the ministry of education." He continues: "I am usually taken for a comparatively pronounced nationalist, and I realize that. But careful observation of historical and contemporary Chinese–Japanese relations shows clearly that Japan's debt to China is larger than the debt of China to Japan; basically, the difference is enough to make me think that the Japanese debt to China is large enough for me to define the war as a war of aggression."

Nakasone also related how he "mentioned clearly in the Budgetary Committee hearings in the Diet that the Sino–Japanese War was a war of aggression. I think I am the first prime minister to call it a war of aggression. Takeshita, my successor, sort of backed out, avoiding making a clear statement."

Actually, it was not in the Budgetary Committee in the Diet, but in a lecture to participants in the Editorial Directors' Conference held by the Kyodo News Service on September 3, 1986, that Nakasone for the first time definitely stated "It was a war of aggression" (according to the *Mainichi Shimbun* of September 4, 1986). It was also on that occasion that Nakasone said: "To have enshrined Class A war criminals together at Yasukuni Shrine antagonizes other nations. I think that war was a war of aggression."

Nihonjin no sensokan (The Japanese people's view of the war), written by Yoshida Yutaka,[3] traces in detail the vicissitudes of Nakasone's statements on Japan's aggression. According to Yoshida, Nakasone replied with some reserve to a question from a Communist Party Diet member in the House of Councilors' Budget Committee soon after the formation of the Nakasone Cabinet: "I believe that the verdict of history should be made by a large number of scholars and historians. But with respect to what Japan did, historians in the nations concerned and elsewhere in the world have rendered their judgment: it was an act of aggression, or an aggressive war." After some meandering, he ended up using the more direct term "war of aggression" himself: in the plenary session of the House of Representatives on September 16, 1986, he stated "The fact of aggression cannot be denied."

To give Nakasone due credit, successive prime ministers before him had also hesitated to categorize Japan's actions as "aggression." Even Tanaka Kakuei, who indicated his deep regret in the China–Japan joint communiqué, didn't make a definite assertion. In reply to a question from Fuwa Tetsuzo in February 1973, Tanaka said: "The fact that at one time Japan did send troops to the Chinese continent, that is a historical fact. On this question, I am not in a position to mention in a straightforward manner whether, as you say, the sending of troops was or was not aggression. This kind of evaluation is for historians of the future to judge."

The first prime minister after Nakasone to state specifically that Japan's involvement in the Pacific war was a war of aggression was Hosokawa Morihiro at his inaugural press conference in August of 1993. There he was replying to a question and his answer was: "I myself perceive it as a war of aggression and a mistake" (*Asahi Shimbun*, August 11, 1993). But this reply was not limited to the Sino–Japanese War and therefore stirred up a storm of controversy. His government considered this reply improper, since it gave the impression that the war in the Pacific as a whole was a war of aggression. In his first general policy speech, quite a while later, Hosokawa amended the above wording to read "acts of aggression."

According to Tanaka Shusei, then the prime minister's special aide, Hosokawa didn't use the adjectival form, "aggressive," which most Prime Ministers before Hosokawa had used, but went one step further, using the balder nominal form, "aggression." On the occasion of the special Diet resolution in commemoration of the fiftieth anniversary of the war's end, bickering about the wording of "acts of aggression" lasted to the very end, when finally the adjectival form (i.e., "aggressive acts") was used. Though it was only a slight difference, it was clearly a step backward.

Incidentally, after Nakasone had given instructions to revise "New Edition: Japanese History," a provocative statement about Korea by Fujio Masayuki, his education minister, caused Nakasone considerable distress. He demanded Fujio's immediate resignation. Later, referring to the incident, he expounded: "He has that conviction in him by nature. That's what made him do that, and he's therefore guilty because of his convictions. I had no choice other than to accept his resignation." In this case, too, Nakasone chose Korea–Japan friendship, restraining the nationalist within him. The year 1985 marked both the fortieth anniversary of the end of the war and Emperor Showa's 60th year on the throne. Nakasone was elated by this opportunity, since he was to be prime minister in a commemorative year and he wanted very much to play the part of a great statesman and prime minister of an internationally open country and to be acknowledged as such at the yearly summit of major industrial nations.

Each time an inconsistency in the simultaneous pursuit of his dual goals surfaced, Nakasone chose in the end to be an internationalist. There was ever some irony in the choices Nakasone, the nationalist, made as prime minister.

In the Yokoyama interview, Nakasone also referred to the traditional pride of the Chinese. The Chinese express their "hearty appreciation, politely" for Japanese ODA, but "they become extremely sensitive when it comes to Communism, the honor of their state institutions, and their ideology. We have to be very aware of this point. Where touchy and vital points are concerned, such as the particularities of their regime or Communism, we

Japanese innocently tend to be quite insensitive, or at any rate we're less aware than we should. We have to learn that China is touchy about those things."

Responding to the question whether this was due to China's traditional Confucianist Sinocentrism or due to the cadres' perceived need for self-respect, Nakasone replied: "It's clearly an issue of prestige—no doubt is possible and no mistake." He added: "It is our duty as neighbors to be as polite as possible vis-à-vis China," but "We want the Chinese to reciprocate by being more sensitive about Japan's monarchy."

When the Miyazawa cabinet was working on the arrangements for a visit by the Emperor to China, Nakasone requested that the groundwork be laid in advance, very carefully, to ensure that the Chinese pay all due respect to the Emperor. This subject is treated in greater detail in Part IV. Suffice to point out for the moment how characteristic of Nakasone it is to make a request of this nature.

As Political Editor of the *Asahi Shimbun* in 1997, the 50th anniversary of the coming into effect of the Constitution of Japan, I arranged and moderated a dialogue between two bigwigs, the constitutional revision advocate Nakasone Yasuhiro and the *status quo* protectionist Miyazawa Kiichi. With substantial additions, the record of the meeting has already been published as *Tairon: Kaiken/Goken* (Constitutional revision or preservation: A debate),[7] and the protagonists' statements are summarized in English in the September 1997 issue of the journal *Japan Quarterly* (The Asahi Shimbun Publishing Co.). In response to my query about their views on the dispute over the term "aggression," Nakasone said:

> This is what I stated as prime minister. First, I do not subscribe to the Imperial view of history. Nor do I accept, secondly, MacArthur's view of history, which dominated the Tokyo Trials. Thirdly, the Greater East Asia War was a conventional war vis-à-vis the UK, the US, and France: there was nothing unusual about it. There were elements of aggression, however, vis-à-vis China and countries in the south of Asia. But the great majority of the Japanese people believed

that Japan was fighting for its survival, in self-defense against the Americans, British, Chinese, and Dutch. Some of them thought Japanese soldiers were fighting out there to liberate colonized parts of Asia. Some leaders in the government and the military believed in Hitler and his Germany and bet on the war, but by and large, the people went to the battlefields in good faith. This I want to live long enough to tell to my grandchildren. When it comes to Korea, whether the unification was based on an international treaty is arguable, but the fact that the treaty was concluded under the threat of military intervention is undeniable. Besides, the Japanization of Korean names, forced visits of worship to Shinto shrines, etc., must have been regarded by the Korean people as an insult and a stain on their honor. For all these things, we owe them an apology.

We have been apologizing, and the act of contrition has been performed. It is all over and done with. It was an act of sheer poor judgment, in the year 1995, to have passed a Diet resolution apologizing for the past. The legislative branch of government does not have the right to dispute history. It was the Cabinet that should have done so instead, precisely because it is the Cabinet, and not the Diet, that has the right to pursue diplomacy. That's what I've been saying all along. In just this sense, I was the first prime minister [in postwar Japan] who admitted to "acts of aggression."

| # The Internal Inconsistencies of the Pro-Koreans

THE ANTI-JAPANESE RHEE SYNGMAN

The special resolution commemorating the 50th anniversary of the end of World War II was being heatedly debated in the Diet in June 1995, which was also the 30th anniversary of the conclusion of the Japan–Korea Basic Treaty.[1] At the beginning of June, on my arrival on my first visit to Seoul in many years, I was told that molotov cocktails had been thrown into the Japanese Cultural Center in Seoul: ex-foreign minister Watanabe Michio, who opposed passage of the special Diet resolution, particularly the incorporation of such language as "aggression" and "colonial rule," had declared that "Japan's annexation of Korea took place smoothly." News of this statement had inflamed Koreans' anti-Japanese feelings to a fiery pitch once again, triggering violent protests by Korean students. For such incidents to occur is not so surprising, given the long history of Japan–Korea relations—but these protests took place thirty years after the Japan–Korea Treaty of 1965 was signed. Thirty years are not yet enough to enable people to forget. . . . I had been in Seoul more than ten years earlier. At that time, I had witnessed the outcry at the Japanese Ministry of Education's textbook inspections. I could not help but heave a deep sigh: history repeats itself.

Watanabe's statement made me feel as if I had been transported back in time. I recalled the rough going of the Japan–Korea negotiations at the time. These talks were aiming at closing the book on Japan's colonial rule over Korean Peninsula once and for all and re-establishing Japan–Korea diplomatic relations, on which talks between Prime Minister Yoshida and South Korean President Rhee Syngman had begun immediately after the conclusion of the Peace Treaty at San Francisco in 1951. In Japan, public sentiment and the logic of rationalizing Japanese colonial rule had been too strong; in Korea, nationalism and anti-Japanese feelings had been too strong, in the years immediately following Korea's regained independence, to permit diplomatic ties to be immediately restored. Thus almost 15 years elapsed from the first preliminary meeting in 1951 until the re-establishment of normal diplomatic ties between the two countries in 1965.

Rhee Syngman, a Korean nationalist revolutionary who had been imprisoned and tortured at the hands of the Li Dynasty and the Japanese military police, fled to exile in Hawaii after the signing of the Japan–Korea Annexation Treaty in 1910; later, he assumed the presidency of the interim government of the Republic of Korea established in Shanghai. Soon after the war ended and Korea was liberated from its colonial status in 1945, he came back to Seoul for the first time in 35 years to be installed with US support as the first president of the Republic of Korea.

His anti-Japanese sentiments had grown considerably in intensity since taking office as president. I once heard that when he was asked by a certain reporter during the Korean War what he would do if the Japanese army decided to come to his country's aid, Rhee replied: "In that case, South and North Korea would join forces to drive out the Japanese." Wondering whether he had actually said this, I checked the *Asahi Shimbun* archives but found no confirmation there. However, according to an article in the *Asahi Shimbun* dated December 3, 1952, carried on the AP wire service from Seoul, Rhee told an NBC interviewer, after criticizing the insincerity of Japan's postwar attitude toward its deeds before the war, that if Japanese troops came to Korea, there would inevitably be a serious conflict with the Korean people. He said: "The threatening influence of this conflict would spill over into East Asia. We must prevent this from happening." This was shortly after authorization of the formation, in the constitutionally demilitarized

Japan, of so-called "Police Reserves" at the request of the United States following the outbreak of the Korean War. (Japan's Self-Defense Forces had not yet been formed.)

The "Rhee Syngman Line," an exclusive fishing zone, was established by Rhee to protect Korean fishery resources; this, too, stemmed from Rhee's antagonistic policy toward Japan. One after another, Japanese fishing boats were captured by the South Korean navy on charges of violating the Rhee Line, heightening and amplifying anti-Korean feelings in Japan. Relations between Japan and Korea were deteriorating in a vicious spiral.

In January 1953, Rhee visited Tokyo at the request of General Clark, Commander of the United Nations Emergency Force. Though an informal one, his visit to Japan was a historic occasion; it led to the first Japan–Korea top level meeting with Yoshida Shigeru. Yet it was curt and cold to the end, testimony to the chilliness of Japan–Korea relations in those days. When Rhee saw minister of foreign affairs Okazaki Katsuo come to meet him at Haneda Airport, he was offended: "I was not invited by Japan," he said. "Therefore, for the Japanese not to greet me at all at the airport would be understandable, indeed preferable. But as a matter of common courtesy, to receive the head of state of a foreign nation, prime minister Yoshida himself ought to have come," and he turned down Yoshida's invitation to a banquet. Rhee's anti-Japanese attitude was beyond Yoshida's comprehension; Yoshida in any event lacked any sense of guilt for Japan's prewar colonial rule of Korea. The only thing the two men had in common was their self-assertiveness. They had talks at General Clark's residence and issued a joint communique, expressing "agreement on readiness to promote the normalization of diplomatic relations between Japan and Korea." But the two leaders' antipathy to each other threw a wet blanket over the talks from start to finish.

The following exchange at their initial meeting is well known: when Yoshida asked Rhee, "Aren't tigers still living in Korea?" Rhee replied "No: Kato Kiyomasa [Toyotomi Hideyoshi's frontline commander during Japan's invasion of Korea (1592–96)] caught them all and carted them off to Japan." Though seemingly too good to believe, this story, which depicts graphically the awkward, strained mood of their encounter, appears to be true. After the meeting, whenever Yoshida was asked which politicians he disliked the most, he used to name Kono Ichiro and Rhee Syngman. Kim Dongjo, who is mentioned in Part II of this book, heard Yoshida's remark in person. Rhee Syngman must have wounded Yoshida's pride just as grievously as Kono had. (Kono Ichiro, one of Hatoyama Ichiro's aides, had tried persistently to overthrow Yoshida.)

"Kubota's Remarks": A setback for Japan–Korea talks

Deeper-rooted even than his personal animosity towards Rhee Syngman, Yoshida must have had a sub-conscious wish to find a historical justification for Japan's colonial rule of Korea. The same can be said of the remarks made later by Fujio Masayuki and Watanabe Michio.

This attitude, moreover, could hardly be said to be limited to Yoshida or to his contemporaries in politics: it was shared to some greater or lesser extent by the Japanese public in general. It was starkly exposed at the third session of bilateral negotiations between the two countries, in October 1953, in the remarks of Kubota Kanichiro, a diplomat and then Japan's chief negotiator. During the talks with South Korea, the Japanese side pressed claims for the estates of dispossessed Japanese residents in Korea; the Korean side countered by demanding indemnification for the harm done to Korea by the Japanese during the Imperial era.

What Kubota said at this stage of the talks touched off a heated controversy. Takasaki Soji's *Mogen no genkei* (The archetype of thoughtless remarks)[2] relates the details of Kubota's remarks. The *Asahi Shimbun* (October 22, 1953) carried the Japanese foreign ministry's record of the proceedings at this bilateral meeting: "Japan built railroads and harbor facilities and developed farmland in Korea, for instance," said Kubota. "In that period, the annual net outlay was as much as 20 million yen from the Japanese treasury, i.e. the ministry of finance. If Korea intends to demand compensation for damages, we might ask Korea to reimburse us for our investment, and our two claims would cancel each other out."

According to Hang Sangil (president of the Social Science Research Institute of Korea), whose account is presumably based on the Korean side's minutes of the talks, the words Kubota used differ slightly from the Japanese record: "If Korea were to claim compensation for colonial rule over 36 years . . . , the Japanese side would be able to offset the Korean claim by arguing for a counterclaim taking into account the positive aspects of the Governor General's rule[, e.g.:] afforestation of deforested mountains, railroad and harbor construction, rice-field expansion."[3] Yet clearly, there is little substantial difference between the two versions.

According to the Foreign Affairs Ministry record quoted in the *Asahi Shimbun*, Kubota prefaced his remarks by saying that what he was about to say was strictly his personal opinion and by asking that it be treated as off-the-record: "Things being what they were in those days, if the Japanese had not been in Korea, probably China or Russia would have stepped in." According to Hang Sangil's account, Kubota said: "If Korea hadn't been annexed, it would have been occupied by China or Russia, and the situation would have been much worse than it was under Japanese rule."[4] Offended by the above remark, the Koreans protested strongly, saying: "If the Japanese hadn't colonized Korea, we ourselves would have built railroads and schools much earlier!" and broke off the talks. The Korean press gave front-page coverage to the incident, and the Korean public vilified Japan.

The Japanese government, however, immediately came to Kubota's defence. Foreign minister Okazaki Katsuo backed Kubota, saying at a press conference that he had "said an obvious thing, the way it should obviously be said" and also in a statement to the Diet, "We have no reason to retract the statement, as we haven't said anything wrong at all."[5] At the time, this attitude, however absurd, was accepted by politicians throughout Japan. The deadlocked negotiations remained in abeyance for more than four and a half years.

As Kubota said, Japanese colonial rule did play a role in Korea's modernization. And in the process leading to Japan's annexation of Korea, internal conflicts in Korea may have played a role, in addition to the hegemonic competition between Russia and Japan. Japan may have simply taken advantage of these circumstances. Nobody can rule out the possibility that either Russia or China would have colonized Korea if Japan had not done so.

Yet only by the ruler's logic can colonial rule be justified based on such circumstantial pleas. Without a doubt, Japan's annexation of Korea was carried out through intimidation, against a backdrop of overwhelming power, which quashed domestic objections. The fact that Japan seized capital goods from Korea, effectively preventing Korea from developing its own modern capitalism, the fact that Japan through its Japanization policy compelled the Korean people to adopt Japan's culture, language, even Japanese names and religion, the fact Japan cruelly humiliated the Koreans by conscripting Korea's men and by abducting young women and forcing them to become "comfort women" (sex slaves) for the Japanese military—these facts cannot be papered over with the ruler's logic of steps on the path to modernization. Kubota's remarks were in reality a calculated maneuver to build a stronger Japanese bargaining position and thereby to reduce the amount of reparations the Koreans would demand of Japan. But by making these remarks he so offended the Korean people that they were taken as nothing more than a reckless and indefensible slip of the tongue.

Forty-two years later, Watanabe Michio made a statement as thoughtless as Kubota's. In the midst of a falling-out with Korea due to Watanabe's gaffe, I paid a visit to Kwon Okie, President of the *Dong-A Ilbo* newspaper company (quoted previously). He had been his newspaper's chief international correspondent in Tokyo and later in Washington DC. As a noted Japanophile and journalist well informed about the inside workings of the Japan–Korea relationship, he had frequently given me thought-provoking suggestions concerning Japanese politics and Japan– Korea relations. Again he succinctly shared with me some valuable insights.

It is a fact that Japanese initiative accelerated Korean modernization. But that initiative was taken by Japan in an authoritarian, imperialistic way, and the Koreans never asked for it. Isn't it on that very point that the perceptions of our two countries diverge?

The Japanese want to stress their achievements contributing to Korea's modernization, while Korea can never forget their deep-seated grudge against the Japanese for having been forced under the yoke of the Japanese Empire. Due to this unfortunate divergence, the two countries continue to fail to see eye to eye. Watanabe's gaffe was a symptom of that gap, and for months it stood in the way of progress in the Japan–Korea talks.

Contacts between Japan and South Korea remained broken off for years. Japanese fishing boats continued to be captured for crossing the Rhee Line. Eventually, the Japanese attitude began to evolve—Kubota's remarks were eventually corrected and an apology was issued—to make life easier for Japanese fishermen. It was Kishi Nobusuke who took the initiative to reopen the completely gridlocked talks, but without success (as we saw in Part II). It was at this juncture that the repatriation to North Korea of Korean residents in Japan took place, a development that cast another long shadow on the talks.

In June 1958, negotiations between Japan and North Korea mediated by the Red Cross in Geneva came to a successful conclusion, and North Koreans living in Japan were repatriated at the initiative of Fujiyama Aiichiro, then minister for foreign affairs, who had been eager to do this. South Korea was furious, and cut off its trade with Japan; again, hostility prevailed for a time. Given Japan's obligation to come to terms with its historical responsibility for colonial rule, the Japanese government could overlook neither the existence of North Korea nor the situation of North Korean residents in Japan. Ironically, that, too, became another wedge driving South Korea and Japan farther apart.

Park Chunghee's pragmatism and a US request

Kishi stepped down in June 1960 after the U.S–Japan Security Treaty was finally, and tumultuously, renewed. Ikeda succeeded him and also took over the task of conducting Japan–Korea talks. In the following year, 1961, the environment surrounding Japan–Korea relations took a dramatic turn when Rhee Syngman was deposed by Park Chunghee, chairman of the Supreme National Council, a junta set in motion by a revolutionary student movement. Park Chunghee, who was later to assume the Korean presidency, stated straightaway that the highest priority should be given to normalization of Korea–Japan relations. Park began to send out feelers to Japan.

In the second volume of *Kiroku Shiina Etsusaburo* (The Shiina Etsusaburo record)[6] by Fujita Yoshiro, a former Diet member, Park Chunghee's brother-in-law Yuk Insu relates Park's thinking as follows.

> The revolution launched on Park's initiative aimed at two targets. One was military: the North Korean menace. The other was Korea's economic reconstruction, i.e. to break out of the country's poverty. . . . Korea faced two enemies. One was a face-to-face confrontation with North Korean communism. The other was the Koreans' anti-Japanese feelings, the nationwide hostility against Japan. "Having enemies both in the fore and in the rear leaves Korea always in an awkward position," was his view. Nothing was needed by Korea more than funds. The US supported Korea, but could not double its aid and could therefore not be relied on. If Korea–Japan relations could be successfully normalized, Korea might be in a position to make a straightforward request for official development assistance funds from Japan. It was, after all, an irreparable loss for Korea to break off Korea–Japan talks on account of anti-Japanese feelings or Korea's sense of national humiliation. Park kept this in mind. . . . He was criticized savagely, called Korea's second "I Wanyon" (the Korean Prime Minister who acquiesced to Japan's annexation of Korea [roughly equivalent to Quisling in Austrian history]).[7]

Prime minister Ikeda's June 1961 visit to the United States was the start of Ikeda's efforts to grapple with the Korean question, according to *Ikeda Hayato to sono jidai* (Ikeda Hayato and his times) by Ito Masaya, then chief secretary to Ikeda. US President Kennedy had made this suggestion: "Reconstruction of the Korean economy with Japanese help would stabilize the unstable political situation in Korea."[8] Ito infers from Kennedy's suggestion that Kennedy was asking Ikeda for Japanese cooperation because, no matter how much the United States spent on Korea, it just fueled corruption there: the Koreans didn't know what to do with the money. In the middle of the seemingly endless Vietnam War, the US wanted very much to strengthen solidarity among the US, Japan, and Korea. The United States was fed up with the persistent bickering between Korea, which was sending troops to Vietnam, and Japan, which was playing the role of logistical rear base.

A visit by Park Chunghee to Japan was arranged in preparation for his visit to the United States at Kennedy's invitation in November of the same year. There began a sudden flurry of developments involving Japan, the United States, and Korea. In advance of the presidential visit, Kim Jongpil, an aide to Park and staff member, came to Japan at the end of October and held frequent and long meetings with Ikeda and other important figures. On November 1, when US Secretary of State Dean Rusk came to Japan to participate in a meeting of the US–Japan Joint Committee for Economic Affairs, he also discussed Korean affairs with Ikeda. According to *Kiroku Shiina Etsusaburo* (The Shiina Etsusaburo record), Rusk strongly urged Ikeda to conclude the Japan–Korea negotiations. "South Vietnam is in a critical situation. If the US stumbles in Korea, US prestige will suffer badly,"[9] said Rusk and stressed that all Japan had to do now was to shore up the deteriorating Korean economy.

Rusk went on to Seoul for a meeting with Korean leaders as soon as he left Tokyo. Following this behind-the-scenes maneuvering, Park came to Japan on November 11 and confirmed at his meeting with Ikeda that Japan–Korea negotiations would rapidly be concluded. He visited Washington DC on November 14. The

US government gave Park its strong backing. The US–Korean summit's joint communiqué contained a passage stating that the USA hoped that Japan–Korea negotiations would proceed smoothly and that friendly relations between Japan and Korea would be established.[10]

As a career military officer of Korea and an alumnus of the military academy of Japan, Park had anti-Japanese feelings of a different sort from Rhee Syngman. As a soldier, he attached more importance to Japan's utility than to excessive ideological considerations. Naturally, Japanese politicians welcomed Park's involvement in Japan–Korea affairs. And interestingly, Ikeda, with his characteristic stress on economics, attached greater importance to the economic significance of Japan–Korea cooperation than to anything else, quite unlike Kishi and quite like Park. Ikeda made every effort to prevent the Japan–Korea relationship from taking on a military hue. According to Ito, he did this because Ikeda thought both that it would prevent Japan–Korea affairs from sowing the seeds of domestic political squabbles and that economic stabilization was the only thing that would bring political stability to Korea.

The Socialist Party was against the Japan–Korea talks because it meant acknowledging the quasipermanent partition of Korea. Ikeda did not share this view. According to *Ikeda Hayato to sono jidai*, Ikeda thought:

> If South Korea succeeded in economic reconstruction, the North would be prodded into doing something. The present situation in South Korea is as close to ruin as Japan's situation was immediately after the war, but this country's riches lie in its industrious and highly educated labor force. Without any doubt, South Korea could enjoy prosperity, if this labor were harnessed to capital. And if South Korea succeeded in achieving economic growth as Japan did, a demographic influx from North Korea would take place, similar to the immigration from East Germany to West Germany. Even in the absence of major migration, however, it would force North Korea to ease the rigor of its totalitarian system.[11]

Though his predictions did not come true immediately, developments in the international situation over the past few years incline one to view his thinking as prescient.

DIVERGENT REASONS, CONVERGENT OPPOSITION TO THE JAPAN–KOREA ACCORD

The crux of the bilateral negotiations, i.e. the issue of Japan's payment of reparations to Korea, was to be settled in the form of economic cooperation, although the Korean side interpreted these disbursements as based on their right to demand restitution for wrongs. Ohira Masayoshi, finance minister and aide to Ikeda, and Kim Jongpil, head of the Korean Central Intelligence Agency and aide to Park, reached a basic agreement on the approximate amount and exchanged memoranda regarding the commitment to transfer funds. The framework of the said memorandum between Kim and Ohira consisted of grants amounting to US$300 million, credits amounting to US$200 million, and something extra (private sector contributions) amounting to US$100 million. Both countries thereupon began to take steps to normalize their diplomatic ties. In both countries, fierce opposition to the accord arose from among the opposition parties as well as among students.

Yet the reasons for this opposition differed entirely. In Korea, students and opposition parties joined forces to resist the accord, fiercely lambasting their government's attitude towards Japan as weak-kneed and humiliating. They insisted that normalization of Korea–Japan diplomatic ties should be unconditionally premised on a Japanese apology and reparations to atone for Japan's colonial past. The opposition parties urged that Korea press much more onerous claims for reparations (on the order of $1,500 million for property damages and $1,200 million for the people's suffering), in addition to rigid maintenance of the Rhee Line. Large-scale student demonstrations took place first on March 24, 1964, and continued intermittently around Seoul and throughout the nation until martial law was declared 70 days later. Incidentally, the generation that engaged in the strife at that time against the Japan–Korea accord now occupies positions of power in every core domain in today's Korea; this generation of South Koreans corresponds to the generation that violently protested against the US–Japan Security Treaty in Japan.

In Japan, the Socialist Party and the General Council of Trade Unions of Japan, together with students, organized protests against the bilateral accord. But as I have already said, the reasoning behind the Japanese protests had nothing in common with the Korean objections: Japanese opponents objected, first, that to establish diplomatic relations with South Korea without duly taking North Korea into account was tantamount to acknowledging and rendering permanent the North-South partition of the Korean Peninsula (the Socialist Party even called the Park regime "the puppet government in the southern part of the Korean peninsula"); second, that to conclude talks with the Park regime was equivalent to lending Japanese support to a military dictatorship; and third, that the proposed tripartite military alliance among Japan, the US, and Korea was a challenge to peace in the Far East. In sharp contrast to Korean objections, the moral issues connected with Japan's colonial past played no part in Japanese considerations at the time.

Ikeda soon stepped down due to illness. Kishi's younger brother Sato Eisaku, who assumed the post of prime minister in November 1964, brought the Japan–Korea negotiations to a conclusion. Shiina Etsusaburo, once called Kishi Nobusuke's right-hand man, took charge of the matter as minister for foreign affairs. On February 17, 1965, Shiina, who had been sent to Seoul to bring the talks to a conclusion, issued a statement on his arrival at Kimpo Airport in which he wished to express his "sincere regret" that there had been "an unfortunate period" in relations between the two countries for which he felt "deep remorse." This apology was so well received in Korea that virtually overnight the talks at last reached their final stage.

Let us leave for later our discussion of the detailed background to Shiina's statement. Due to the two countries' difference of positions, the treaty handled very ambiguously both the impropriety of

Japan's colonizing rule and related reparations. On the Japan–Korea Annexation Treaty of 1910, for instance, the Koreans took the position from the start that, because it was signed under duress, it should be interpreted as null and void. Japan refused to concede this, maintaining that the treaty had been valid in light of international law at that time. In the end, as I mentioned earlier, the two parties decided to compromise, stating simply that they "acknowledge the said treaty to be no longer valid."

In his publicized comments at the treaty's signing, Sato Eisaku said merely, "It is extremely natural for Japan and Korea, neighbors with only a narrow strip of water between them and a long and ancient history of exchanges, to maintain good neighborly and friendly ties with each other, with mutual respect for their respective positions." He made no mention of the phrases used in Shiina's statement, "unfortunate past experience," "sincere regret," and "deep remorse."

Why then, despite the wide discrepancies between their positions as well as fierce domestic opposition, did both governments conclude the accord? One can point out the following decisive factors: first, the perceived need to form a united front against "the Communist threat"; second, the need to develop the Korean economy with Japanese support; and third, strong pressure from the United States (the most decisive factor).

Though Shiina expressed his sincere apologies outwardly, he had not changed his mind inwardly. And like Shiina, almost all conservative politicians in Japan at the time seemed to want to find some justification for Japan's colonization of Korea. Even seven years later, when for example Tanaka Kakuei became prime minister, this attitude prevailed. Upon forming his cabinet, Tanaka answered questions at the plenary session of the House of Representatives in January 1974 as follows: "The past period of annexation between Japan and the Korean Peninsula was very long. After that period ended, by asking individual Koreans and listening to other people, I have learned that, in the long history of Korea and Japan brought together as one nation, the things remaining most deeply implanted in the Korean people's hearts include the transfer of knowhow related to the cultivation of nori [laver seaweed] and the introduction of the Japanese educational system, in particular compulsory education; these spiritual things, rather than economic influences, stand in the Koreans' estimation as valuable contributions to Korean culture, things that the Koreans regard as worth preserving even today. They have taken root in their lives, and that is what is so important." This— though almost as provocative as Kubota's remarks—was almost overlooked, simply because it was not said at the negotiating table. At the time, apparently, beliefs of this kind were not considered so out of place.

THE TEXTBOOK INCIDENT DILEMMA

The Japan–Korea Treaty of 1965 was hammered out by the Ikeda–Ohira lineage of politicians descended from Yoshida Shigeru, most of whom were members of the conservative mainstream Kochikai group. This group based its actions on Japan's economic interests. From the pact's conclusion on, however, it was not they but the right-wingers of the LDP, sympathetic to the political heirs of Kishi, Sato, and Shiina, or the pro-Taiwan group, who formed the core of the pro-Korean group in Japan and became the most friendly to Korea.

Yet most members of the pro-Korean group were weighted down by onerous contradictions. Most (notably Kishi Nobusuke himself) were dyed-in-the-wool nationalists, a trait that led them to attempt to justify Japan's presence in Korea's history. That is to say that, while their anti-communist stance brought them closer to South Korea, the rest of their political makeup made them incompatible with Koreans' often violently inimical feelings toward Japan.

The inconsistencies in the pro-Korean group's views were exposed in 1982, while Suzuki Zenko was prime minister, when another incident drew public attention. It concerned history textbooks. In the process of the ministry of education's inspection of high school history textbooks (required in Japan before texts receive official approval), it transpired that the ministry had instructed the editor to rewrite a passage that originally referred to Japanese "aggression" overseas, ordering it to be changed to "advance." Similarly, the ministry ordered another passage referring to "the March 1st independence movement" in Korea to be changed to "rioting." This unleashed a torrent of clamorous protests from both China and Korea.

During my one-year stay in Seoul as a student, I was drawn into the maelstrom of the Korean public's outrage against Japan. The phrase "distortion of history" became a buzzword, not only in news reports but even on entertainment programs on TV. Distortion became a leitmotiv in discourse everywhere. Restaurants and taxis put up signs saying "No Japanese, please!" The controversy led to the opening in a Seoul suburb of Independence Memorial Hall, a museum where exhibits realistically depicted or reenacted the barbarous acts committed by Japanese during Korea's colonization.

This situation was eventually brought under control by chief cabinet secretary Miyazawa Kiichi, who released an official statement declaring "The Japanese government is keenly aware that our country's acts caused great hardship and extensive harm to Asian nations, including Korea and China." Amidst vehement criticism from Korea or China, minister of education Ogawa Heiji gave a straightforward reply to a question in the House of Representatives Committee for Educational Affairs when he described the Sino–Japanese War as an "act of aggression." Ogawa was the first cabinet minister to categorically call Japan's wartime acts "aggression" in the Diet.

On this occasion, most of the LDP's right wing bristled at these Chinese and Korean attacks, calling them "interference in Japan's internal affairs." But many were members of the Japan–Korea Parliamentarian League and of the pro-Korean group, and this flare-up exposed their ideological inconsistencies. Several parliamentarians were caught on the horns of a dilemma, unable to be completely faithful to their beliefs due to their pro-Korean commitment. When accusing Japan of responsibility for wrongdoing in the past, Korea and China tend to rise above their ideologies and form a common front against Japan. If China had been the only country to accuse Japan on the textbook issue, the LDP's right wing would have resisted their criticism with more determination. Their internal inconsistencies and divisions came to the fore in debate on the Diet resolution commemorating the 50th anniversary of the end of the war. Parliamentarians opposing the resolution included many members of the Japan–Korea Parliamentarian League. This so upset their Korean colleagues that some Korean parliamentarians even called for the League's dissolution.

Sometime after the furor over the textbooks gave signs of having died down for the time being, I asked Kwon Okie what he thought about the curiously close Korean ties of yet unrepentant Japanese nationalists. Kwon answered: "The pro-Korean group in Japan call themselves right-wing, but they aren't pure nationalists: they're pro-US nationalists. If you watch Mr. Kishi's actions carefully, you can see the reason: Japan and Korea were reconciled as a result of US mediation in the cause of anti-communism. The Korean side has also made use of the other party without regard to its fundamental beliefs."

The Chun Doohwan regime, which came into existence after Park Chunghee's assassination, asked Japan for aid totaling $6,000 million as "economic cooperation for security." This aid turned out to be a political entanglement. The Korean side argued as follows: Korea provides for Japan's defense against a military threat by confronting North Korea on the 38th parallel; Korea is therefore naturally entitled to ask Japan to shoulder its share of the burden; after all, the amount of economic cooperation granted under the Japan–Korea Treaty of 1965 was paltry. This line of reasoning led directly to the possibility of Japan–Korea defense cooperation, and in any event the South Koreans were requesting more than Japan could readily accept, but the textbook incident had put Japan in an awkward position.

Nakasone Yasuhiro, Suzuki's successor as prime minister, reached a settlement with the Koreans, promising $4,000 million, and on his first official foreign tour as prime minister, he chose to visit South Korea. Partying with president Chun in January 1983 on his visit to Korea, he even sang a song in Korean to deepen friendship and to accelerate the establishment of a new bilateral relationship. At the time, three hard-liners used to be spoken of in one breath: Reagan–Nakasone–Chun Doohwan. Nakasone deliberately tickled the Koreans' pride to promote the formation of a closer relationship, revealing his strategy of laying the foundations of a framework for coexistence between Japan and other Asian countries without upsetting Japan's relationship with the USA.

This led Nakasone to pave the way for a Korean presidential visit to Japan. During Chun Doohwan's visit, Emperor Showa apologized to the South Korean president for Japan's colonizing rule in Korea, with the first use (by the Emperor) of the expression "regret." (I will describe the details later on.) Prime minister Nakasone then expressed his contrition, using phrases that addressed the issue as if to fill in the gaps in the Emperor's apology. In this as in his other acts, he took great pains to bolster Japan–Korea ties and cement his ties of friendship with Chun Doohwan. As I pointed out earlier, Nakasone was very adaptable, despite his strong nationalistic roots, as a result of his strategic perceptions of the East–West cold war. His arrangements for Chun's visit to Japan and his clear-cut statements about Japan's "aggressive war" are evidence of this adaptability.

The "Pro-US Nationalists" Versus the "Pure Nationalists"

Nakasone ran into the worst difficulties in coping with nationalism in his own camp in September 1986, when minister of education Fujio Masayuki published a controversial magazine article. Nakasone, who had herded the cabinet together and marched them off to worship officially at Yasukuni Shrine the previous year, backed down from further shrine visits in the face of fierce protests from China. This retreat was repellent to the right wing, and notably to Fujio. As mentioned in Chapter 10, a textbook edited by the right-wing National Conference for Defending Japan brought matters to a head when it touched off 'the second text-book incident.' Nakasone brought the situation under control in person by postponing the official decision to have the textbook read in schools. This the right wing also found repellent. Fujio wrote the offending article mentioned above for the October 1986 issue of *Bungei Shunju*, a monthly. His argument runs as follows. The Japan–Korea annexation was agreed upon bilaterally and legally, in both form and substance; Korea bears some responsibility for the annexation; is there any guarantee that China or Russia would not have intervened in the Korean peninsula, had Japan not annexed Korea?

Nakasone had to scramble to patch up relations with Korea. Fujio, like Nakasone, was once a member of Kono Ichiro's faction: they had roots in the same political soil. After Kono's death, Fujio joined the faction of Fukuda Takeo, Kishi's successor. Fujio was a noted hard-liner in the LDP at the time. Nakasone urged Fujio repeatedly to retract his article, but Fujio wouldn't budge. Finally Nakasone, judging him irredeemable, removed him from the cabinet. Fujio's remarks appear to have been a deliberate provocation, issued in full cognizance of the foreseeable Korean reaction.

On the very day Fujio lost his cabinet job, I was put in the awkward situation of having to write an interpretive article on the background to this incident. Certain insightful remarks by Kwon Okie ran through my mind repeatedly and gave me a clue to how to start. Kwon had pointed out that Kishi and Nakasone were nationalists, but that both had become pro-American nationalists. Fujio, on the other hand, was a pure nationalist who remained resolutely anti-American. Fujio was therefore less committed to the new Japan–Korea relationship, which the pro-American factor had catalyzed. Moreover, the pro-Taiwanese Fujio felt indebted to Chiang Kaishek, who had pardoned Japan, "repaying violence with virtue"; he was much less sympathetic to the Koreans, who had remained staunchly anti-Japanese since Rhee Syngman. I used this line of reasoning as the backbone of what I wrote in my interpretive article.

Ishihara Shintaro, author of 'No' to ieru Nihon (A Japan that can say 'No') and a man who basks in controversy for the anti-American tone of his sayings and doings, could be counted in the same category as Fujio. When prime minister Hosokawa Morihiro called the war a "war of aggression" at his press conference after assuming office in August 1993, Ishihara challenged Hosokawa to a debate in the House of Representatives Committee on the Budget the following October, intending to argue that Japan need make no apology to Korea for the previous war. In his rebuttal, Ishihara said what Fujio had written: "In the light of the disordered situation in Korea at that time, Korea would, without any doubt, have been annexed to neighboring China or Russia (had no annexation to Japan been concluded)." Thus, the archetypal LDP right-winger Ishihara's weak influence in Japan–Korea affairs can be explained in the same way as Fujio's.

Chapter 12

The Anti-Pro-South Koreans and the Diet Delegation to North Korea

THE KOCHIKAI'S AVERSION TO SOUTH KOREA: THE MILITARY DICTATORSHIP ERA

It was the Sato cabinet that brought the negotiations with South Korea to a conclusion, as I mentioned, and the Ikeda cabinet also played a major role, thanks to talks between Ikeda Hayato and Park Chunghee, as well as an agreement on economic cooperation hammered out by Ohira Masayoshi and Kim Jongpil. However, once the treaty had been concluded between Japan and South Korea, close ties with South Korea were actually maintained by politicians in Kishi Nobusuke's lineage, not Ikeda Hayato's political heirs in the Kochikai, which kept its distance with respect to the South Korean regime.

There were several reasons for this. For a start, the Kochikai had always been cool to South Korea partly because of its founder's (i.e. Yoshida Shigeru's) personal dislike for Rhee Syngman. While the LDP's strongly anti-Communist rightwingers had no qualms about ties to South Korea's military dictatorship, the leftwing Kochikai did, and wanted to remain relatively impartial toward both North and South Korea. Kishi and the pro-South Koreans close to him were constantly wreathed in rumors involving their interests in economic cooperation with South Korea; factional resistance also contributed to the Kochikai's antipathy to South Korea. The most clearcut case was the scandal surrounding the bilateral loan to

South Korea for construction of a subway in Seoul, which led to hearings in both countries' parliaments.

Because the Kochikai had a traditional Japanese view of China and wanted to restore diplomatic relations, this, too, inclined them to put ties with South Korea on the back burner. During the Korean War, China had sent reinforcements to North Korea and stood staunchly by it. Exchanges between China and South Korea were still pipe dreams in those days. Ohira Masayoshi, who became foreign minister in the Tanaka cabinet, played an important role in pushing for normalization of diplomatic ties between Japan and China.

It was also during the Tanaka premiership (in 1973) that the South Korean opposition leader Kim Daejung was kidnapped by South Korean operatives while on a visit to Japan and hustled back to South Korea. Only a few months later, on August 15, 1974, at a ceremony celebrating South Korean Independence Day, a Japanese resident of South Korean origin attempted to assassinate Park Chunghee but killed the president's wife, Yuk Yongsu, instead. Foreign Minister Ohira found himself working overtime in the aftermath of both shocking incidents.

Incidentally, during World War II, when Korea was a Japanese colony, Tanaka Kakuei owned and operated an airplane parts manufacturing plant in South Korea's Taejon. According to Hayasaka Shigezo, when the war ended, Tanaka left Taejon for Japan, feted with cries of "banzai" by representatives of his former workers, to whom on parting he had handed over ownership and a catalogue of all the factory's assets, "a gift, gratis, to you who inherit the newborn Korea." Hayasaka recalls a time after the war when Tanaka arrived uninvited in a room where talks were being held with a South Korean businessman and volunteered insights from his personal experience with Koreans. His relaxed attitude and respect for the Koreans was unusual in the Kochikai.

On one occasion, for example, when Tanaka became the LDP's chief secretary, he called his personal secretary and right-hand man Hayasaka into his office and said, "Listen: from now on, people from all kinds of intelligence agencies like the CIA and the KGB are going to be trailing you, trying to get information. You don't have to avoid them: you know what you can say and what you can't. But when you're with people working for South Korea or North Korea, be very, very careful: each and every one of these guys is smarter than you. The Korean people have been treated rotten for centuries, first by the Chinese, then by the Japanese. What they've gone through is no picnic."

Now let us return to the subject of the Kochikai: Miki was prime minister in the next cabinet and Miyazawa Kiichi, also a member of the Kochikai, was foreign minister. The Miki cabinet had a hard time reaching a definitive "political solution" to the Kim Daejung kidnapping affair. But they did, and at the same time, they managed also to solve the problem of some Japanese journalists who had been arrested for "assistance in rebellion and subversion" because they had helped anti-establishment activists. During the Chun Doohwan presidency, Japanese prime minister Ohira died suddenly and was succeeded by Suzuki Zenko, a Kochikai member. At that time, I was about to go to Seoul to study Korean, and before my departure when I paid a visit to Suzuki, whom I had known for a long time, he warned me with great apparent concern: "South Korea is a dangerous place; make sure you don't get arrested for anything." It was a fitting send-off message for a Kochikai member, and I remember I had mixed feelings about it.

During Suzuki's premiership, the Chun Doohwan regime made a bid for $6 billion dollars in economic aid from Japan on the grounds that Korea was shouldering the burden of Japan's defense, demanding economic aid for security. The controversy over Japan's history textbooks also flared up during Suzuki's premiership. Miyazawa was chief cabinet secretary and Ogawa Heiji, also a member of the Kochikai and a relative of Miyazawa's to boot, was education minister; theirs was the task of smoothing over the affair. Ito Masayoshi, Ohira's direct heir, was foreign minister, and this was a man whose very face betrayed an obvious dislike for South Korea, a fact that did not remain unnoted by the South Koreans. When Miyazawa later visited South Korea as prime minister, he encountered fierce protests over the involuntary enlistment of Korean women as sexual slaves for the Japanese military in World War II. The men of this political stripe were by no means friends of North Korea, but their total lack of sympathy for South Korea (which South Korea reciprocated) was nonetheless extremely apparent.

Kono Yohei left the LDP at one point to join the Shinjiyu (New Liberal) Club and when that group dissolved, he returned to the LDP fold and quickly joined the Kochikai; he, too, for a long time kept South Korea at arm's length. He made his first visit—ever—to South Korea when he was deputy prime minister and foreign minister in the Murayama cabinet. He had never visited South Korea before, but this was not so much because he belonged to the Kochikai but because he, together with Utsunomiya Tokuma, had been a prominent supporter of Kim Daejung. As a general rule, dyed-in-the-wool pro-China politicians likewise remained aloof from South Korea.

RESPONSIBILITY FOR THE PARTITION OF NORTH AND SOUTH KOREA

Without any doubt the military dictatorships of Park Chunghee and Chun Doohwan contributed to giving South Korea a scary image. Notable is the massacre in Kwangju in 1980 (before Chun Doohwan came to power), in which the army was called out to repress demonstrations against Kim Daejung's arrest and hundreds of demonstrators were killed. As a result, both the Socialist Party and the LDP tended to avoid seeking more comprehensive ties with South Korea. The most overt criticism of the South Korean regime came, however, not from the Kochikai with its predominantly conservative former bureaucrats, but from Miki Takeo's faction and other party left-wingers.

The best example is Utsunomiya Tokuma, a disciple of Ishihashi Tanzan. Tokuma was the eldest son of Utsunomiya Taro, a general of the Imperial Japanese Army and commander of Japanese forces in Korea. The son had been a Marxist who was jailed as a subversive before the war; after the war, he made a fortune on the stock market and ran Minofagen Pharmaceuticals before entering politics. In word and deed, he remained consistently the left-most member of the conservative camp. In 1964, he opposed the creation by Kaya Okinori, Nadao Hirokichi, and the LDP's right wing of the Asian Affairs Study Group; he cooperated to create the counterveiling Asian and African Affairs Study Group in the bosom of the LDP with Matsumura Kenzo and Fujiyama Aiichiro as advisors. He pushed energetically to establish friendly relations with China and North Korea, and he was one of the few LDP Diet members who strenuously opposed the signing of the treaty with South Korea.

In 1967, two years after the treaty's signing, Utsunomiya was invited to the University of Tokyo's May Festival, where he delivered an address on North Korea and Japan. His message about the Korean peninsula could be summarized in terms of three concerns: first, Korea is the nation closest in kinship to Japan; second, if tensions on the 38th North parallel should heat up to the point of boiling over, the consequences for Japan would be extremely serious; and third, Japan had responsibility for the Korean peninsula's being divided today into North and South Korea.

It follows from these points, he said, that establishing relations with only one of Korea's two halves was improper and that Japan should have peaceful ties with the entire Korean nation. Making a fuss about spies and plots whenever the question of North Korea came up was an intelligence-agency-bureaucratic type way of thinking and extremely worrisome. Diplomacy and politics must play greater roles.[1]

What is this "responsibility for the divided Korea" that Utsunomiya talks about? Japan annexed Korea and turned it into a military stronghold, giving the Soviet Union, when it finally declared war on Japan, a pretext to advance southward into Korea "to disarm the Japanese army." This led to today's divided Korea, says Utsunomiya. Many years after this statement by Utsunomiya, namely in January 1995, Socialist Party head and prime minister Murayama Tomiichi mentioned Japan's responsibility in the course of Diet deliberations, saying: "Korea's division into North and South Korea and its present unhappy condition are, in some measure, I think, the historical responsibility of the Japanese people." Earlier, in July 1994, at a US–Japan summit shortly after he became prime minister, in the course of discussions about North Korea's nuclear arms program, Murayama had expounded on the close historical ties between Japan and the Korean peninsula, mentioning Japan's responsibility for the partition of Korea.

The day following the Diet session, however, Murayama had to retract his statement, saying "What I said yesterday in the Diet referred to responsibility for the historical circumstances of Japan's former colonial domination of Korea, which was in no way partitioned by the Japanese government at any time, but rather by the victors after World War II, who divided it amongst themselves. . . . I wish to make it clear that Japan has no responsibility for the division of Korea into North and South Korea." This correction was made in accordance with foreign ministry instructions. In the past, the Japanese government had always taken the view that Korea's division resulted from the balance of power between the United States and the communist states; Japan was not involved and bore no responsibility.

The "responsibility" that the foreign ministry denies refers to direct responsibility and legal accountability. Korea's division stems from the separate occupations by US and Soviet forces, and the line of demarcation is the truce line established at the end of the Korean War. Korea's partition results from military dynamics having nothing to do with Japan. And in that sense, Japan certainly bears no responsibility. But as I mentioned already, it is also indisputable that there would have been no separate US–Soviet occupation of the Korean peninsula had it not been a Japanese colony. And if Japan's unconditional surrender had occurred slightly earlier than it did, the Soviet Union might not have been able to declare war on Japan at the last minute and send its troops south into North Korea.

Whatever the case, Japan, Korea's colonial master, was defeated and occupied, but not partitioned; when the Korean War broke out, Japan was able to take advantage of the cold war balance of power to supply the United States with materiel and prime its own economic growth. Yet Japan's colony, Korea, was not as fortunate: scarcely had it time to celebrate its liberation before it became a nation divided against itself, a battlefield where Koreans fought against Koreans. I think it is natural for the Japanese to feel a moral responsibility for this disparity in the two countries' destinies.

Murayama's amended statement of course drew criticism from South Korea. The Foreign Ministry held that for the prime minister to acknowledge Japan's responsibility could not fail to make future negotiations with North Korea more difficult and add to the cost to Japan when North and South Korea were eventually reunified: best to leave the whole thing unsaid.

UTSUNOMIYA TOKUMA'S VIEW OF ASIA: HIS FATHER'S WILL

We return now to Utsunomiya Tokuma, whose view of Korea and of Asia was strongly influenced by his father, Utsunomiya Taro, the general who commanded the Japanese army in colonized Korea. Utsunomiya Taro was among the most enlightened officers in the Japanese military, and he felt a deep attachment to Korea's common people. On March 1, 1919, while he was commander in Korea, erupted the famous "banzai" incident, which marked the emergence of the Korean Independence movement. The Japanese army crushed the uprising, killing many people, and Utsunomiya Taro was branded from that time on as a cruel and repressive commander, but according to his son (in Utsunomiya Taro, published in the *Asahi Journal*, June 14, 1964), the general called out the troops but expressly forbade them to use live ammunition under any circumstances. Officials in the army ministry believed Taro's leniency was inciting the Korean masses to insurrection and put pressure on him to take a harder line to quash the uprising, but Taro resolutely refused, calling their demands nonsense. Later, when the affair was brought before the League of Nations, Taro's attitude and the documented existence of his express orders not to shoot at demonstrators turned out to be advantageous to Japan. In the same *Asahi Journal* article, Utsunomiya Tokuma writes the following:

> My father's affection for Korea was part and parcel of his feelings for China and all of Asia. You can call it the ideology of the Meiji Japanese. When the slogan "Respect the Emperor and Expel the Barbarians!" was replaced by "Overthrow the Feudal Government and Open Up the Country to the Rest of the World!"—in other words, when Japan decided to end its isolation and modernize, opening its doors and eyes to the rest of the world—the world was under Western domination, almost all of Asia and Africa had been colonized, and China and Korea were on the verge of subjugation, too.

> Yet the antiquated and corrupt governments of China and Korea and inefficient political systems were virtually incapable of maintaining their independence. For this reason, Japanese of goodwill naturally lent support to revolutionary forces in both countries (which was in Japan's own interest) and hoped that completely modernized independent governments would emerge in China and Korea. Sun Yatsen, Huang Xing, Jin Yujun, and other Asian revolutionaries came to Japan, and Tokyo became a center of the modernizing movement in East Asia.

> My father apparently had close contacts with these people. And the country that was exerting the most blatant repression to stamp out independence movements in China and Korea was Imperial Russia.
> . . .

> My father used to say to people: Japanese should marry Koreans. One day when I was just a little boy, he had me kneel stiffly in front of a low desk and read a booklet aloud to him. In a loud voice, I declaimed an essay he had written whose message was "Japanese should marry Koreans." My mother was listening nearby and laughed that I was still a bit too young to be reading stuff like that. My father, however, was sternly serious: I'm sure that he wanted me to have a Korean wife when I was older.

Tokuma witnessed the massacre of Koreans in Japan after the Great Kanto Earthquake of 1923; it was the year after his father Taro's death. Tokuma was 16, and he tells how he would never forget the sight of people (Japanese) organizing vigilante gangs that trooped around hunting for Koreans. His father left a will, the gist of which was "Asians, people of color, non-Christians! You must unite and resist the invasion of the Western powers! I pray that you of the same mind and intent will fight for this cause!" Utsunomiya Tokuma ends his article with the following words:

> In retrospect, this is the ideology of the Greater East Asian Co-Prosperity Sphere as well as the spirit of the Asian and African Affairs Study Group, but for my father, this was a broader, deeper, very, very keenly felt emotional thing. Through the window of the Meiji Restoration [by which direct Imperial rule was restored], the Japanese were seeing the contemporary world for the first time; these were their feelings and the feelings of fellow Asians; against the backdrop of Japan's rise to prominence and prosperity, this spirit spread to Asia and to Africa. Although I do understand the desire to justify the "Greater East Asian War" [World War II in the Pacific] as a step in its spread, is this not at the same time meaningless, unless efforts are made to improve relations with China, North Korea, and the former French Indo–China and to banish American meddling in Asia?
>
> For unless this is done, the Great East Asian War will have had as its ultimate result only to open the doors decisively to American influence in Asia and to put continental China, North Korea, and North Vietnam under Russian influence. At this point in time, it is indeed meaningful to ally oneself to my father's cause, but by no means is it an easy task.

The thinking of Utsunomiya Tokuma's father, who made contact with Kim Okkyoon and other Asian revolutionaries, appears to reflect the hopes for Asia's modernization that permeates the early thinking of Fukuzawa Yukichi. At the same time, elements of Greater Asianism influenced by Sun Yatsen are also apparent.

There are hints of overembellishment in Tokuma's image of his father, but the son certainly inherited his father's dream of weaning Asia from America's bosom and of Asian people's devoting themselves, whether anti-communist or not, to the construction of Asian solidarity.

Utsunomiya Tokuma appeared in a dialogue with the Sinologist Takeuchi Yoshimi published in the May 27, 1966, issue of the *Weekly Asahi*. They argued that both the United States and Japan should open their eyes to China as a step toward Tokyo's reestablishing diplomatic relations with Beijing. Utsunomiya held that the Greater East Asia War was started by totalitarian forces and that Sino–Japanese relations should be normalized as quickly as possible in order to deal definitively with the aftereffects of the war. But (as we see from the article I quoted earlier) due to his resistance to Western imperialism, Utsunomiya was unable to completely detach himself from justifications of the Pacific War, and Takeuchi largely echoed and applauded his Greater Asianism. Takeuchi indeed preached the duality of the Greater East Asia War: on one hand, an aggressive imperialistic war against Asia, on the other, a war of resistance against Western imperialism.

In his *Asahi Journal* article, Utsunomiya even writes that "in the very midst of the Russo–Japanese War, some Japanese newspapers openly preached anti-war themes, and Yosano Akiko wrote poems loudly proclaiming her hatred of war," lamenting that the breath of Meiji era freedom turned gradually militaristic. Utsunomiya's opposition to violent domination by national authority is what led him, he said, to criticize South Korea's military regime and to actively support the Korean opposition leader Kim Daejung.

Utsunomiya's opposition to the Japan–Korea Treaty was principally a question of maintaining a balance in Japan's attitude between North and South Korea. The need to maintain this balance was behind Utsunomiya's strenuous efforts to maintain friendly relations with North Korea. An advocate of friendship with North Korea of the same prominence as Kuno Chuji, Utsunomiya Tokuma visited the North several times and built close ties to its leader, Kim Ilsung. In Utsunomiya's eyes, Kim Ilsung was more of an Asian leader and Third World representative than a Communist. Needless to say, Utsunomiya was severely rebuked for this by the South Korean government. That he was on such friendly terms with North Korea and also a steadfast supporter of Kim Daejung had the unfortunate consequence of making Kim Daejung look even more dangerous in the eyes of the South Korean government. It happened that when Kim Daejung was kidnapped in Tokyo, he was there precisely to meet Utsunomiya and other Japanese supporters. Utsunomiya demanded permission to visit South Korea to plead for Kim Daejung's freedom to be restored, but quite predictably, South Korea refused even to let him into the country.

It has never been widely understood in South Korea why opposition politicians and even LDP members like Utsunomiya Tokuma, as well as other political and media figures in Japan, actively led the movement to support Kim Daejung. Kim Daejung's repeated criticisms of the South Korean regime, from overseas and especially from Japan, helped in a strange way to inspire mixed feelings in other South Korean critics of the Park regime, politicians and media figures alike, who largely blamed Japan for allowing these criticisms, alleging that the Japanese were still treating South Korea like a colony. These criticisms boiled down to saying that Japan's deliberate refusal to take into account South Korea's present stage of historical development and progress toward democracy and its measuring of Korea by Japanese standards differed in no wise from the prewar Japanese attitude toward Korea. Similar in some ways to American criticisms of China for human rights abuses, Japan's criticisms of South Korea are all the more likely to fall on deaf ears because Japan once colonized Korea. Whether of the left or of the right, all Japanese who criticize South Korea appear equally anti-Korean to Koreans.

FAR-REACHING CONSEQUENCES OF KOREA'S DEMOCRATIZATION

Yet for this very reason, the steps toward greater democracy taken by South Korea since Kim Youngsam became president in 1993 have helped greatly to advance Japan–South Korea relations. Not only for the LDP, but also for the Socialist Party, which had been waiting for an opportunity to change its South Korea policy, this shift was a signal to act and a cause that they could rally to. The advent of a civilian government in South Korea was clearly connected to the removal of the threat from China and the Soviet Union, North Korea's patrons. First came South Korea's "Northern policy": South Korea successfully established diplomatic relations with both China and the Soviet Union; the decisive next step was prompted by the collapse of the Soviet Union.

As the cold war ended on the international arena, so did the LDP's postwar monopoly of power end in Japan. The first non-LDP cabinet in decades was formed, followed closely by a tripartite coalition government composed of the LDP, the Socialists, and the New Party Sakigake. The chairman of the Socialist Party, who once railed against South Korea, had no sooner taken his seat in the halls of power than he prepared to visit South Korea, where in talks with the President of South Korea, the two nations confirmed each other's intention to cooperate. The unimaginable had now become reality. This arrangement permitted a shift to natural neighborly ties, without catalysts: neither cold-war strategic considerations, nor anti-communism, nor avowal of friendship with the United States to facilitate the rapprochement. For the same reason, Japan's view of its own history was about to be put to the test.

All this is not to say that Japan–Korea relations improved steadily and smoothly under the Kim Youngsam administration. Pro-Japanese when assuming office, Kim soon found himself stalemated in the domestic political game and constrained in his possible range of measures vis-à-vis North Korea, and gradually assumed a harsher posture toward Japan, prodded no doubt by an apparently unending series of problematic statements by Japanese politicians. He whipped up nationalistic sentiment by dispatching troops to boastfully occupy the territorially contested Takeshima/Tokdo islands. Toward the end of his administration, he went so far as to arrest former presidents Roh Taewoo and Chun Doohwan on charges of past crimes, prompting a response in some quarters in Japan that "as we always suspected, the Koreans are inscrutable."

As it happened, the rivalry between Japan and Korea for the privilege of hosting the upcoming 2002 World Cup Soccer Games was acute at that time. An all-or-nothing outcome would leave whichever party that lost the contest carrying a bitter grudge. Should Japan carry off the palm, anti-Japanese sentiments in Korea would be rekindled and were not likely to be extinguished until years ahead in the 21st century. Fearful of such an eventuality, I concurred with those in both countries who suggested an eclectic proposal for the two countries to co-host the quadrennial event, and penned an *Asahi Shimbum* editorial (June 23, 1995) in support of it on the 30th anniversary of the Japan–Korea Treaty. In May the next year FIFA ruled favorably, translating a wishful proposal into a reality. Entrusted with a joint project they could not afford to fail in, Japan and Korea were now bound together by a future-oriented bond. The whole turn of events was pregnant with historical implications.

That Kim Daejung, the tragic dissident, should have been elected president in December 1997 after Kim Youngsam was an epoch-making incident marking a great turnabout in Japan–Korea relations. In August 1973, when Korea was under the rule of Park Chunghee, Kim Daejung was kidnapped by "unidentified agents" during a visit to Tokyo and later found half-dead in front of his own house in Seoul. Investigations by the Tokyo Metropolitan Police Department encouraged the suspicion that the Korean CIA had been involved, but the investigations were not followed up, and the case was shelved in a political settlement by the two governments concerned. The case's lack of closure left a nasty aftertaste, an irritant to the palates of both Japanese and Koreans for over a score of years.

After Park Chunghee's assassination, Kim Daejung briefly emerged as the hero of a series of events marking "the Seoul spring," only to be arrested again, sentenced to death, and otherwise persecuted under the Chun Doohwan administration. Both the Japanese government and politicians took action through official and private channels to ask for his life and/or release. From the Park through the Chun years, however, it was Doi Takako, Den Hideo, and other JSP members, as well as Utsunomiya Tokuma, Kujiraoka Hyosuke, Kono Yohei, and other "left-wing" conservatives who consistently acted in support of Kim Daejung. Invited naturally to Kim's inauguration ceremony in February 1998 as old friends from Japan were Kono, Doi, Den, and others who represented a strand of personal connections poles apart from the traditionally entrenched network of Japan–Korea interpersonal relations.

In his bid for power, however, Kim Daejung had to team up with Kim Jongpil, a former close associate of Park Chunghee, and could no longer afford to continue playing the dissident card. In addition to his old friends from Japan, he officially invited to the inauguration ceremony, of all people, Nakasone Yasuhiro and Takeshita Noboru, the Japanese partners of his archenemies in Korean politics. The gesture was taken to show his desire to open wider channels of communications between Korea and Japan, because it had been none other than prime ministers Nakasone and Takeshita who, during their respective tenures of office, had extended official invitations to presidents Chun Doohwan and Roh Taewoo. Presumably this diplomatic ploy was also designed to solicit Japan's aid in reinvigorating the Korean economy, which was in a serious recession at that time. Somewhat uneasy at first about the rise to power in Korea of the former dissident, Japanese conservatives appreciated Kim's gesture and heaved a great sigh of relief. Japan–Korea political ties were now on a much firmer, broader, and stabler basis than ever.

THE NARROW CHANNEL BETWEEN JAPAN AND NORTH KOREA

The Socialist Party had for a long time been on friendly terms with the North Korean Workers' Party, but for all that, it had no monopoly of contacts with North Korea. Even the LDP had Utsunomiya Tokuma and the Asian and African Affairs Study Group, as well as Kuno Chuji and a few other members of the Japan–North-Korea Parliamentarians' Friendship League. Most of the LDP Diet members who maintained contacts with North Korea were at the same time, like Utsunomiya, partisans of friendly relations with China, but their contacts with the North undeniably lacked breadth and scope compared to their contacts with China. North Korea exerted less influence on the rest of Asia than China, and was sinking deeper and deeper into international isolation. Originally the Komeito had been close to North Korea, but beginning in the 1980s it began to assign more importance to ties with South Korea, and even the Socialist Party, when Ishibashi Masatsugu became chairman, began to explore the possibility of overtures to South Korea.

Behind this coolness toward North Korea lay the decisive impact of serious acts of international terrorism imputed to North Korean operatives (although North Korea continues to deny any involvement): the Rangoon bombing in 1983 and the bombing of a Korean Air Lines passenger plane in 1987. The independent Japanese Communist Party entered a phase of bitter opposition to North Korea. In the LDP, Kuno Chuji had been engaged in Japan–North-Korea ties for decades as head of the non-partisan Japan–North-Korea Parliamentarians' League, but after his retirement from politics the league entered a period of dormancy.

Kanemaru Shin, head of the LDP's Takeshita faction and reputed to be a political king-maker (as well as a pro-Taiwan and influential pro-South-Korea Diet member), and Watanabe Michio, who headed his own LDP faction, together with certain other influential people who formerly had no pro-North-Korea connections, began to make high-profile visits to North Korea more recently. Kanemaru visited the peninsula in September 1990 to parley for the release of Japanese fishermen captured as "spies" by North Korea. He headed a mission whose members included the Socialist Party Diet member Tanabe Makoto; the mission signed an agreement to begin talks leading to the normalization of diplomatic ties between Japan and North Korea. When these talks later foundered, Watanabe Michio visited North Korea in March 1995 at the head of a tripartite delegation representing the three parties in the Murayama coalition cabinet and agreed to resume talks. This paved the way for later donations of Japanese rice to North Korea.

Watanabe's problematic statement about the "smooth" annexation of Korea that triggered such an outcry was made later, but his statement was witness to his identity as a strongly nationalistic, right-wing politician with very strong anti-communist tendencies who had always turned a jaundiced eye to North Korea. Persuaded to make the trek to North Korea by the LDP's Kato Koichi, who had made the preliminary arrangements, Watanabe, like Kanemaru, was motivated not by any affinity to North Korea but by the patriotic desire to leave his name in the history books.

North Korea is now the only nation with which Japan does not have diplomatic relations. Together with a Japan–Soviet-Union peace treaty that would return the Northern Territories to Japan, the opening of talks with North Korea leading to the establishment of diplomatic ties was, and is, a political task of dimensions too vast for the purview of bureaucrats. It is, moreover, a job that only an accomplished politician can do, but for one with an eye to the premiership, the risks are just too great. Hence as a fitting challenge for seasoned veterans, the task devolved either to Kanemaru, who had no chance or hopes of becoming prime minister, or to Watanabe, whose failing health had forced him to withdraw from the race.

In the fall of 1999, Japan–North Korea relations were at an impasse. They had thawed briefly in 1997 when Pyongyang complied with Tokyo's request to let Japanese wives of North Koreans (who had gotten married in Japan and gone back to North Korea after the war) visit their homes in Japan. It was hoped for a time that their homecoming might lead to talks to normalize diplomatic relations between Japan and North Korea. At precisely that time, however, suspicions, confirmed by statements by refugees from North Korea, grew that a certain number of Japanese nationals who were reported missing one after another in 1980 had in fact been abducted by North Korean operatives.

Then on August 31, 1998, North Korea launched a Taepodon-class ballistic missile over Japan into the Pacific Ocean. In March

1999, two North Korean spy boats masquerading as Japanese fishing boats approached the coast of Niigata prefecture. Both the Maritime Safety Agency and Maritime SDF dispatched vessels to chase them away, firing warning shots; they outstripped the Japanese vessels and got away. These provocations, combined with suspicions that North Korea is attempting to develop nuclear weapons, amplified the sense of threat and of enmity that the Japanese have toward North Korea.

The normalization of North Korea's relations with Japan would generate substantial economic aid in the form of reparations for Japan's colonial rule, and to a country with a dire food shortage and an economy in catastrophic shape, the prospect must certainly be attractive. Herein obviously lies the key to a breakthrough. But North Korea has stonewalled Japan's requests for clarification about suspected abductions and adamantly denies any involvement; it rebuts accusations by reminding Japan how many North Koreans it abducted during the colonial years. As things now stand, the two nations are tuned to entirely different wavelengths, gridlocked and working at cross-purposes, and getting nowhere. In December 1999, former prime minister Murayama Tomiichi led a nonpartisan delegation to North Korea on a visit intended to restore diplomatic relations, signaling the first step toward normalization of bilateral ties, but in all likelihood the path leading to the final phase of reconciliation is still a long and arduous one

Chapter 13 | Japanese Leaders' "Ego Trips" to Southeast Asia

TAKING THE ROUNDABOUT ROUTE BACK TO ASIA

In August 1994, Murayama Tomiichi, freshly inaugurated as prime minister of Japan, visited Malaysia in the midst of a round of visits to Southeast Asian countries. In a meeting with prime minister Mahathir, he was completely taken aback when Mahathir remarked:

> I really can not understand why Japan continues to apologize for what happened fifty years ago. Though it is true that one has to learn lessons from the past, relations between nations should primarily focus upon the present and the future. If we were to demand compensation for what happened fifty years ago, the question might arise whether similar demands should be made to the suzerain states of all the ex-colonies. It's time for Japan to stop apologizing. We are ready to support Japan's bid for permanent UN Security Council membership. I want Japan to play every possible role for the sake of Asia's peace and prosperity.[1]

Murayama had every reason to be surprised. During this tour, which included preceding visits to the Philippines and Thailand, the Socialist Party leader heading Japan's coalition government had tried to express Japan's apologies to Asia in clear terms. But now, in the face of his counterpart's totally unexpected statement, calling for "no more apologies," then announcing his support for

Japan's bid for permanent membership in the Security Council of the United Nations (an issue which Murayama had hesitated to put on the meeting's agenda) he could hardly find words with which to respond.

Voices of opposition to Mahathir's call for "no more apologies" erupted immediately, even from among Malaysians, not to speak of elsewhere in Southeast Asia. Recalling his wartime experiences, Lee Kwan Yew, the former prime minister of Singapore, explained in an *Asahi Shimbun* interview: "Mr. Mahathir, a young student then, was a Malay by race and Muslim by faith. I, too, was a young student then, but Chinese. The way I suffered during the wartime and the way he suffered were different. The Japanese treated Muslim Malays rather well, Malay and Singapore Chinese harshly. Thus the two experiences were different."[2]

This notwithstanding, Mahathir's comment was welcomed, and exploited, by certain Japanese, such as those who opposed the 50th end-of-war anniversary resolution and who felt "That is exactly what we think."

It is true that Southeast Asian countries, in contrast to the reluctance shown by China and Korea, have in general shown support for Japan's bid for permanent membership in the Security Council. Mahathir's statement was an extreme case, but it seems generally that Southeast Asian countries were more tolerant of Japan's wartime misdeeds than China and Korea were. Certainly, Southeast Asian countries are no exception in that abominable memories of the invading Japanese army remain there, too, but it is not surprising that their rancour is not as deep as in countries that Japan colonized or where it set up a puppet state.

In fact, it was precisely the countries of Southeast Asia and other countries like India that were first to reconcile themselves with postwar Japan and established friendly relations in return for reparations and economic cooperation. This breakthrough—coming as communist regimes established themselves in China and North Korea on the one hand and Japan groped with difficulty to open diplomatic relations with South Korea on the other—might be called Japan's roundabout return to Asia, a detour via Southeast and South

Asia. What's more, Japan began to feel more and more at ease in the role of aid donor, seated at the head of the table and increasingly enjoying, as it were, the place of honor: reparations, whose original purpose was to compensate for damages inflicted during the war, began to assume the character of economic aid to developing countries (and to the regimes in power there as well).

Many of Japan's successive postwar prime ministers therefore availed themselves of the chance to boost their egos by making the rounds of Southeast Asia. Contrastingly, China and Korea initially withheld their consent to visits by Japanese prime ministers, and on several occasions when such visits eventually took place, Japanese official visitors to China and South Korea were made to feel distinctly uncomfortable. They therefore preferred to make trips to Southeast Asia, knowing that their stay there would be a pleasant one.

Kishi's Rounds: Testing the Waters

As I wrote earlier, Kishi Nobusuke's first round of visits to Asian countries was designed to prepare his subsequent visit to the United States. This was not, however, the only significance Kishi attached to this trip: to Kishi, a former proponent of Greater Asianism, this round of visits—calling on India first, then on Pakistan, Sri Lanka, Thailand, and Taiwan—was meant to help him achieve his Greater Asian ambitions. An extensive quotation from Kishi Nobusuke's *Memoirs* demonstrates this:

> Nowadays visits by Japanese prime ministers to Southeast Asian countries are not rare at all. But back then, my tour was, to begin with, not only the first of its kind in the postwar years, but also the first ever since the Meiji Restoration; secondly, I had attached a special meaning to this trip, which was planned so that I could visit all the major countries in Asia before my departure to the United States.

> Before World War II, every country in Southeast Asia except Thailand had been colonized by Western powers. Indo-China, com-

prising Vietnam, Laos, and Cambodia, was French territory. Burma, India, Pakistan, Malaysia, Singapore, and Sri Lanka were British possessions. Indonesia and New Guinea were both under Dutch rule. And the Philippines was a US territory. Soon after the war, one after another, they all became independent. At the time of my visit to this area, these fledgling nations had just won independence and were all struggling hard to build themselves up.

I therefore thought it appropriate first to take this opportunity to express our sense of regret for having inflicted much trouble and damage during the war and, second, to ready our government to enter as a representative of "the Asian Japan" into discussions with the United States, by acquiring a thorough knowledge of the state of affairs in those nations and also by seeking to comprehend fully what their leaders expected Japan to do, through a frank exchange of opinions with them.

Needless to say, the realization of peace and prosperity in Asia is a significant contribution to world peace, and consequently, it was incumbent upon Japan, located in Asia with a people sharing the same roots as people throughout the rest of Asia, to conduct active Asian diplomacy to this end. I therefore thought that for us to do so, it was necessary for me to be fully informed of the actual circumstances in those newly born nations and to learn, through person-to-person conversations with their leaders, what they had set as their goals, what they aspired to, what they rejected. I believed that the best way to make my visit to the United States a fruitful one was to speak on the basis of such knowledge and experience at discussions with American leaders. In my judgment, if I could succeed in establishing Japan's status in Asia, that is, if I could succeed in showing clearly that the center of Asia is Japan, this would strengthen my negotiating position in my efforts to persuade Ike to transform the Japan–US relationship into one based upon an equal partnership.

Naturally, my agenda also included the expression of our gratitude for their warm backing of Japan's application for membership in the United Nations, as well as efforts to sound out which specific areas of cooperation might be promoted in the field of economic and cultural exchange.[3]

Kishi deserves due credit for his effort through this round of visits to Southeast Asia to address problems attributable to the war but left unattended since its end and for paving the way for the solution of the reparations issue. But at the same time, he goes so far as to say that "showing clearly that the center of Asia is Japan" by deepening mutual understanding with the leaders of newly born nations would "strengthen [his] negotiating position" in his talks with the United States. He mentions that to express his regret for "having inflicted much trouble . . . during the war" was one of the purposes of his visits to Southeast Asia. But at the same time, immediately after describing in detail how Southeast Asian countries were once colonized by Western powers, he emphasizes that Japan should help them with their nation building. Here we can sense, can we not, a lingering odor of prewar calls for Japan as the "leading power of Asia" to promote "Asian liberation."

I am, of course, not the only one who has noticed this. Referring to this part of Kishi's memoirs, Hara Yoshihisa, author of *Kishi Nobusuke*,[4] wrote as follows: "It must be remembered that Kishi's recent approach to Asia is not necessarily contradictory to his commitment in earlier days to the philosophy of the Greater East Asia Co-Prosperity Sphere or Greater Asianism, theories justifying Japan's role as Asia's leader." In an interview with Hara, Kishi said that his concern with Asia in the postwar years was not only "definitely connected" with the Great Asianism ideals he cherished in the prewar days but also "related to my experience of being posted in Manchukuo." Furthermore, when asked about the prewar and postwar aspects of his own personality, he asserted that there was "probably no gap between them," and that they were "consistent." Hara refers to these remarks in the same context as mine.

Kishi's first destination was India. Prime Minister Jawaharlal Nehru, who received Kishi in New Delhi, was known as a leading figure of the global non-alignment movement. According to *Kishi Nobusuke's Memoirs*, Nehru said, referring to the Russo–Japanese War in his speech at the welcome meeting, that the victory of Japan, a tiny island country in Asia, over Russia, reputed to have the strongest army in the world, had greatly encouraged him and made him decide to join the Indian independence movement, which he had originally thought a cause without hope of success.

It could not be a coincidence that Kishi chose to visit first India, Pakistan, and Sri Lanka (Ceylon at that time), countries which escaped from becoming battlefields during the Greater East Asia War and consequently where people did not have as much ill-feeling toward Japan as in other parts of Asia. Kishi described his impressions of these visits as follows:

> I had been concerned with the feelings of people in the countries of Southeast Asia about the Pacific War, which Japan had begun, but I was told everywhere, "Japan, with nothing but paper and bamboo, made airplanes and tanks, drove the British and the Dutch out of this area, and enabled us to achieve independence."
>
> Though these words were spoken in diplomatic language over glasses of champagne at welcome receptions, it did not seem to me that they were merely lip service. Rather, seeing the remarkable revival of the Japanese people, who were totally beaten and crushed in a war against the whole world only ten years ago, but are now well dressed and even have television sets at home, my hosts seemed to be saying that the Japanese are a great nation and that they themselves should follow the Japanese example.[5]

From these experiences, Kishi drew a self-seeking conclusion, writing, "Though we need to have a sense of remorse [about the war], behaving too humbly will do more harm than good in our postwar efforts for peace and reconstruction."

Southeast Asia's sentiments toward Japan were not, however, as simple as Kishi contends. Kishi ought to have felt this keenly throughout his second round of visits, made in the same year, to the countries of Southeast Asia and the Pacific. In Australia, where the veterans' association had strongly opposed his visit from the beginning, Kishi was unexpectedly handed a document by an elderly woman during his visit to the tomb of the unknown soldier to lay a wreath. She wrote in the document a detailed account of her son's ordeal, to the effect that he had been taken prisoner on the war front in Burma and died of forced labor in the construction of the Thai–Burma Railroad built by the Japanese army, cutting through jungles, to transport war supplies. A large number of prisoners of war as well as locally commandeered laborers were put to work on this railroad, and tens of thousands died from exhaustion, disease, and other causes. Her son was one of them. "The circumstances were such that, naturally, the atmosphere at the welcome reception held by the parliament was not a warm one."[6]

Kishi's reception was not warm in the Philippines either, but Kishi did not describe it in detail. In his *Memoirs*, Kishi Nobusuke writes only, "In Australia and the Philippines, there remained ill feeling toward Japan that had grown during the war. I thought that, although it will diminish gradually with the passage of time, Japan should make every effort to remove it as soon as possible."[7]

Kishi had special ties to the Philippines originating from his wartime experiences. According to Fukuda Takeo's *Kaiko kyujyunen* (Reminiscences of ninety years), it was an extremely complicated relationship, which he described as follows.

> The president of the wartime government of the Philippines backed by the Tojo cabinet was a man named Laurel who, among other things, attended the Greater East Asia Conference presided by prime minister Tojo. At Japan's defeat, he fled to Japan to seek a place of safety, having lost a haven in his homeland. He arrived in Nara with his son, Laurel III, who was a graduate of Japan's military academy, but Laurel Senior was arrested later by the American Military Police and sent to Sugamo Prison, where he came to know Kishi, who was also being detained there. When diplomatic ties between Japan and the Philippines were restored, Laurel III returned to Japan as his country's first ambassador to Japan.[8]

Naturally, he often turned to Kishi for help. The Laurel regime was a puppet government installed within the framework of the Greater East Asia Co-Prosperity Sphere. Kishi's encounter with Laurel Senior in the Sugamo Prison is therefore somehow symbolic. Incidentally, when the Philippine–Japanese Friendship Association was founded, Kishi became the first chairman (he was later succeeded by Fukuda).

Kishi's experiences in Australia and the Philippines apart, successive prime ministers of Japan after Kishi enjoyed similar experiences, going on similar ego-boosting jaunts to countries in Southeast Asia. In November 1961, Ikeda Hayato, after completing a meeting in Tokyo with Park Chunghee of Korea, began a tour in which he visited four countries: Pakistan, India, Burma (now Myanmar) and Thailand. According to *Ikeda Hayato to sono jidai* (Ikeda Hayato and his times), written by Ito Masaya, who accompanied Ikeda as a secretary, Ikeda addressed his counterpart rather triumphally at his meeting with president Ayub Khan of Pakistan as well as at the later meeting with prime minister Nehru of India, declaring "Japan has learned, at the time of the Meiji Restoration and also since the end of the war, that development of a free economy is effective for nation-building. Let me talk about our experience with you."[9]

Nehru spoke eloquently on political matters as a Third World leader, but when the focus was narrowed to economic issues, his tone would turn to entreaty. Typically, among other things, he would say "Buy our cotton!" or "Buy our sugar!" Ikeda countered these pleas, saying equally earnestly "We wish we could, but the quality of your commodities is too poor and your prices are too high. Yesterday, when I visited one of your model farms, I realized that as long as you stay with such an out-of-date system, there will be no future. You should promote economic development more intensively and make your economy more competitive internationally."[10]

In Burma, Ikeda received a grand welcome, despite the pending issue of re-negotiating reparations. Ito wrote that "most of the leaders in the movement for Burma's independence were trained by the Japanese army and, at the time of independence, they admired the

Meiji Restoration, calling it their model."[11] Ikeda, likewise, talked mainly about the course of Japan's development since the Meiji reforms. He went on to express his doubts about Burma's socialization policy, saying, "You keep refusing to allow foreign capital in, simply out of fear, but what then are you producing, other than the electric lighting around here, with the electricity generated by the power plant financed with the reparations we paid you?"[12] These remarks ought to have been regarded as a little too self-serving to address a nation where thousands of lives were sacrificed in the construction of the Thai–Burma Railway, and the Burmese people for that reason still harbor mixed feelings toward Japan. At any rate, according to Ito, "During his visit to the United States the previous year, Kennedy had taught Ikeda more than what Ikeda could teach Kennedy. This time in Southeast Asia, however, it seemed as if Ikeda was in the teacher's role all the time."[13] His psychological predominance was apparently partly due to Japan's economic superiority. The issue of reparations to Burma was finally settled in 1963 after long negotiations, marking the end of Japan's attempts to settle war-related issues concerning Southeast Asia. Japan thus acquired a free hand in Southeast Asia once again, in contrast to the unresolved onus of its relations with China and the Korean peninsula.

The perks and perils of aid diplomacy: Reactions to "economic aggression"

Kishi wrote in his *Memoirs* how struck he was during his first visits to Southeast Asia by the poverty in these countries. Ikeda was also to have this impression later. Ito writes in his book as follows:

> There were modern buildings along all the main streets of the cities, but once I stepped into the narrow back alleys, I saw how commonly people everywhere in Asia lived in the most abject poverty. . . . Ikeda, I am sure, felt as I felt and realized clearly that Japan's role in Asia would be an extremely important one, since the route we Japanese were to take in our own advancement would serve as

a guidepost for the people of Asia in charting the course of their development.[14]

It is noteworthy that Ikeda recognized that Japan, unlike Europe and America, was not encumbered by historically complex ties with the countries of Southeast Asia, and he viewed this difference as a blessing. According to Ito, Ikeda used to say in those days:

> Most of Southeast Asia was once a British possession; relations between those countries and Britain and the rest of Europe have been entangled for a long time by, for example, inherited questions of debts and credits and by the conflict between their sense of duty and the dictates of simple humanity. Though it came along later, the United States has also gotten increasingly snarled in these cobwebs from the past. Japan in this respect is a newcomer. Japan is neither as rich as the United States, nor is its diplomacy as mature as that of the United Kingdom, but Japan has a freer hand in dealing with matters related to Southeast Asia.[15]

By the time of Ikeda's second tour in November 1961, this time visiting the Philippines, Indonesia, Australia, and New Zealand, inspired by the conception of the EEC (European Economic Community, the prototype of the EU), Ikeda had been dreaming of one day establishing an "Asian EEC"—a unique stance toward Asia which only a politician like Ikeda, "the man of the economy," could take.

Yet while Japan's diplomacy towards Southeast Asian countries was evolving in this way, Southeast Asian public opinion was gradually growing hostile to the penetration of their markets by Japanese firms, which went hand in hand with the expansion of economic aid; this opposition was mixed with their ill-feelings against their own governments, which were often too authoritarian and prone to corruption. Such a situation became manifest in January 1974 on the occasion of the round of visits to Southeast Asia by Tanaka Kakuei. All through his visits to the Philippines, Thailand, Singapore, Malaysia, and Indonesia, Tanaka encountered fierce anti-Japanese demonstrations.

In Thailand and Indonesia in particular, his arrival was greeted by crowds shouting "No to Japanese Economic Aggression!" and "Down With the Economic Animals!" In Indonesia, anti-Japanese demonstrations escalated into riots, and a curfew was eventually proclaimed. The situation was such that Tanaka had to be evacuated from the presidential palace and transported to the airport by an air force helicopter to catch his flight back home. It would be unfair to impute this to Tanaka's responsibility, as the surge of such anti-Japanese movements was driven partly by the rise of nationalism in these days. Yet Tanaka's public image coincided closely with the public image of Japan as a nation that cared about nothing but business and development. Tanaka's image was the perfect symbol of such a nation.

Fukuda Takeo used this bitter experience to good advantage when he visited Southeast Asia in August 1977. In the Philippine capital Manila, the last stop of his tour, he announced the so-called Fukuda Doctrine comprising three basic principles of his Asian policy, drawn up with emphasis on the importance of "heart-to-heart ties." The three principles were the following: (i) Japan will devote itself to peace and never become a military power; (ii) Japan will promote cooperation as an equal partner, upholding the value of "heart-to-heart ties" among members of Asian society and affirming ethnic diversity; and (iii) Japan will cooperate energetically in voluntary efforts by members of ASEAN to enhance the organization's solidarity and strength, in the expectation that mutual understanding and co-existence can eventually be achieved in Indochina. Fukuda's aim was on the one hand to soothe the perturbed feelings of the countries of Southeast Asia arising from the fall of Saigon in the Vietnam War and on the other to demonstrate Japan's readiness to correct its past policies, in which too much importance was attached to economic considerations.

Although it was Kishi who had first paved the way for establishing postwar relations with the countries of Southeast Asia, Fukuda, too, had been working under Kishi in this process, engaged in activities to support students from abroad, for example.

Fukuda could proclaim with confidence that "With the Philippines as well as with Indonesia and other countries like Malaysia, Singapore, and Burma, I established much deeper relations than other prime ministers, and not only in my official capacity as cabinet minister and premier."[16] The Fukuda Doctrine formed the basis of Japan's diplomacy toward Southeast Asia from that time on. Fukuda can rightly have been satisfied that he succeeded through his visit to Southeast Asia in making up for the failure of Tanaka's diplomatic efforts, though Tanaka had gone far ahead of Fukuda in dealing with China–Japan issues.

THE VIETNAM WAR: FIRST SIGNS OF SYMPATHY FOR ASIA

Meanwhile, the Vietnam War, clearly one of the biggest cold war era events in Southeast Asia, complicated Japan's perceptions of the region. The United States continued to warn that Vietnam's "falling to the communists" would result in the domino-like fall to communism of the rest of Southeast Asia. The Japanese government tended to be supportive of this view, as evidenced by Sato Eisaku's visit to South Vietnam in 1967. The opposition parties, however, were harshly critical, arguing that it was "intervening against national self-determination in Asia" reflecting "American imperialism." According to various public opinion surveys, the Japanese people, no matter whether conservative or reform-minded, were inclined to support national self-determination rather than to uphold freedom.

Even within the LDP, there were voices tenaciously opposed to US involvement in Vietnam. A basic pattern was apparent: the pro-Chinese group was generally against intervention, while the pro-Taiwan group supported it. Belief in the domino theory was virtually synonymous with hostility to mainland China, which was backing North Vietnam. Miyazawa Kiichi, while showing a certain degree of comprehension for the martyr's sense of duty to protect liberty revered by the American people, remonstrated against an excessive fear of the Chinese revolution and severely criticized the United States, writing in his *Shakaito tono taiwa* (Dialogue with the Socialist Party):

> I think that, to many Asian countries, whether liberalism or communism prevails is only a secondary choice. In other words, the principal question in this area is which system is more conducive to the establishment of their national state and to industrialization, their primary goals. . . . The United States needs to better understand this reality. . . .

> Vietnam's becoming communist, if this happens, will do nothing to harm the United States, because the Vietnamese have never had, and will never have, the audacity to try to become a source of worldwide revolution. . . . If we succeed in making Vietnam neutral, I do not think that Vietnam will become a tributary state of China. Historically, Vietnam has incessantly resisted invasions from China. The Vietnamese people are therefore very cautious of China, in their heart of hearts. . . . The problem is that the United States is not thinking this way. Americans believe strongly that the Vietnam War is a proxy war against Beijing.[17]

This is yet another example of Miyazawa's calm view, not only of Vietnam but also of Asia as a whole, complementary to his view of the Chinese revolution, referred to earlier. The acuity of Miyazawa's insight has been well proven by such subsequent events in Asia as Vietnam's war with China after winning the war against the United States and the recent normalization of US–Vietnam diplomatic ties. Even Miyazawa, however, could not foresee the rapid pace of industrialization in Vietnam, which he once termed a "primitive communist state."

A drastic post-cold-war redrawing of the map of Asia is now in progress. The Association of Southeast Asian Nations was founded in August 1967, in the midst of the Vietnam War. The situation in Cambodia degenerated into total chaos after the war, and Vietnam stepped in but payed a high price for invading Cambodia. When peace eventually came to Cambodia, Vietnam became a member of ASEAN, in the summer of 1995.

Chapter 14 | The Political History of
Japan's Apology
Diplomacy

Japan's first official apology: The unexpected effects of Shiina's statement

There has always been one political issue Japan cannot avoid when it tries to establish friendly relations with other Asian countries: the "apologies" of Japanese heads of government for Japan's prewar colonial rule and wartime aggression in Asia. This chapter analyzes the history of the Japanese leadership's major apologetic statements.

As explained in Part II, then prime minister Kishi Nobusuke sent Yatsugi Kazuo to South Korea as his personal special envoy in May 1958. It was reported that Yatsugi apologized to South Korean president Rhee Syngman for "the wrongs committed by Ito Hirobumi." If Yatsugi's apology had truly been issued by prime minister Kishi, it would be recorded as Japan's first official apology to South Korea. However, its credibility was fatally undermined by Kishi's subsequent denial. This episode is described in detail in Part II, but it was Shiina Etsusaburo, then foreign minister, who publicly overcame the Japanese people's strong aversion to making any apologies to South Korea. When talks to normalize bilateral diplomatic relations between Japan and South Korea reached their final stage in February 1965, foreign minister Shiina read a statement aloud at Kimpo Airport in Seoul. His statement has been regarded as the first official apology by Japan to South Korea. His words are as follows.

. . . It has long been my cherished desire to come into contact with your country's beautiful natural scenery and to see how you are engaged in building a dynamic nation. Now that my wish has been fulfilled, I am deeply enthused. . . . Japan and South Korea are separated only by a narrow strip of water and have maintained close cultural and economic ties throughout the ages, not to speak of the contacts between the people of our two nations. We feel great regret and deep remorse over the unhappy phase in the long history of relations between the two countries. Now I believe that, with our eyes to the future, it is our mutual desire this year to establish everlasting friendship between Japan and South Korea, based on the thousand-year-long history of our bilateral ties, and also to form a new historical starting point from which our two nations can join forces to prosper together.

I sincerely hope that my visit to your country will contribute to realizing the goal of friendship between our two countries and in particular that it will help to rapidly normalize Japan–South Korea diplomatic relations, a goal which we both earnestly aspire to achieve.[1]

The key points of this statement are the following three phrases: "unhappy phase," "great regret," and "deep remorse." Their wording accelerated the negotiations on the Treaty on Basic Relations between Japan and the Republic of Korea, culminating eventually in the initialing of the treaty in Seoul. Japan's intention to express its "regret" and "remorse" was included in the joint communiqué issued by both Japanese and South Korean foreign ministers.

South Korean opposition parties and students were violently opposed to signing the treaty with Japan. It was in such an atmosphere of tension that Shiina read his statement. The language had been worked out through many twists and turns. According to *Kiroku Shiina Etsusaburo* (The Shiina Etsusaburo record),[2] the South Korean government had wanted Yoshida Shigeru himself to visit Seoul as a special envoy and apologize by saying that Japan was sorry for what it did to the Korean people during its 36-year colonial rule of the peninsula. The Korean government truly be-

In February 1965, after having read aloud his historic statement expressing regret for Japan's past actions, Foreign Minister Shiina Etsusaburo (left) paid a courtesy call on South Korean President Park Chunghee at the Blue House in Seoul.

lieved that a visit and apology by Yoshida would, at one stroke, reverse the tide of popular sentiment against Japan and eliminate any remaining obstacles to a breakthrough in the two countries' face-off. On the other hand, if the Japanese government decided to send a special envoy only to apologize, public feeling in Japan would erupt with anger. As Kishi's denial of his earler apologetic message indicates, the anti-South Korean feelings of opposition parties and a major segment of the Japanese press had been incensed by the unilateral imposition of the Rhee Syngman line establishing Korean territorial fishing waters [Part II, P. 40]. The Japanese government was fiercely criticized in Japan for yielding too much, too easily, to South Korea. There was also some nervousness that South Korea might present more extensive claims for reparation if the Japanese government admitted that its colonial policy had been wrong.

Under the circumstances, the Japanese government promptly turned down South Korea's request that it send Yoshida to South Korea as a special envoy and decided to send Shiina instead. The South Korean government had insistently demanded that Shiina express deep regret in a statement to be read when he arrived at Kimpo Airport. Japan's Ministry of Foreign Affairs worked out the draft statement in response to this request. Ushiroku Torao, then chief of the Asian Bureau and later Japanese ambassador to South Korea, together with other foreign ministry officials, inserted the following passage: "there were regrettably unfortunate incidents between Japan and South Korea in the past." Ushiroku sent the draft by telegraph to Maeda Toshikazu, who had been dispatched beforehand to South Korea as a researcher and would later become Japanese ambassador to South Korea. Maeda took a look at the manuscript and immediately asked Ushiroku for a more straightforward statement, because, in its present form, the draft would be insufficient to quell anti-Japanese public sentiment in South Korea.

Ushiroku and Maeda give a full account of the rest of the story in *Kiroku Shiina Etsusaburo* as follows:

> USHIROKU: But . . . I pushed the original draft through and distributed advance copies at a press conference when the chief of the Asian Bureau left for South Korea. Some members of the press club then came to tell me that the statement would backfire. They were adamant that, if the statement did not include a clear-cut apology, it should not touch upon the issue at all, or if it touched upon the issue, the statement should say more clearly that Japan regretted its conduct in South Korea. On top of that, a couple of telegrams came from my colleague Maeda, who was stationed in Seoul, asking me earnestly to do something more decisive. . . . So I rewrote the "regrettably" part, changing it to "We feel great regret . . . over the

unhappy phase." Finally, I also added the following phrase to the statement: "and deep remorse." Foreign Minister Shiina did not make an issue of these modifications at all, saying merely, "OK, so let's go with this." . . . Shiina read the statement aloud exactly as it was at Kimpo Airport. It turned out that the speech had unexpected effects. . . . Overnight, the mood in South Korea changed dramatically. It was unbelievable. A single statement can make such a difference! . . .

MAEDA: I remember that the speech was broadcast live. The event attracted a great deal of public attention in South Korea. . . . Later, on the same day, in the evening, South Korean foreign affairs minister Lee Tongwon hosted a welcome banquet in honor of Shiina. The party was attended by a large number of guests, including the American and German ambassadors. I was really delighted to hear everyone at the party praising the phrase "deep remorse."[3]

South Korean Foreign Minister Lee Tongwon reminisces about Shiina's statement in the same book.

Later, when I had an opportunity to go to Japan, I said to prime minister Sato Eisaku, "Japan's colonial rule of the Korean Peninsula lasted for 36 years and Japan subdued South Korea with guns, but your country never captured the Korean people's hearts even once. Mr. Shiina did not bring a large army of a million soldiers and guns to South Korea—but he captured our hearts with just a few words.
. . .

At the moment of that speech, South Koreans got the impression that Mr. Shiina was different from the typical Japanese politician. We believed that he was a great man, a statesman worthy of veneration. He was a man who could understand the importance of reflecting on his own country's past conduct and who knew how to express his remorse for the past. So we thought he would handle well whatever problems arose in the future. South Koreans therefore began feeling tremendous warmth toward Shiina, regarding him as truly "a man, a human being."[4]

These memoir notes show how impressed the South Korean people were by Shiina's statement. Yet according to *Kiroku Shiina Etsusaburo*, the beauty of the statement is that the subject of the sentence—"We feel great regret and deep remorse"—cannot be determined. It is impossible to determine who "we" is. It may be the Japanese government, the ministry of foreign affairs, or foreign minister Shiina himself. The statement is so ambiguous that it is impossible to determine whether the apology was offered by Japan as a nation or not. Another important and noteworthy point is that it is highly doubtful that Shiina truly expressed this apology from the bottom of his heart.

Double-dealing: Political expedients

Shiina Etsusaburo wrote a book titled *Dowa to seiji* (Fairy tales and politics)[5] that was published by in 1963, just two years before his visit to Seoul. In it, Shiina praised the achievements of his uncle, Goto Shinpei, writing,

> Japan administered Taiwan, annexed Korea, and tried to realize the ideal of harmonious coexistence among five ethnic groups in Manchuria. From the Meiji era on, the purpose of these attempts was to defend Asia and maintain Japan's independence against the threat of Western imperialist might. If it is true that these acts were acts of Japanese imperialism, that imperialism was glorious. Goto Shinpei was a pioneer of Asian liberation. I firmly believe this.[6]

Goto Shinpei's birthplace was Iwate Prefecture, where Shiina also was born and brought up. Goto held various ministerial posts such as interior minister in the Katsura cabinet and minister for foreign affairs in the Terauchi cabinet, as well as serving as mayor of Tokyo. After the Great Kanto Earthquake of 1923, he headed the Imperial Capital Reconstruction Organization and is remembered even today for his distinguished service in this area. After the Sino–Japanese War of 1894 to 1895, he was engaged in administering Japanese-occupied Taiwan as its first director in charge of civilian affairs. After the Russo–Japanese War of 1904 to 1905, he was president of the South Manchuria Railway Company. While Foreign Minister, he was in charge of Japan's military expedition to Siberia. In this way, he played major roles during the era of Japanese imperialism.

In *Dowa to seiji*, Shiina wrote that some people regarded Goto as a pioneer of Japanese imperialism. Refuting this view, Shiina continues, "When Asia was under the menace of Western imperialism, none but Japan among the Asian and African nations was able to stand up to Western imperialism. The Sino–Japanese War was never a war of imperialism. The Russo–Japanese War was a marvelous counterattack against Russian imperialism. I count myself as a student of history, and I have no hesitation in declaring this to be a fact. I want to draw attention to the Russo–Japanese War in particular as heralding the dawn of Asian and African independence movements in the light of world history. Even now, we must not forget that Asian and African countries and Japan, *nolens volens*, share a common destiny. Japan must support these countries' liberation and independence and aim to achieve coexistence and co-prosperity with them." After this passage comes the passage stating that, in his opinion, "that imperialism was glorious." His book reveals Shiina to have a view of history typical of Japanese conservative politicians of the Pan-Asian school (e.g. Kishi Nobusuke).

Just before Shiina's visit to Korea, Ishino Hisao of the Japan Socialist Party questioned Shiina on his view of history in a session of the Lower House Committee on the Budget, and quoted this passage from *Dowa to seiji*. Shiina answered that his view had been revised somewhat since that time and added that, in his opinion, even well-intentioned imperialism could make mistakes. This question and answer session ended with wry smiles on the faces of those who witnessed the exchange. But Shiina's answer reveals that his apology in Seoul was based on a calculating political judgment.

Shiina and Kishi had been close for a long time. Shiina followed the same career path as Kishi from the Imperial University of Tokyo to the ministry of commerce and industry. During this period, Shiina became one of Kishi's protégés. Kishi sent Shiina to Manchuria before he went there himself. When Kishi was appointed minister of commerce and industry in the Tojo cabinet, Kishi nominated Shiina as the ministry's vice-minister. Upon Kishi's arrest as a Class A war criminal after World War II, Shiina submitted to General MacArthur a petition requesting Kishi's release.

Shiina filled the important position of chief cabinet secretary in the Kishi cabinet, a fact indicating better than any other the close relationship between the two men. There is no way to know whether Shiina was directly involved in the sending of Yatsugi as a special envoy to South Korea, but his pragmatism closely resembled Kishi's, in that Shiina suppressed his real feelings when he apologized to South Korea. The difference between Kishi and Shiina is that Kishi later denied Yatsugi's apology, while Shiina directed and performed his own. The difference also seems to be due more to the Japan–South Korea treaty's fate hanging in the balance than to a change in the climate of the times.

But when Shiina's apology is compared with his statements in his book, his "double-dealing" attitude becomes unmistakable. Several interesting episodes shed light on Shiina's personality. He had a sharp mind, but he was also good at feigning ignorance. These talents were displayed frequently in his answers to questions by opposition party members during the Diet sessions. In the above-mentioned session of the Lower House Committee on the Budget, Togano Satoko of the Japan Socialist Party grilled Shiina with a question about the meaning of his words "we feel . . . deep remorse." Shiina answered with a serious look, "What I meant is that we express remorse quietly," and the whole audience burst into laughter.

The following episode also took place when Shiina was foreign minister. When he answered a question on the US–Japan Security Treaty, he said bluntly that the United States was "Japan's watchdog." Even the opposition party member who was questioning him could not overlook the offensiveness of this term. He rebuked Shiina, saying, "How dare you say such a thing?" Shiina rose again to answer and said, "Pardon me, I made a mistake: it is our beloved watchdog." Everyone burst out laughing. Both these episodes are well-known, indeed famous, true stories. They belong among the treasury of Shiina's legendary sayings, still talked about today.

THE PERMUTATIONS OF THE EMPEROR'S WORDS

Shiina's apology has been used as a model not only by the Japanese government but also by Japan's emperors. When Chun Doohwan made the first official visit of a South Korean president to Japan in September 1984, the greatest attention was focused on what Emperor Showa would say in his statement. His speech was based on the exact words spoken by Shiina in 1965.

Chun's visit was heralded as an epoch-making event, even in the light of the long history of the two countries' relations, simply due to his meeting with Emperor Showa and a dinner banquet hosted by the Emperor in President Chun's honor. His visit was regarded as different from those made by Rhee Syngman and Park Chunghee, because his was the first official visit of a South Korean president. Koreans had been forcibly made the Emperor's subjects under Japan's colonial assimilation policy. For Koreans, therefore, the Emperor was none other than the most prominent symbol of Japanese imperialism. That is the reason why so much attention was paid, in both Japan and South Korea, to how the Emperor would express Japan's apology for its actions in the past.

At the time, Japan was in a difficult situation. Japan's new postwar constitution does not permit any political involvement by the Emperor. So if the Emperor had crossed the line and made an openly political statement, his statement would probably have been criticized in Japan as an unconstitutional exploitation of the Emperor for political purposes. The Japanese government therefore explained to its South Korean counterpart that there was an inevitable limit on what the apology statement by the Emperor could include. South Korea did not fully accept this explanation. In the mood then prevailing in South Korea, South Koreans who remembered what they had suffered during Japan's colonial rule could never fully accept this excuse, even if Japan insisted that the Emperor had nothing do with politics under the new constitution.

I covered president Chun's visit to Japan as one of the reporters assigned at the time to the ministry of foreign affairs. Together with my colleagues, I was eager to be on the scene and report the news, knowing that South Korea had high expectations of hearing a satisfying "Emperor's statement" during unofficial preparatory meetings between the two countries. I could scoop the news, I hoped. The news was reported in the morning edition of my newspaper on the day before president Chun's visit to Japan. Its headline declared, "Emperor's Statement to Express 'Regret'." The word "regret" had lost its novelty, but at the time I had no experience gathering preliminary news about the Emperor's state- ments. I was therefore very nervous until I could confirm the news. The following day, the Emperor delivered his speech at the dinner banquet welcoming president Chun. The text of the speech was made public, and it contained the word "regret." I was hon- estly relieved to find the word. The text stressed the long history of close relations between the two countries as neighbors and con- tinued as follows.

> I feel great regret that there was an unhappy phase in relations be- tween our two countries in a certain period of this century despite the close ties between us. I believe that such things should not be repeated.[7]

Some of the passages in the speech, such as "unhappy phase" and "feel great regret" are identical to those used in Shiina's state- ment. When the Emperor went to the United States in 1975, he re- ferred in a statement to "the unfortunate war for which I feel deep sorrow." It is certain that, compared with the remark to the United States, the Emperor's statement to president Chun went one step further toward the use of more straightforward expressions. Responding in his speech to the Emperor's statement, Chun Doohwan said:

© Asahi Shimbunsha

In September 1984, the late Emperor Showa (right) expressed his deep regret for "an unfortunate past" at a dinner banquet welcoming South Korean President Chun Doohwan (left).

I and the people of the Republic of Korea listened, with great solemnity, to Your Majesty referring to the unhappy phase in the history of the relationship between our countries.

After quoting a proverb known to the people of both countries meaning that after a storm comes a calm, he said, "I believe that the unfortunate past must be used as a precious foundation stone for building a closer relationship between our countries in the future."[8]

Chun Doohwan in his capacity as South Korean president welcomed the Emperor's statement. But unlike Shiina's statement, the Emperor's did not mention "remorse." And like Shiina's statement, the Emperor's speech did not specify who was responsible for the "unhappy phase." On top of that, the original meaning of the Japanese word for "regret" is "disappointing." It is a convenient word, one often used when people lodge protests. And this is also true of the Korean word equivalent to "regret." Therefore, although South Koreans were moved by the historic event, some of them criticized the Emperor's statement, complaining that it was ambiguous.

It was Japanese Prime Minister Nakasone Yasuhiro who tried to compensate for the lack of clarity of the Emperor's statement with his own language. On the following day, he delivered a speech at a luncheon where he said the following.

> Japan has been deeply indebted to you in the long history of our bilateral relationship. Yet unfortunately the fact cannot be denied that Japan caused great suffering to your country and your people during a certain period during this century. I would like to announce that the Japanese government and people express deep regret for the wrongs done to you and are determined to strictly caution themselves against repeating them in the future.[9]

The statements by Nakasone and the Emperor were prepared as a two-piece set by the ministry of foreign affairs. The distinctive feature of Nakasone's statement is its clear specification of who caused the "great suffering" and its inclusion of "wrongs" in it.

When Roh Taewoo, who succeeded Chun as South Korea's President, visited Japan in 1990, he was welcomed by the current Emperor, Akihito. The Emperor's expression in his statement was more straightforward than Emperor Showa's, giving careful consideration to the complaints about his father's remarks. It reads as follows.

> When I think of the sufferings your people underwent during this unhappy phase, bought on by my country, I cannot help feeling the deepest regret.[10]

Like this, the statement said clearly that "the unhappy phase" was "brought on by my country" and included the passage "feeling the deepest regret." But the word "remorse" was not included in it.

POSTWAR-GENERATION PRIME MINISTERS SPEAK CLEARLY

Apart from the Emperors' pronouncements on the subject, among the statements regarded as "epoch-making" in South Korea was the apology Japanese prime minister Hosokawa Morihiro offered during his visit to South Korea in 1993. When Hosokawa met with South Korean president Kim Youngsam in Kyongju, he apologized as follows.

> During Japan's colonial rule over the Korean Peninsula, the Korean people were forced to suffer unbearable pain and sorrow in various ways. They were deprived of the opportunity to learn their mother tongue at school, they were forced to adopt Japanese names, forced to provide sex as "comfort women" for Japanese troops, forced to provide labor. I hereby express genuine contrition and offer my deepest apologies for my country, the aggressor's, acts.[11]

Hosokawa apologized straightforwardly, citing specific examples of reprehensible acts by the Japanese, such as the attempt to force Koreans to change their names. It was the most explicit apology ever made to South Korea by a Japanese government leader. It impressed and touched South Koreans deeply. Later, I had an opportunity to interview Hosokawa and confirmed details of the statement's genesis. I had taken it for granted that the statement was the result of long deliberations. His answer to my query was unexpected:

> At the time, I had no time to prepare for the visit until just before the departure. So I worked out what to say in Kyongju with foreign ministry staff on the airplane until about 10 minutes before our arrival in Pusan. A draft had been prepared in advance for my speech, but it was much the same as the statements by Mr. Nakasone and Mr. Miyazawa. So I said, "That's no good at all: I want to be more straightforward and to talk about more specific things." Then Ambassador [to South Korea] Goto replied, "If that's what you think, how about mentioning how Japan forced

Koreans to change their names to Japanese-style names." So that's what I decided to say in my speech. It was all improvised on the spur of the moment.

In this way, the text of his historical statement in Kyongju was worked out impromptu, but once it had taken form, it was decided on without any resistance. The process of drafting the statement was similar to that of Shiina's remark because both men, at the eleventh hour, accepted the advice of the Ambassador to South Korea, who knew exactly what atmosphere prevailed there.

It was Hosokawa's idea, however, that the statement should be much more straightforward. He also told me: "I had wanted to do this since I took office as prime minister. The previous statements were unsatisfactory, so I wanted to give a speech with more sincerity."

His statement did not have the oppressive tone and traces of double-dealing that characterized Kishi's and Shiina's remarks. He obviously accepted without question the need to apologize. It is well known that Hosokawa's grandfather was Prince Konoe Fumimaro, whose responsibility for pushing Japan into the Pacific War was incontrovertible. Hosokawa demonstrated a pragmatism in his words and deeds that apparently only a postwar-generation prime minister is capable to develop. The passage of time seems to be the key ingredient.

Understandably, Hosokawa's statement struck a chord in the hearts of the South Korean people. When he visited South Korea in February 1995 after he resigned as prime minister, he jokingly referred to his popularity in Korea saying: "My apology made me so famous in Seoul that I think if I ran for public office here I'd be elected." If it hadn't been for subsequent offensive statements by several cabinet members on Japan's colonial rule over Korea and various insensitive remarks made in opposition to the 50 Year Post-War Diet Resolution, Hosokawa's statement might have become a major watershed in the relationship between the two countries. It could have ushered in a new era in their bilateral ties. I regret to say that events did not turn out that way.

The Democratic People's Republic of Korea also suffered under Japan's colonial rule. At present, Japan and North Korea do not have diplomatic relations. In 1990, a delegation of members of the Liberal Democratic Party and the Socialist Party headed by Kanemaru Shin and Tanabe Makoto visited North Korea and reached an agreement with North Korea to start talks on the normalization of diplomatic relations. Pyongyang made an issue of Japan's apology. The question was included in the joint communiqué announced by the two Japanese political parties and the North Korean Workers' Party.

> The three parties acknowledged that Japan should officially make a full apology and offer compensation to the Democratic People's Republic of Korea for the misery and suffering inflicted by Japan on North Koreans for 36 years of colonial rule as well as for the losses suffered by North Koreans for 45 years since World War II.[12]

In these terms, Japan promised to officially apologize in the future for the "misery and suffering" inflicted during Japan's colonial rule; this part was accepted as a matter of course. But the joint declaration stirred up criticism that Japan had yielded too much, because it also mentioned "the losses suffered by North Koreans for 45 years since World War II." At the time, the crews of a Japanese fishing boat, the 18th Fujisanmaru, had been captured by North Korea on suspicion of spying activities. The problem of obtaining their release demanded a humanitarian solution, complicating the delegation's job. Yet even when this is taken into account, it is difficult to fathom what "the losses suffered by North Koreans for 45 years since World War II" means. The joint statement was criticized for unacceptable language in the light of Japan's treatment of South Korean claims. Though the diplomatic normalization talks between the two governments went ahead on the basis of the joint communiqué signed by the three parties, the controversial phrase became a heavy burden to Japan.

Another delegation to North Korea was formed by members of the three ruling parties in the Murayama coalition government. They were the Liberal Democratic Party, the Social Democratic (formerly the Socialist) Party, and New Party Sakigake. The delegation, headed by Watanabe Michio, went to North Korea in March 1995 and tried to "shelve" the 1990 joint statement. North Korea gave evasive answers, and the delegation's attempt went nowhere. None can deny the possibility that this joint statement will remain a thorny issue in future talks between the two countries.

"MEIWAKU": DIFFERENT DEGREES OF TROUBLE IN THE CHINA–JAPAN JOINT COMMUNIQUÉ

Apology also played a crucial role in normalizing diplomatic relations between Japan and the People's Republic of China. Apologizing was only a matter of course, since Japan had left scars of ruthless aggression in China and had not reestablished diplomatic relations with China for nearly 30 years after the war.

Eventually, the Japanese prime minister at the time, Tanaka Kakuei, was to make a visit to China in September 1972 and offered to normalize diplomatic relations between the two countries. In March of the same year, before he became prime minister, he made an important statement as minister of international trade and industry in the Lower House Committee on the Budget. In reply to a question from dietman Kawasaki Hideji of the Liberal Democratic Party, he said, "In my opinion, the first precondition for the normalization of diplomatic relations with China is our understanding that Japan caused China enormous trouble and that we truly want to offer an apology from the bottom of our hearts. This belief of mine is now unshakable and will never change in the future." According to *Seijika Tanaka Kakuei* (Tanaka Kakuei, politician), the statement was a clear sign to China.[13] As described in Chapter 9, Tanaka did not necessarily perceive Japan's acts clearly as aggression against China. But he emphasized his seriousness and determination to embark on the task of normalizing diplomatic relations with China by repeating again and again that Japan had caused "trouble." This heightened China's expectations of him.

During Tanaka's historic visit to China, Chinese Premier Zhou Enlai welcomed Tanaka and in a meeting with him emphasized the importance of the normalization of diplomatic relations between the two countries. Zhou said, "We know the crippling hardships of war reparation. We do not want the Japanese people to suffer these hardships." He then hinted that China would abandon its claims for reparations from Japan. The crushing reparations that Japan had demanded after the Sino–Japanese War (1894–95) were doubtlessly foremost in Zhou's mind when he mentioned "the crippling hardships of war reparation."

Premier Zhou declared furthermore that China would not interfere with the US–Japan Security Treaty and would not seek to export its revolution to Japan. At a dinner banquet to welcome Tanaka, he straightforwardly referred to Japan's past "aggression against China." In his speech, he said:

> China and Japan had a 2,000-year history of friendly personal contacts and cultural exchanges between their peoples. The people of both countries had maintained a close friendship. . . . However, Japanese militarists invaded China in 1894, and their invasion lasted for half a century, causing terrible damage to the Chinese people and inflicting huge losses on ordinary Japanese people as well. It is often said that we must not forget the past and learn lessons from it. So must we engrave these experiences and lessons deeply in our memories.[14]

In response to Zhou's remarks, Tanaka said the following.

> Japan and China are located in close geographic proximity to each other and share a 2000-year history of exchanges in many fields. Yet, regrettably, the relationship between the two countries went through an unfortunate period over dozens of years in the past. So, once again, I would like to express my deep remorse for the huge trouble which Japan caused to the Chinese people.[15]

When Zhou mentioned "in 1894," he had the Sino–Japan War in mind. But Tanaka did not offer his opinion on the war and conveyed his remorse only for the "trouble" caused by Japan "over dozens of years in the past." So he apologized to China without clarifying which of three related incidents was the starting point of the trouble caused by Japan: the Sino–Japanese War, the Russo–Japanese War, or the Manchurian Incident.

However, amidst all this imprecision, what China made an issue of was the meaning of "trouble." The Chinese version of Tanaka's statement was prepared by the Japanese government. And the part reading "meiwaku o kaketa" in Japanese, which means "caused trouble," was translated as "tianle mafan" in Chinese. But the Chinese expression is merely a casual expression. On the following day, Zhou Enlai mentioned this in a meeting with Tanaka and pointed out that the expression was usually used by Chinese to excuse themselves when they have, for example, carelessly splashed water on women standing by the side of the road. Tanaka was doubtlessly embarrassed by Zhou's unexpected response to his statement.

Learning a lesson from the episode, the correct expression was used in the China–Japan joint communiqué signed by the two Premiers. Part of the statement is as follows.

> Japan feels heavy responsibility for having caused grave harm to the Chinese by waging war against China in the past and expresses its deep remorse.[16]

The joint statement clearly stated the following three decisions on the basis of this understanding. First, the joint statement put a definitive end to the "abnormal circumstances" of the bilateral relationship. Second, Japan recognized therewith the People's Republic of China as the sole legitimate government of China. Third and last, China relinquished its claims against Japan for war reparations. The current relationship between the two countries continues to be based on these decisions.

Exactly 20 years later, in October 1992, Emperor Akihito visited China. His statement on that occasion also touched upon the past. The wording was as follows.

In the long history of ties between our two countries, there was an unhappy phase in which my country inflicted great suffering on the people of China. I deeply deplore this. When the war came to the end, the Japanese people, believing with a sense of deep remorse that such a war should never be repeated, firmly resolved to tread the path of peaceful nations and addressed themselves to national reconstruction.[17]

This statement was written on the basis of a series of remarks addressed to the president of South Korea. Its distinguishing characteristic is the use of "the Japanese people" as the subject and the addition of the word "remorse" for the first time in an Emperor's statement.

Japan also issued apologetic statements in Southeast Asia, for example, when Kaifu Toshiki went to Singapore as prime minister in May 1991, the year marking the fiftieth anniversary of the beginning of the Pacific War. Kaifu's statement is Japan's most explicit accounting for its wartime behavior in the Asia-Pacific region. His words are as follows.

This year marks the fiftieth anniversary of the beginning of the Pacific War. Once again, I look back over the history of the early half of this century, and I solemnly express our sincere remorse for Japanese actions in the past which inflicted unbearable suffering and sorrow upon multitudes in the Asia-Pacific region.[18]

HOW MURAYAMA'S REMARKS PLAYED A SIGNIFICANT ROLE

As I have described above, apologies have played a significant role in Japan's postwar Asian diplomacy. They were important because issuing an apology was the indispensable first step toward establishing normal diplomatic and friendly ties with Asian countries, especially with those that had suffered Japanese aggression and colonial rule.

Even the speeches at the National Memorial Service for the War Dead organized annually by the Japanese government on August 15 have changed a great deal over the past several years. In 1993, newly-elected prime minister Hosokawa was the first Japanese prime minister to refer to war victims in other Asian countries at the memorial service. He said, "On this solemn occasion, I would like to offer my condolences again, across national borders, to all war victims and their families in neighboring Asian countries and all over the world." Lower house speaker Doi Takako, a Socialist, said at the same memorial ceremony, "We have not yet been fully reconciled with the Asian people who were forced to endure terrible sacrifices caused by the wrongs committed by Japan."

The next year, in 1994, prime minister Murayama Tomiichi made a speech at the annual memorial service. Murayama was, like Doi, a member of the Japan Socialist (now the Social Democratic) Party. Just before this memorial service, one of his Cabinet members, Sakurai Shin, had resigned due to an offensive statement regarding Japan's wartime behavior. This led Murayama to pay more attention than usual to his speech: he even made corrections in the manuscript himself. In it, he said: "The war inflicted horrific, indescribable suffering upon many people in Asia and throughout the world. Reflecting deeply on the agony and sorrow of these people, I wish to express my deep remorse and humbly offer my heartfelt condolences."[19]

The National Memorial Service for the War Dead is a ceremony established by cabinet decision in 1963. It is dedicated "to the war dead (soldiers; civilian employees of the armed forces and members of army civilian employee families; those who died an unnatural death outside Japan; those killed by warfare in Japan; others) in the wars following the China Incident." In brief: until Murayama, the organizers of the memorial service did not have in their mind the Asian victims of the Japan military machine. They became aware they had been ignoring the non-Japanese war dead at a very late date.

On August 15, 1995, the fiftieth anniversary of the end of World War II, prime minister Murayama issued a statement in which he stated clearly that "aggression" and "colonial rule" were the result of a "mistaken national policy." Whereas in the Diet resolution, under threats from the opposition, the term "aggression" had been deliberately replaced with a more ambiguous word and the phrase "mistaken national policy" was not mentioned at all, Murayama offered a clear-cut apology to the non-Japanese Asian victims as follows.

> During a certain period in the not-too-distant past, Japan, after adopting a mistaken national policy, marched down the path to war and provoked a crisis jeopardizing the very survival of our people. Japan's colonial rule and aggression inflicted immense harm and suffering upon people in many countries, especially in other Asian countries. I humbly acknowledge these irrefutable facts of history, express my deep remorse once again, and offer an apology from the bottom of my heart, in the hope that no such mistake will ever be made in the future. I also offer my sincere condolences to all the victims of this period of history in Japan and abroad.[20]

Analysis of Japan's apologies reveals that over the past 50 years Japan has apologized to other Asian countries in small doses. I agree that it is not normal for prime ministers, representatives of a sovereign State, to offer one apology after another seemingly without end. Yet it is also true, as I pointed out earlier, that Japan's apologies have always been followed by fellow Japanese politicians' verbal and behavioral displays of insensitivity, nullifying the effects of any apology. Moreover, many of these statements had an element of double-dealing; sometimes, they were mere attempts to pass off ambiguous phrases as apologies.

Under the circumstances, Murayama's statement is the definitive apology. I earnestly hope that other politicians will not again step forward and, through their acts or words, defile the spirit engendered by Murayama's remark, arousing suspicions that his statement was yet another episode of duplicity in the annals of Japanese diplomacy.

This said, I unfortunately have to cite still another gaffe. Eto Takami of the LDP, who served as director general of the

Management and Coordination Agency in the Murayama administration, talked to the press and said, "Prime Minister Murayama
was wrong when he said that the annexation of Korea had been an
act of coercion. . . . In those years, the weak got taken advantage of,
and nothing could be done about it. . . . Not all that Japan did during the colonial years was bad." His was a classical rationale of
justification in the same vein as the gaffes of Fujio Masayuki and
Watanabe Michio described above.

Eto's statements were made off-the-record and were not reported
in the Japanese press. They surfaced later in a magazine article, hit
the headlines in Korea, and inevitably became politicized. Some
would-be defenders in Japan suggested that "off-the-record comments should be treated as such," while Koreans felt that Eto "gave
himself away precisely because it was off-the-record." In the end,
Eto was forced to resign—a symbol of diehard conservative opposition to the Murayama statement.

KIM DAEJUNG AND JIANG ZEMIN: A STUDY IN CONTRASTS

As mentioned in the Introduction (pp. 1–6), Korean president Kim
Daejung and Chinese president and head of state Jiang Zemin paid
official visits to Japan in close succession in the fall of 1998. With
the turn of the century just around the corner, their visits were
equally memorable and significant, but as different as day and
night.

Given his past record and previous association with Japan, Kim
Daejung's visit to Japan in October 1998 was fraught with historical implications. Several of his predecessors had stage-managed
ceremonies to bury the hatchet between Korea and Japan, but Kim
Daejung was best qualified to work out a definitive settlement of accounts between Korea and Japan from the colonial years to the lat-
est phase of postwar bilateral relations, with all their ups and
downs. It was natural that a great number of Japanese extended to
him a much more eager and enthusiastic welcome than had ever
been accorded to his predecessors.

In October 1998, at the official guest house in Tokyo, Prime Minister Obuchi Keizo (right) and South Korean President Kim Daejung (left) signed a joint communiqué declaring a reconciliation between Japan and South Korea.

Prime minister Obuchi Keizo was no exception. He readily complied with Kim's suggestion on the wording of an apology to be included in the text of the Joint Declaration:

> Reviewing bilateral relations between Japan and Korea in the present century, and recognizing with profound humility the historical fact that, for a time in the past, Japan by its colonial rule inflicted great damage and pain on the Korean people, Prime Minister Obuchi Keizo expressed deep remorse and most sincere apologies for this. President Kim Daejung in good faith accepted and appreciated Prime Minister Obuchi's expression of his view of history and stated that the current of the times was such that the two nations are required now to live down the unhappy phase of their past history and to make their best efforts for reconciliation and for good neighborly and friendly relations.[21]

The draft text of the Joint Declaration, however, was longer in the making. The Japanese officials at first balked at the Korean demand that an explicit apology be included. They protested once again that an apology had been made explicitly in the Murayama statement of 1995, on top of all the apologies to the Koreans that had been repeatedly made over the years, and it made little sense to keep doing the same thing over and over again. The Korean side insisted on the significance, to the Korean audience in particular, of an explicit reference to "apologies" and the Japanese side had to capitulate in the end. In return, Kim Daejung proposed to have the two nations' reconciliation expressly stated in the Joint Declaration, thereby committing himself to the position that henceforth Korea would not again try to politicize the past.

At the bilateral summit meeting, Kim Daejung said that he wanted to see the unhappy past of the 20th century accounted for before the turn of the century, and that the agreed text of the Joint Declaration was the first documented evidence of an explicit awareness of the past. He went on to promise that Korea, as a gesture of relinquishing its grudge over the past wrongs, would now open its doors to Japanese movies, popular songs, and other cultural assets that had been denied entry for many years.

Kim Daejung began his speech at the joint plenary session of the Diet by saying, "I nearly lost my life in my struggle for democratization, and I feel deeply moved by the sheer fact of my being here today as president of the Republic of Korea." Reminiscing on his past struggle, he expressed his gratitude to "the Japanese people, the press, and the government for their sustained efforts to defend my life and safety—an obligation I shall never forget." He appealed to the Japanese people to have the courage to face up to their past and expressed his appreciation for the consolidation of democracy in postwar Japan, Japan's economic growth, its peaceful Constitution, and its economic aid to developing countries. His speech was widely admired in Japan.

Soon after Kim's return to Korea, president Jiang Zemin of China arrived in Japan in November. His visit was meant to return the courtesy of the Emperor's visit to China in 1992, and to celebrate the 20th anniversary of the conclusion of the Treaty of Peace and Friendship between Japan and the People's Republic of China. As it was the first visit to Japan of a Chinese head of state, it was hoped it would provide a good opportunity to consolidate the two nations' frienship. At the bilateral summit meeting, at an audience with the Emperor, and at public appearances at Waseda University and elsewhere, however, Jiang Zemin put a damper on such expectations by repeatedly referring to Japan's "aggression" as a matter of historical fact. His preoccupation with past wrongs differed markedly from Kim Daejung's bid for reconciliation, and in no small measure took the Japanese people by surprise.

In negotiations prior to the visit, China demanded, as did Korea, that an "apology" be expressed explicitly in the prospective Joint Declaration. The Japanese side agreed to include explicit references to "aggression" and "remorse," but did not agree to have "apologies" expressly mentioned in the text. The Japanese position was firstly that the 1972 Joint Communiqué explicitly referred to Japan's "responsibility and regret for the past wrongs," and the Emperor's visit to China in 1992 marked a break with the past, and secondly that the Chinese side refused to have "reconciliation" expressly stated in the text of the Joint Declaration, hinting that China, unlike Korea, would continue to be concerned with problems of the past. Prime minister Obuchi instead made his "apologies" by word of mouth at his meeting with Jiang Zemin, who was distinctly displeased. The following exchange ensued:

> JIANG ZEMIN: I am opposed to the view that an extensive oral discussion of historical problems should make superfluous an explicit expression of apologies in writing. To China, problems of history and of Taiwan represent the roots of China–Japan relations, and can on no account be bypassed. I don't mean to carry a grudge over the past, but the two problems should be rightly understood and treated so as to open the door to the years ahead. Our 2,000-year history of bilateral relations has been predominantly marked with friendship and cooperation. Only in the recent past did Japanese militarism start a war of aggression that inflicted a calamity upon

© Asahi Shimbunsha

An austere Chairman Jiang Zemin (second from the left), attired in a Mao jacket, addressed the dinner banquet at the Imperial Palace welcoming him to Japan in November 1998. He is flanked on the left and right by the Emperor and the Empress.

the Chinese people. Prime minister Murayama's statement and those by other leaders are adamantly opposed to the revival of militarism, and China appreciates their commitment. But from time to time, diametrically opposed views are aired in speech and in action. Our neighborly hope and advice is that you learn your lesson and enlighten the nation.

OBUCHI KEIZO: For a time in the past, there were unfortunate relations between Japan and China. The then prime minister's statement issued in 1995 expressed deep remorse for the acts of colonial rule and aggression by Japan for a time in the past, and registered most sincere apologies for them. The government of Japan takes this opportunity to again express such feeling of remorse and apologies to China.[22]

The text of the Joint Declaration after the bilateral summit reads as follows:

The Japanese side stated that Japan is painfully aware of its responsibility for a great deal of damage and pain that its acts of aggression for a time in the past in China inflicted on the Chinese people, and expressed deep remorse for them.[23]

As Obuchi indicated, the wording was based on the 1995 Murayama statement, and represented the most candid and straitforward forms of expression to be found in any document exchanged between Japan and China. No mention of "apologies" however was to be found anywhere in the text.

In his after-dinner speech at the prime minister's official residence, Jiang Zemin again referred to Japanese militarism starting wars of aggression on China, inflicting great calamity on the Chinese people, and leaving painful lessons for the Japanese people. In his lecture titled "The Mirror of History to Open the Way for the Years Ahead" at Waseda University, Jiang maintained his tough posture, citing statistical data as he said, "Japanese militarism started an all-out war of aggression against China, causing 35 million casualties and over $600 billion in economic damages."

As I have pointed out already in this book, Jiang Zemin's hardline position was undoubtedly motivated by his strong objection to repeated attempts by certain Japanese politicians and celebrities to justify the country's past wrongs and by his apprehension at the way the history of aggression tended to be whitewashed in school textbooks and classroom lessons. The political community in Japan in a sense invited Jiang's outspoken barrage. Yet Obuchi's refusal to mention an apology explicitly in the text of the Joint Declaration was strongly supported in the Japanese political community, and the Japanese people in general, whether of the right or left, found it objectionable that China should aim at military hegemony in Asia and, at the same time, exploit the "Japan card" as it were by harping on Japan's responsibility for past aggression. In contrast to Kim Daejung's ploy to tickle the vanity of the Japanese, Jiang Zemin's persistent warnings apparently rubbed Japanese nationalism the wrong way and were generally counterproductive.

IMPERIAL VISITS: YARDSTICKS OF OUR SENSE OF DISTANCE

The Emperors' travels abroad, as we have seen already, have had a considerable political bearing on the question of apologies. The Emperors have made trips abroad in the following order: Europe, the United States, Southeast Asia, and finally China. They have yet to visit the Korean Peninsula. Their foreign destinations began with the countries with the least anti-Japanese public sentiment and were followed by those where hostility was progressively greater. This is hardly a coincidence, and how much their visits achieved and how much remains to be done are yardsticks that permit us to measure the psychological distance between Japan and other Asian countries.

Emperor Showa's first postwar trip abroad was a tour of seven European countries in 1971. He visited the United States in 1975. The purpose of both journeys was to heal the wounds caused by World War II. He passed away without realizing his wish to visit other Asian countries; he had been especially eager to visit China. It is obvious that he voluntarily abandoned his hope to visit China because of his advanced age and the perennially unresolved issue of his responsibility for the war.

Long-pending visits to other Asian countries were realized by Emperor Akihito. To begin with, he made a tour of Thailand and other Southeast Asian countries in September 1991; no one in Japan raised any objection to this voyage. In other words, the Emperor's travels in Asia began in the same way that successive prime ministers' visits to the region had begun, with Southeast Asia.

The Emperor's trip to China then sparked a major political controversy. The 1992 visit was intended to mark the 20th anniversary of the normalization of diplomatic relations between Japan and China, in response to a pressing invitation from the Chinese government that had been accepted by the Miyazawa Cabinet.

The announcement touched off protests in Japan. Although those who were against the visit were few in number, right-wing groups and Diet members, as well as some sectors of the mass media, mounted an aggressive campaign against it. Their opposition can be summarized in three points: the People's Republic of China is a communist country, anti-Japanese feelings continue to run strong there, and the Emperor's visiting China might be interpreted as acceptance of sinocentrism (in effect, Japan's paying symbolic tribute to China). Prime minister Miyazawa had recently canceled a visit to Yasukuni Shrine, and the emotional response to this retreat further complicated the situation. Nationalism and antipathy to communism combined to ignite an outburst of opposition to the visit. Notwithstanding these protests, however, the Emperor went to China. His trip is described in detail in Part IV.

An imperial visit to South Korea is now emerging as an issue. By the criterion of the country's political system (i.e. whether free-economy or communist), the Emperor ought to have visited South Korea before visiting China. Yet the Japanese government continued to tread lightly on this issue, and it seemed the time was not yet ripe for an Imperial visit to South Korea.

It is not that nothing has changed: on the contrary, South Korea's progress toward democracy and the Japan Socialist Party's change of policy toward South Korea have softened the opposition from left-wingers in Japan. But there remain two major obstacles to a visit by a Japanese Emperor. First, anti-Japanese sentiment is still deeply rooted in the South Korean general public. The visit could easily be spoiled by demonstrations or other unforeseen incidents. (It is ironic that in China, the Emperor's security was more securely ensured by the government's strict control). Second, because the Koreans are a divided people, a visit to South Korea automatically means that the Emperor owes a trip to North Korea. The Nakasone cabinet had at one point arranged a visit by the Crown Prince (the current Emperor) and Princess (now Empress), but the visit was canceled. The ostensible reason was the Crown Princess's illness. The real reason was reportedly a possible surge of protests from South Korean opposition parties.

In the summer of 1995, South Korean president Kim Youngsam met the president of the Asahi Shimbun Publishing Co., Nakae Toshitada, and talked about an imperial visit to Seoul. President Kim indicated at that meeting that the time was not yet ripe. He said to Nakae, "The visit should be celebrated by the people of both countries. So both peoples must continue their efforts to create such an atmosphere. Efforts on Japan's part are especially vital. It is extremely unfortunate that some Japanese, including politicians, continue to make offensive statements that rub South Koreans the wrong way. Whether the Emperor visits South Korea depends entirely on the attitude of the Japanese people."[20]

In contrast to Kim Youngsam in the summer of 1995, Kim Daejung on his historical visit to Japan in 1998 went out of his way to promote friendly Japan–Korea relations and displayed an unprecedented eagerness to extend an invitation to the Emperor to visit Korea. He stated at a press conference that "it is unnatural for diplomatic relations to have been normalized 33 years ago without the Emperor of Japan's even once having visited Korea during that time." He committed himself to ensuring that the invitation was acted on before the World Cup Soccer Games in 2002, which will be jointly hosted by Korea and Japan. Though Japanese officials have become slightly more positive about the visit, they still tend generally to prefer that the visit be scheduled after the presumably resounding success of the World Cup Games has generated a genuinely friendly ambience. The Emperor's visit will in any case be the last card to play in the consolidation of friendly relations between Japan and Korea.

PART IV

THE EMPEROR'S ROAD TO CHINA

The welcome reception held for the Emperor and Empress in Beijing. Where the Emperor spoke of his "deep sorrow" for the "great suffering" caused to the Chinese people, this was translated into Chinese as [深感痛心] *"shengan tongxin" (deep sorrow). In the center stands reception host President Yang Shanghun.* (October 1992)

The Visit's Real Meaning

In the summer of 1995, I was suddenly struck by a discouraging thought: when the Japanese government filed a strong protest over the string of nuclear tests China was conducting and hinted at cutting down on its grant aid, China retorted that Japan was in no position to preach, given its own lack of remorse over past invasions. This was despite the fact that three years before, the Miyazawa cabinet had finally managed to arrange a visit to China by the Emperor, an event proclaimed as solidifying amicable relations between Japan and China and signaling "a major break with the past." In other words, die-hard right-wing politicians' continuing attempts to justify Japan's militaristic past gave the Chinese a convenient excuse to justify China's nuclear tests. Fifty years after the end of the war, Japan–China relations were still uneasy. I was not alone in seeing no light at the end of the tunnel.

I have already noted how a succession of imperial visits has done much to salve wartime scars elsewhere. Of these, the 1975 visit to the United States by Emperor Hirohito and the reigning Emperor's visit to China have attracted the most attention in Japan and abroad. The latter was arranged in response to China's strong desire for proof of the amity of the bilateral relationship, but the stiff opposition thrown up within Japan from right-wing groups and conservative forces such as the LDP led to an interval of some eight months between the unofficial and official decisions.

That was the year in which, after great commotion, the Diet finally passed the Law Concerning Cooperation for United Nations Peacekeeping and Other Operations (the International Peace Cooperation Law) and sent a unit from the Self-Defense Forces to Cambodia; it was also the year in which the issue of the return of the Northern Territories emerged with an unprecedented sense of reality. The Emperor's China visit became interwoven with these underlying currents, imbuing it, for better or for worse, with enormous political significance.

Three years later, groups opposed to the Emperor's visit were to form a chorus of opposition to the Diet resolution marking the fiftieth anniversary of the end of the war. This was probably due in part to a heightened sense of alarm triggered by recent statements by prime ministers Hosokawa Morihiro and Murayama Tomiichi. Opponents were highly concerned that if the Diet resolution was passed on top of these, their cause would be lost.

As it happened, I was working then as a political correspondent handling Cabinet affairs, which put me in a position to gather information and report on the decision process involved in the Emperor's China visit. Analyzing information from front-line reporters and collecting my own information, it was my job to make a comprehensive judgement. A year later, I contributed to *Chuo koron* (September 1993 issue) a piece of reportage entitled "Inquiry: The Emperor's China Visit," which was based on this earlier work as well as new research on matters that could not be studied at the time. Here I would like to revisit that "inquiry," reviewing my own thoughts as to the significance of the visit.

CHINA'S FERVOR

The opening days of 1992 were a period of frantic activity for the ministry of foreign affairs. Welcoming US President Bush, due in Japan on January 7, would have been demanding enough, but his visit was preceded by minister for foreign affairs (and deputy prime minister) Watanabe Michio's trip to Beijing on January 3, when everyone was still tipsy or hung over from their New Year's cups. Watanabe, appointed second in command when the Miyazawa cabinet was inaugurated in November the preceding year, had chosen China as the destination of his first official visit to mark the twentieth anniversary of the normalization of relations between Japan and China. A major proposal had been readied for this occasion.

The foreign ministers met on January 4, 1992, in the Diaoyutai guest house. After some discussion on the twentieth anniversary issue, Chinese foreign minister Qian Qichen broached the subject. "We would like Their Majesties the Emperor and Empress to visit China this fall."

While this was hardly the first such invitation to be issued by China, the specific indication of a date, "that fall," was a first. Watanabe responded: "We greatly appreciate your repeated invitations. The government will give serious consideration to your proposal."

The "serious consideration" offered by Watanabe was also the first definite statement on the subject by the Japanese government. This was subsequently announced to the press, who were told that it "effectively signaled confirmation of the Emperor's visit," but in fact, Watanabe had added the following words in the foreign ministers' talks, surprising senior officials on both sides: "In terms of timing, could we suggest October 22–27?"

Foreign ministry personnel had anticipated that China would press for such a visit, and had worked out this date beforehand in line with circumstances of the Imperial Household and the Chinese side. It was a proposal well beyond the scenario for the talks. "Certainly," responded a delighted China, but this portion of the talks was suppressed in the press statement and remained off the official record thereafter.

As the straight-talker of the Seirankai, the LDP's most hawkish faction, Watanabe had adamantly opposed the normalization of Japan–China relations and the Sino–Japanese Air Traffic Agreement. Watanabe could well have been impressed by his own metamorphosis: who would have thought that he would ever be playing this particularly responsible role?

The Emperor's China visit had of course been a long-pending question. Emperor Hirohito, who toured seven European countries in 1971 and then the United States in 1975, commented on his return from America that he would be very happy to have an opportunity to visit China once the Treaty of Peace and Friendship between Japan and the People's Republic of China had been signed. And in fact it was immediately after conclusion of this treaty, October 1978, that Deng Xiaoping, visiting Japan as Chinese vice-premier, issued an invitation to the Emperor.

Apparently Emperor Hirohito wanted very much to visit China. Whereas the Korean Peninsula had been annexed during the reign of Emperor Meiji, Hirohito had been on the throne from the Manchurian Incident to the end of the Asia-Pacific War, and the Emperor's eagerness has been interpreted as stemming from a sense of personal responsibility.

In any case, his wish was not to be granted, and the question of a China visit was inherited by his heir, the reigning Emperor Akihito. Li Peng, visiting Japan in April 1989 as Chinese premier, invited the Emperor to visit China at "a convenient time," However, this was immediately followed by the Tiananmen Square incident, which triggered a barrage of criticism directed at China from the international community. Japan–China relations cooled by several degrees, and talk of a visit vanished.

It was revived in June 1991 when Qian Qichen visited Japan as foreign minister. Qian again pushed for a visit by the Emperor, suggesting "a convenient time next year." "Next year" meant 1992, exactly twenty years after the 1972 normalization of Japan–China relations. Qian added, "A visit by the Emperor would be greeted with great enthusiasm by the Chinese people and would prove a major milestone in the history of Japan–China relations." When prime minister Kaifu Toshiki visited China in August that year to patch up diplomatic relations after the Tiananmen incident, premier Li Peng himself mentioned the "twentieth anniversary of the normalization of ties," proposing that the Emperor visit the following year. China's invitations were becoming more insistent.

The Kaifu cabinet dissolved that fall, leaving the question of whether or not Japan could permit such a visit as a task for the succeeding Miyazawa cabinet, and it was Watanabe, the new foreign minister, who, urged by Hashimoto Hiroshi, Japanese Ambassador to China, and Yano Sakutaro, director-general of the Asian Affairs Bureau in the ministry of foreign affairs, went ahead and gave the go-sign for the visit. This was also supported by Miyazawa. After working out the finer details with the prime minister, Watanabe flew to Beijing, where the issue became the subject of the opening exchange in talks with his Chinese counterpart.

The foreign ministers also agreed on an April visit to Japan by general secretary Jiang Zemin, head of the Chinese Communist Party. The arrangement was that the Emperor's visit would be officially decided at the April Summit talks. Where Watanabe had proposed beginning the visit on October 22, subsequent criticism from opposition forces resulted in a one-day delay, but China was nevertheless able to launch into steady preparations as of January.

BUSH AND ROH TAEWOO

The twentieth anniversary was a felicitous occasion also for the Japanese government. Architect of the Emperor's visit as Japanese Ambassador to China, Hashimoto was to vacate this post soon afterwards to become a special advisor to Kobe Steel. The visit was to be his parting gift, as it were. But in retrospect, he noted that "I thought a milestone such as the twentieth anniversary would be sufficiently persuasive not only within Japan but also abroad, and particularly to Korea." With Korea's history of colonial rule lending great historical significance to an imperial visit, Japan needed a solid reason for the Emperor to visit China first.

This aside, when Miyazawa met with George Bush during the latter's January 7 visit to Japan, he quietly informed Bush of Japan's intention to send the Emperor to China. The scars from the Tiananmen incident had yet to heal internationally, and the human rights issue had created particularly strained relations between China and the United States. Japan had accordingly gone to the trouble of informing the United States in advance, but the casual acceptance of this news by the US President set the Prime Minister's mind at ease.

Not only that, but when President Bush visited the Emperor on the 10th to pay his respects before returning home, he said to the Emperor, "I hear you will be visiting China." As the visit had yet to be officially decided, the Emperor was somewhat taken aback, but parried that, while he had heard about the possibility, it was up to the government to decide. Hearing of this later on, the prime minister admitted to breaking out in a cold sweat, noting that the Emperor had saved the day.

The prime minister flew to Korea on the 16th. While this visit was in response to a strong appeal from president Roh Taewoo, another reason why the Prime Minister chose Korea as his first official destination was to pass on the details of the Foreign Minister's January visit to China, as well as to play up Japan's Asian alignment. This was immediately after the PKO bill had been thrown out of the Diet due to the opposition parties' staunch opposition at the extraordinary session the previous fall, shortly after the new cabinet's formation. The same bill was to be put before the Diet again during the regular Diet session beginning January 24, and the government must have regarded easing Asian countries' fears as an essential step.

What the government had miscalculated, however, was the comfort women issue, which had suddenly come to a boil, souring relations with Korea. The Prime Minister plunged headlong into this whirlpool. Legislation to permit the dispatch of troops abroad, quarrels over compensation for ex-comfort women—the unfortunate conjunction of these controversies with the timing of Miyazawa's trip stirred memories of Japanese militarism. At their talks on the 16th and then the 17th, Miyazawa made deep apologies to Korea about the comfort women, and when Roh Taewoo extended the usual invitation to the Emperor, the atmosphere was evidently such that Miyazawa could not produce his explanation of the Emperor's visit to China.

The government next chose Takeshita Noboru, former prime minister and chair of the Japan–Korea Parliamentarians' League, to explain the situation to Korea. As Japan's prime minister, Takeshita had cooperated toward the success of the Seoul Olympics, Roh Taewoo's pet project, and had even attended the opening ceremony. If Chun Doohwan was Nakasone's partner, Roh Taewoo was Takeshita's. A frequent target of right-wing criticism over his Chinese connections, Takeshita hesitated to accept the government's request, but after much thought, he yielded at the urging of Watanabe Michio and chief cabinet secretary Kato Koichi. Timing his visit with the end of the Korean general elections, he landed in Seoul on March 30.

In response to Takeshita's courteous explanation, Roh Taewoo chose his words carefully, indicating his understanding of the situation and asking that the Emperor visit Korea when he was in a position to do so. The press was told that discussion had centered on such issues as the fisheries cooperation agreement between Korea and Russia. Takeshita continued to conceal the truth, even after his return home. Miyazawa was much relieved over this course of affairs. The understanding of the Korean government was not the only boon: the kingpin of the largest faction supporting the government had involved himself in this matter. When opposition to the Emperor's China visit later began to spread within and outside the party, this must have been a source of considerable comfort.

Let us wind back the clock a month. The "PKO Diet" opened on January 24. And on the 31st, attending an emergency UN Security Council Summit held in New York, Miyazawa met Russian president Boris Yeltsin face to face for the first time. This was where the two agreed on the Russian president's September trip to Japan, which was later suddenly canceled. Miyazawa lost no time in launching into territorial diplomacy, later telling reporters that he had "made some inroads" over the Northern Territory negotiations, and that "there was such a thing as timing."

The Emperor's China visit, the return of the Northern Territories, the assignment of Self-Defense Forces personnel to peace-keeping operations abroad—these three major issues arrived on the table simultaneously, ready for action in the fall.

EXPLOSIVE PROTEST

Gradually, however, the omens for the Emperor's China visit began to worsen to the extent that, looking back long afterward, then-chief cabinet secretary Kato shook his head in disbelief at the government's miscalculation of the mounting domestic opposition.

The spark that touched off the explosion was kindled by the LDP's own Fujio Masayuki, on January 17, the very day that prime minister Miyazawa was apologizing in Korea for the Japanese military's treatment of the comfort women. At an LDP general council meeting, Fujio raised the possibility that the issue of war responsibility might come up in China, too. "How can you say the Emperor won't become entangled in politics in the end?" he asked. (As you remember, Fujio was a hard-liner who, while in the Nakasone cabinet, had refused to back down from his stand on Korea's shared responsibility for its annexation by Japan, resulting in his removal from the post of minister of education. His strong connections to the hawkish right-wing group Daitojuku made the above rhetorical question ring all the more ominously.)

Perhaps sensing the danger, an increasing number of party members started to express opposition or to urge caution. At a general council meeting on February 21, Itagaki Tadashi, an Upper House member from the Japan Association of the Bereaved Families of the War Dead, also stated his opposition. Reading the writing on the wall, party secretary-general Watanuki Tamisuke had suggested to Miyazawa the previous day that they tread carefully.

At that very moment, China began to send provocative messages to Japan. First were warnings against sending Japan's Self-Defense Forces on peacekeeping operations abroad. For example, at a press conference during his visit to Singapore, president Yang Shanghun declared: "Historical causes have made the dispatch of Japanese troops abroad in whatever form an extremely delicate issue. Not only are many people within Japan opposed to this, but China and the other Asian countries are also on the alert. We hope that Japan will proceed with caution."

There was also a sudden spate of public statements seeking, it would seem, an apology from the Emperor. At a February 22 press conference, Chinese Ambassador to Japan Yang Zhenya expressed the hope that "Japan would indicate its attitude toward the unhappy phase in the history of relations between our two countries." While his feelings were quite understandable, he was clearly jumping the gun by making such a statement at so early a stage.

Japan and China also found themselves in a face-off on the shelved Senkaku Islands territory issue. On February 25, China put into effect legislation on its territorial waters claiming as Chinese possessions both the Senkaku and the Spratley Islands, over which China and Vietnam were at loggerheads. This law included the right to remove invaders using military force. Some victims of the Sino–Japanese War also began to seek civilian reparations. The Chinese government ignored these moves, but those opposing the Emperor's China visit grew increasingly alarmed with the emergence of one issue after the other.

The Japanese government nevertheless remained committed to having the Emperor visit China. The government planned officially to accept the Chinese invitation when Jiang Zemin made a visit to Japan for talks between the leaders on April 6. The events of the evening of March 18 preceding the scheduled visit, however, threw a major spanner in the works. The prime minister had called together the LDP's senior advisors for an informal meeting at a Tokyo hotel. Though it was not announced to the press, former prime minister Nakasone Yasuhiro called a halt to the Emperor's visit at this meeting. Then as well as later, Miyazawa wondered why: normally, Nakasone should have been in favor of the visit. Perhaps Nakasone, who nursed special feelings for the Imperial Household, was put out that he had not been consulted. In any case, deciding that not enough groundwork had been done, Miyazawa shelved his plans.

What was Nakasone really after? When Miyazawa later sounded him out, Nakasone said that he was concerned in particular about public opinion in Korea and the response from the right-wing in Japan. That made some sense, as Nakasone had experienced trouble in both these contexts during his time as prime minister.

Firstly, Korea. Nakasone had worked actively to develop relations with Korea, and had responded to then-president Chun Doohwan's earnest request by scheduling a visit to Korea by the Crown Prince (the current Emperor) and Princess. However, rising anti-government sentiment in Korea eventually led to the visit's cancelation (and the Crown Princess Michiko's illness was given as the ostensible reason). Nakasone had learned the hard way that even when the Korean government gave its blessing, the response of opposition groups and the mass media was another matter entirely. This cancelation during his own time in power would certainly have made him reluctant to see a visit to China go ahead while the Korean visit was still pending. He believed that serious thought needed to be given to the response of the Korean mass media.

His scuffles with the right wing were related to his frustrated visit to Yasukuni Shrine and strong opposition from the right over his dismissal of Fujio Masayuki as minister of education. After making one visit to Yasukuni Shrine in 1985, Nakasone gave up the whole idea the next year after a sharp reproach from China, and this policy turn-around drew rightists' cries of faint-heartedness and betrayal. Conservatives were strident also in their condemnation of Fujio's dismissal, demanding that Nakasone "protect our patriotic warrior." He was frequently accused of being a traitor, not least because of his original sympathy and personal connections with the conservative right.

In fact, when Nakasone called a halt to the Emperor's visit that March, the conservatives were spearheading a mounting opposition in the form of a national protest campaign. On the 31st, a people's meeting seeking postponement of the Emperor's China visit was held at the Tojo Hall in Tokyo. This was convened by such members of the intelligentsia as Uno Seiichi, Eto Jun,

Mayuzumi Toshiro and Muramatsu Tsuyoshi. The hawkish Daitojuku, its de facto organizer, announced the meeting in its organ *Fuji*, noting that they were engaged in full-scale preparations. The meeting addressed a petition to prime minister Miyazawa listing reasons for opposing the China visit.

JIANG ZEMIN'S SHOCK

On April 1, a month before his visit to Japan, Jiang Zemin met with Japanese reporters in Beijing. With his visit just around the corner, he spoke with the usual earnestness, voicing his conviction that the Emperor's visit to China would contribute to the development of amicable relations between the two countries. Summit talks took place on April 6 in Tokyo. Topics ranged widely from the economy to human rights issues, the Korean Peninsula, and the overseas peace-keeping operations issue, but Miyazawa was not forthcoming with the critical reply. Growing impatient, Jiang Zemin broached the issue himself, saying that "a visit to China by the Emperor this year would be sincerely welcomed."

Miyazawa's response deflated his expectations. Miyazawa said only that the Japanese side was "currently giving serious consideration to this issue." Continuing, he said: "A visit in the year marking the twentieth anniversary of the normalization of Japan–China relations would be extremely significant in the development of friendly relations between our peoples in the years to come. We would like to continue considering the matter." This was the strongest commitment that Miyazawa was able to make, but according to Kato, who also attended the meeting, it threw the Chinese side into a panic. Director of Japanese Affairs in the Chinese Ministry of Foreign Affairs Wu Dawei blanched.

The circumstances that had made it difficult for Japan to accept the invitation for an imperial visit had already been communicated to China through diplomatic channels. China should have been aware of the tone of the Japanese press. Yet the Chinese side undoubtedly believed, following talks between foreign ministers in

January, that this question involved a high-level political resolution which went beyond any scenario developed by the ministry of foreign affairs. "That was probably exactly what they thought the Summit meeting was for," says Kato.

Kato, as it happened, was a former diplomat who had studied Chinese in Taiwan before ties were normalized between Japan and China. He had worked under Hashimoto Hiroshi, Ambassador to China, when Hashimoto was Director of Chinese Affairs. As such, he was able to read the Chinese reaction particularly clearly.

At talks with key politicians in Japan, Jiang Zemin had continued to respond gently but firmly to Japanese requests for understanding over the overseas peace-keeping operations bill, which was entering a critical stage at precisely that time. He had acknowledged to Miyazawa as a friend that peace-keeping operations were a sensitive issue, and he hoped Japan would take a cautious stance. He had advised Kanemaru Shin, the LDP's vice-president, that Japan should learn from its mistakes in the war. These statements had received wide press coverage, but it was understood that these were the stock responses he was obliged to give when asked. When Ouchi Keigo, chairman of the Democratic Socialist Party, mentioned his concern over the Emperor's China visit given the Senkaku Islands issue and civilian reparations, Jiang Zemin denied that any difficult issues would be raised, displaying all possible consideration.

Visiting the Emperor at the Imperial Palace on the 7th, Jiang Zemin again noted that China was hoping to be able to welcome the Emperor and Empress. However, the Emperor was powerless to respond. Jiang Zemin returned home amidst whispers from China that the Chinese government was offended and had lost face because the Japanese government had postponed its decision.

THE AMBASSADOR'S SECRET MISSION

The momentum of the Emperor's China visit had diminished. On April 23, young LDP Diet members proposed to party executives that the visit was premature. When reporters asked for his response,

Miyazawa said, "It's important to undertake such a visit with the blessing of the Japanese people. If public opinion ripens in that direction, the Emperor will go to China. This will require a little more time."

Back at square one, Miyazawa used the string of public holidays in early May known in Japan as 'Golden Week' to visit France and Germany. He wanted to make prior arrangements with these countries to ensure that the Northern Territories issue would be brought up at the July Munich Summit ahead of Boris Yeltsin's visit to Japan. Almost simultaneously, foreign minister Watanabe set off for Russia. For a brief while, Japan's foreign policy objectives centered on the return of the Northern Territories. Takeshita visited China within the same time-frame. Chairman of the National People's Congress Wan Li came to Japan at the end of May, but no discussion on the China visit is recorded. Around that time, Miyazawa announced a "cooling-off period" to those around him.

With the cooperation of Komeito and the Democratic Socialist Party, the overseas peace-keeping operations bill, the government's greatest political challenge, was beginning to look as though it would be passed, but an unforeseen event was lying in wait on May 31. Watanabe was suddenly hospitalized with gallstones. The Emperor's China visit was losing vital momentum, seemingly adrift with no one at the helm.

Yet the prime minister had in fact devised a plan: he would entrust Hashimoto in Beijing with two important secret missions. One was to speak with key figures in China, explaining why Japan was unable to clear the Emperor's visit, and to ask for their cooperation in creating a climate conducive to this visit, which meant that he was asking them to refrain at least for the time being from words and actions that might inflame conservatives in Japan. The other was, if that went well, to explain China's intentions in detail to key LDP figures upon his return to Japan, nudging the domestic climate in the right direction. These were his two special missions.

Hashimoto Hiroshi had been involved in the negotiations for normalization of relations as Director of Chinese Affairs when the

Tanaka cabinet was in power, and he was known as a man of principle who in no wise fit the mold of the stereotypical bureaucrat. His relationship with Miyazawa also went back a long way, with the two working together on policy when the Suzuki Zenko cabinet was caught up in the textbook issue, Miyazawa as chief cabinet secretary and Hashimoto as director of the ministry of foreign affairs' Information and Cultural Affairs Bureau. Feeling personal responsibility as part of the driving force behind the Emperor's visit, he was someone on whom the prime minister could rely.

Motives for domestic conservatives' opposition to the China visit could basically be summarized as follows:

(a) China was a communist state now ostracized by the West over human rights issues in particular. The Emperor should not visit such an essentially alien country, which could also draw criticism from the United States and Europe;

(b) China was meddling in Japan's internal affairs by, for example, criticizing Japan over the peace-keeping operations issue, had taken a provocative stance on issues such as the Senkaku Islands, and was displaying a general unfriendliness;

(c) During the Emperor's visit, China might demand an apology from him in regard to war responsibility or throw claims for civilian reparations in his lap;

(d) A visit at a time when true friendship did not exist between the two countries would amount to political use of the Emperor, which was unconstitutional.

The undercurrent to these protests was nationalistic sentiment: the historically unprecedented event of the Emperor's visit to China could be seen as the diplomacy of a tributary state resigned to Chinese suzerainty. Hashimoto commented that "Both prewar and postwar public opinion in Japan was never unanimous in regard to China policy. It came down to either liking or hating China, and this situation is unlikely to change."

Ignoring the outright hostile elements, Hashimoto focused his attention on those who were simply chary of the risks of the visit, who, he believed, undoubtedly understood the importance of friendly relations between Japan and China. He saw them as basically concerned that China still nursed hostility toward Japan. Should stone-throwing or similar incidents occur, this would ignite Japanese nationalism and damage bilateral relations beyond redemption. It was Hashimoto's task to win over these fence-sitters.

WHILE DENG XIAOPING IS ALIVE AND WELL

So how did the government read the Emperor's China visit? First of all, they saw China's eagerness to invite the Emperor as a desire for tangible evidence of friendly relations between Japan and China. Miyazawa was Japan's tenth prime minister in the twenty years since the re-establishment of Japan–China diplomatic relations (and prime ministers since Miyazawa have continued to change at a dizzying pace). Tanaka Kakuei, who had played a leading role in the normalization of relations, was now under arrest. It was natural for China to conclude that no matter how many of Japan's rapidly changing prime ministers they visited, none could present definite proof of the solidity of Japan–China relations. The reaction verging on excess displayed by some Japanese during Emperor Hirohito's battle with illness and subsequent passing away might well have confirmed irrevocably China's belief that, for Japan, the Emperor's authority was still absolute.

Behind this lay objective consideration of China's self-interest: friendly ties with Japan, an economic superpower, were essential to China's efforts to promote a more open economy. China might also reasonably regard the Emperor's visit as a golden opportunity to polish its tarnished international image in the aftermath of the Tiananmen incident. The Japanese government was clearly aware of these Chinese aims and motives, but rather than impugning them, the Japanese government led the developed world by launching moves to restore its own ties with China, believing that to assist China's economic development was to hasten it along the path to greater democracy. The government saw the Emperor's visit as an effective way to make China more democratic.

Naturally, the government also viewed the China visit as a chance to put the postwar period behind it. With the world poised on the verge of a major transition set in motion by the end of the cold war, Japan wanted to form an unshakable friendship with China, an enormously powerful, albeit potentially unstable, Asian power. Without China's understanding on the sending of Self-Defense Forces overseas on peace-keeping operations and the Northern Territories issue, this would be difficult to achieve. A member of the prime minister's inner circle, deputy chief cabinet secretary Kondo Motoji pointed to relations with China and the restoration of the Northern Territories as evidence that, in a different sense than Nakasone, Miyazawa, too, was seeking a final settlement of accounts in postwar politics.

There was also concern that Deng Xiaoping's death might throw China into chaos again. The ministry of foreign affairs thought it wise for the Emperor to visit China while its supreme leader was still alive and well. And in any event, given the major stakes involved in bilateral relations, it appeared to be very risky to continue to snub China's repeated advances.

Unquestionably various political calculations were being made; critics' accusations that the Emperor was being used for political ends were therefore in a sense quite justified. This was the Japanese Communist Party's reason for its vigorous opposition to the visit. The government reiterated that the visit's intent was to improve amicable relations and therefore not political, but the Emperor's very existence is essentially political in nature, and everyone knows that amicable relations between states are inseparable from politics. Still, it was difficult for senior government officials to come out with the truth; instead they complained that if opposition to efforts to achieve peace was "political use," then the Emperor could never go anywhere: to allow the visit to go ahead was simple common sense, to oppose it was the pot calling the kettle black: using the Emperor for political ends by accusing the other side of doing the same thing. A joke went around that played on the "peaceful use" of nuclear power: "Oh, so it's not political use, but peaceful use of the Emperor!"

PASSAGE OF THE INTERNATIONAL PEACE COOPERATION LAW

Let us return to the Hashimoto maneuver, stage one, whose purpose was to defuse this changed situation. The Chinese turned out to be surprisingly easy to persuade: Beijing promised to do nothing that would put the Emperor in an awkward position. China would make no requests regarding statements by the Emperor and was confident it could control its people's behavior. China would do nothing that could be interpreted as exploiting the Emperor's visit politically.

Permit a slight digression on the subject of Chinese sensitivity to the problems of the Japanese government: China's leaders went to great lengths to ensure that the topics brought up in the various talks during the Emperor's visit to China were strictly non-political. Casual conversation exempt of political overtones is no easy matter for a politician, however: "Studying up on the Emperor's beloved biology apparently gave president Yang Shanghun and premier Li Peng quite a headache," laughs Hashimoto.

Chinese criticism of the peace-keeping operations bill also subsided just as deliberations in the Japanese Diet were entering a critical stage. Director of the Asian Affairs Bureau Yano was apparently told by a Chinese diplomat that "China is essentially opposed to the assignment of Japanese troops abroad, not operations where the Self-Defense Forces are dispatched for tasks such as road repair. We would appreciate your understanding of this distinction." When Yano pressed for a written statement, however, he was turned down.

The Law Concerning Cooperation for United Nations Peacekeeping and Other Operations (the International Peace Cooperation Law, as it became known) was passed on June 15 amidst an unusual level of chaos in the Diet, including exhaustive use of delaying tactics by the Socialist Party and Diet members tendering their resignations en masse. A Chinese government-run paper, the *Xinhua* (New China News Agency), flashed the news from Tokyo when the bill was passed, but no harsh comments followed in its editorials. The spokesman for the Chinese ministry of foreign affairs merely reiterated China's basic stance, namely the desire that Japan proceed with caution, and refrained from further criticism.

Observing this mild response, Miyazawa brought up the issue of the Emperor's China visit during his address at a general meeting of the Japan Newspaper Publishers' and Editors' Association two days later, seeking again to build the right mood. "Having the Emperor visit China would be in Japan's interest. Though we are now in the midst of a cooling-off period in our relations with China, we would now like to begin to explain the Chinese position to permit the Emperor to visit China with the people's blessing." Unbeknownst to many, this statement actually marked the transition to the second stage of the Hashimoto maneuver. When Hashimoto came home at the end of the month, he began to make the rounds of key LDP figures. He took his tale to main party executives, former prime ministers such as Fukuda Takeo, Nakasone, and Takeshita, and even to business leaders and some influential media figures.

Hashimoto would start by saying, "Because of the constraints of my position, I will limit myself to explaining the current situation in China," and go on to present China's case, namely that the recent Chinese legislation on the status of the Senkaku Islands was merely a matter of China's tidying up its domestic legislative institutions: the Chinese government had no intention of reviving the quarrel over these islands, and the dispute would remain shelved, as previously agreed; the Chinese government regarded the war compensation issue as having been resolved, and calls for civilian reparations would be limited to appeals by specific groups who would receive no Chinese government backing; the Chinese situation made it unthinkable that the comfort women issue would flare up as it had in Korea; and China was aware of the Japanese feelings for the Emperor and would do nothing to embarrass him or place him in a difficult position. Being able to quote key Chinese figures in regard to all of the above lent the weight of authority to Hashimoto's points.

Hashimoto's verve and dedication contrasted sharply with the apparent inertia of the prime minister, who remained mum. Yano and other foreign ministry officials did the rounds of LDP members. Protests began to surface not only from within the LDP but also from the ministry itself that bureaucrats should not be made to do what was really the task of politicians. Looking back on his role, Hashimoto comments: "It was only possible because of the trust which Miyazawa placed in me and because the prime minister had issued instructions that it should be done in this way," an admittedly irregular state of affairs. This was the Miyazawa style at work, an approach diametrically opposed to the high-handed and forceful leadership displayed by Tanaka Kakuei in the bilateral talks to normalize Japan–China relations twenty years before. Hashimoto continued his pilgrimage.

RIGHT-WING MOVES

The International Peace Cooperation Law, the Emperor's China visit, and the Northern Territories issue. Interestingly enough, antithetical political dynamics were at work on these three issues. For one thing, where it was the opposition parties that stood between the government and the International Peace Cooperation Law, the barrier in the case of the Emperor's China visit came from the conservative LDP's right wing. And where the bitter experience of sending troops into Asia acted as a brake in regard to the peace-keeping operations issue, the momentum behind the Emperor's China visit was the desire to heal the wounds resulting from that experience.

These two issues were therefore enmeshed just below the surface like colliding tectonic plates, and the Northern Territories issue added to the momentous friction. The impediment of the side issue arose not from domestic quarters but from Russia (and the uninterested West), Japan being seen as the victim of this particular postwar accommodation. Unlike the other two issues, the Northern Territories issue functioned to fuse widely divergent strands of public opinion. I even began to suspect that the reason the government was so heated up over the restitution of the

Northern Territories, a hopeless cause from the outset, was to distract right-wing attention from the Emperor's China visit. I cannot say to what extent the government exploited this factor consciously. In any case, the Munich Summit held on July 6–8 closed with the successful incorporation for the first time of a reference in the political communiqué to the Northern Territories' retrocession.

The time for a decision on the Emperor's China visit drew closer, but amidst the turmoil of the July 26 Upper House elections, the government had little time to think of anything else but the elections. Where the media began to predict with increasing frequency during the election that the prime minister would decide in favor of the visit, the July 17 edition of the *Sankei Shimbun* ran a protest advertisement with a banner headline declaring opposition to the Emperor's China visit. It was signed by more than a hundred names, including representatives from the worlds of business, academia, and entertainment.

A public opinion poll conducted secretly by the government revealed that 72 percent of the population was now either for, or more for than against, a China visit by the Emperor. With the exception of the *Sankei*, the editorials of most major newspapers were also giving the thumbs-up. However, as Miyazawa hinted at the time, this was no issue to determine simply by majority vote. Faced with a hard decision, he saw the conclusion of the Upper House elections as the dreaded moment.

The protest advertisement in the *Sankei* had again been organized by Daitojuku. Involved in a number of pre-war terrorism attempts, Daitojuku was a hard-core right-wing group, fourteen members of which had staged a group suicide when the war ended to "apologize to the Emperor with our deaths." After the war, the group also played a front-running role in movements such as the reinstatement of Empire Day, legislation on era names, and state guardianship for Yasukuni Shrine. Group founder and long-time leader Kageyama Masaharu also chose to take his life in 1979 to draw attention to these efforts. The deputy cabinet secretary in charge of administration at the prime minister's official residence at the time, Ishihara Nobuo, watched the group closely, noting: "While Daitojuku was unlikely to return to terrorism, the government's keeping it under control was a prerequisite to controlling other right-wing groups."

Key government and LDP figures had been receiving anonymous threats through the mail, and the police were very much on edge. Secret police details guarding chief cabinet secretary Kato and other public figures were reinforced, and police boxes were set up temporarily in front of the homes of certain senior foreign ministry officials. A right-wing extremist had fired pistol shots at the LDP fixer Kanemaru Shin just that March to protest his active involvement in Japan–Korea relations. The atmosphere was tinged with tension. We can laugh about it now, but several senior government officials took out massive life insurance policies on the eve of the Emperor's fall visit to China.

MAKING COMMITMENTS AND GOING THROUGH THE MOTIONS

The Upper House elections, the central issue of which was the passage of the International Peace Cooperation Law, ended in an LDP victory. Once again able to move freely, the prime minister decided to announce the decision by the time of the mid-summer Bon festival and moved quietly into action. First of all, he met with Nakasone at a restaurant at noon on July 28th. In response to the prime minister's request for cooperation, Nakasone stressed that Miyazawa had to move carefully in developing the right climate, taking personal responsibility. This could well have been a sarcastic reference to the Hashimoto maneuver. Nakasone advised that "one gunshot and it will all be over, but there's no point in brooding over it." He recommended taking particularly great care in handling Daitojuku and Yasukuni Shrine officials.

Under attack from the right wing of his party, Kanemaru announced that he would make himself less conspicuous. The very same day he fired a metaphorical salvo in support of the prime minister. In a speech before the Asian Affairs Research Council, he spoke in typically opaque Kanemaruese: "To the greatest extent possible, the Emperor should not be used as a tool in regard to neighboring countries and those countries that Japan had caused trouble for, but as he is the symbol of the people, thought should naturally be given to Korea and China."

The next day, Miyazawa called for the cooperation of top LDP officials, brandishing the banner of peace in Asia. Seeing how far matters had already developed, LDP secretary-general Watanuki, general council chairman Sato Koko and Policy Affairs Research Council chairman Mori Yoshiro pledged their help. On the 30th, Miyazawa visited former prime minister Fukuda Takeo, who had some sway over Fujio and other hawks, and asked for his support too. Vice-minister for foreign affairs Owada Hisashi, who had served as private secretary to the prime minister when Fukuda was in power, had already played his card in seeking Fukuda's cooperation; incidentally, this was shortly before rumors again began to circulate of marriage between Owada's eldest daughter, Masako, and the Crown Prince.

"The outer moat had been filled" (i.e., Miyazawa had secured the perimeter), but he had yet to deal with the LDP. On the 28th at an executives' meeting, the chair of the Diet Affairs Committee and right-wing representative Murakami Masakuni denounced as "sneak-thievery" the barrage of media reports of a decision in favor of the Emperor's visit while politicians were busy with the elections. He accused the government of guiding the hand of the press. Voices of protest were raised in the LDP's general council as well. Members of the intelligentsia who were against the visit held a public meeting on the same day as the general council meeting to seek the Imperial visit's cancelation; Fujio and Itagaki lashed out at Japan's "tributary diplomacy" and "weak-kneed foreign policy." On the 30th, first-year Diet members such as Eto Seiichi formed a group of Diet members opposed to the visit and began collecting signatures seeking a postponement. Tension mounted as the impending final decision by the prime minister's office grew near.

The Yasukuni Shrine issue also reared its head as the anniversary of the war's end approached on August 15. Those against the China visit had always been bitter over China's forcing Japanese prime ministers to renounce their visits to the shrine. Moves to have the prime minister visit Yasukuni Shrine arose every year around this time, from both within and outside the party, but pressure that year was particularly intense. Certain party executives even proposed that a visit to Yasukuni Shrine by the prime minister would weaken opposition to the China visit, and that the prime minister should do so in a private capacity if it was impossible to do so officially. This was seen as sufficient to persuade even Daitojuku. Some members of the government even urged sounding out China on the matter, a proposal that was dismissed as simply preposterous.

Miyazawa showed himself to be terribly naive in the matter of the Yasukuni visit. He continued to equivocate in response to reporters' questions, saying that a decision had yet to be made. Suddenly, on August 9, he announced that he would visit Yasukuni Shrine "in a private capacity at an appropriate time." While he was not specific about the timing, he is said to have actually made a secret visit in a private capacity long after that announcement.

On August 5, Miyazawa conferred with the party's senior advisers. He pointed out that the United States and Korea understood the situation, and asked for the party elders' cooperation. Suzuki Zenko, who considered himself to be a kind of private patron to Miyazawa, did some pushing behind the scenes. Close to five months after their March meeting, even Nakasone was raising no objections, and a definite momentum was gathering.

Such was the atmosphere permeating the LDP's general council when it met on August 5. There were the usual clashes, but ears pricked up at Fujio's throw-away comment that he was against the visit, but if it was already decided, whatever he said at this point would be in vain. Some speculation arose as to his intention, but the general view was that he was concerned that any further protest might be against the Emperor's wishes.

The fact that the Emperor wished to go to China had long since been communicated to opposing groups. Fujio had high-handedly told Kato and company that even so, this was not a matter that could be decided on the basis of the Emperor's wishes: the Emperor had to steer clear of politics. At the same time, it was a development that must have weighed heavily on Fujio's mind. He may have come to the conclusion that if the Emperor's China visit was unavoidable in any case, it would be unwise to oppose it too tenaciously.

What the government was afraid of was that "one gunshot." Even if the government was to decide in favor of the Emperor's China visit, one single thing amiss could unravel the whole plan. That meant somehow managing to procure Daitojuku's acquiescence. Kato and Ishihara were considering this when, on August 7, they received a visit from Daitojuku representative Suzuki Masao.

Avoiding the prime minister's official residence by meeting at Kato's office in the Diet Members' office building, Suzuki handed over an offer addressed to the prime minister. After laying out the problematic nature of the Emperor's visit to China, the document proposed the establishment of a council of eminent persons and implementation of a number of public hearings around the country. It made the peculiar declaration that "If the government goes ahead with the Emperor's China visit without first taking the above steps . . . , the primary responsibility will lie with the government for anything untoward that might occur." Despite the threatening language, the tone did not suggest all-out obstruction. Kato and Ishihara saw it as a way out.

Of course it was too late to hold council meetings and public hearings. They could, on the other hand, sound out the views of eminent persons. The Cabinet decision on the Emperor's visit was postponed accordingly until the end of the month and interviews were set up over the mid-summer Bon vacation. Representing a balance of opinions for and against the visit, fourteen eminent persons paid visits to the prime minister's official residence one after another over the 17th and 18th. This was the reason for a move generally viewed as a pure formality coming far too late to have any meaning.

In the evening of August 10, the day the International Peace Cooperation Law officially went into force, the prime minister conveyed his decision to the party machinery. The Cabinet would work to create the right climate, and once this had come into being to some extent, the Cabinet would make its decision. In other words, they would go through the motions of creating the right climate over the Bon vacation. The Cabinet decision was made on the 25th.

Incidentally, while the prime minister was resting in Karuizawa over the Bon vacation, an incident occurred that was kept completely hidden from the press for a time. Miyazawa unexpectedly received a phone call from Korean president Roh Taewoo. Korea, he announced, was about to conclude diplomatic relations with China. Signatures were to be put to this lightning normalization of relations in Beijing on the 24th.

This was August 1992, a month of dramatic realignment in East Asia. With China and Korea engaged in a major rapprochement, the Korean opposition to the Emperor's visit feared by Nakasone and others vanished into thin air. Yeltsin's scheduled visit to Japan in September was abruptly canceled four days before Yeltsin was to arrive. Though this was a setback for Northern Territories diplomacy, that autumn, a Japanese Self-Defence Forces unit was sent without incident to Cambodia on a peace-keeping mission.

Finally, on October 23, Their Majesties the Emperor and Empress set foot on Chinese soil for the first time. In his reception speech, the Emperor expressed "deep sorrow" and "regret" for the "great suffering" caused to the Chinese people.

PART V

REPORT: THE POST-COLD WAR ERA AT THE KOREA–JAPAN FORUM

The end of the Cold War brings together Japanese and Korean leaders. Summit talks between Prime Minister Hosokawa Morihiro (left) and President Kim Youngsam (right) in Kyongju produced historic results, but . . . . (November 1993)

THE KOREA–JAPAN FORUM

It was December 1993 when the Korea–Japan Forum was launched as a talkshop centering around Japanese and Korean politicians and private sector representatives from economic, media and academic circles. In October of the same year, prime minister Hosokawa Morihiro visited Korea, and in their talks in Kyongju, he and president Kim Youngsam reaffirmed their commitment to building future-oriented ties between Japan and Korea. The Korea–Japan Forum grew out of this atmosphere. The model for the forum was the Japan–US Shimoda Conference, a forum with a long history of private sector exchange. The aim was not to seek some kind of conclusion, but rather to provide an arena for open and wide-ranging debate, broadening understanding on both sides.

The Japanese chair was Owada Hisashi, who had retired from the post of administrative vice-minister for foreign affairs (and who was later appointed Ambassador to the UN), while the Korean side chose Pae Jaeshick, professor emeritus at Seoul University. (Former foreign minister Choi Kwangsoo has taken over Pae's seat since the sixth meeting.) Owada had spent the first five years of his foreign ministry career in the Treaties Division enormously busy with the negotiations for the normalization of diplomatic relations between Japan and Korea. As a scholar of international law, Pae at that time had taken an antagonistic stance toward the treaty in newspapers and other media, declaring that Korea should not create "a treaty that was no more than a statement of political compromise and did not stand up in law." In addition to these two chairs, there was also a number of Korean members who looked back with nostalgia on their participation in fierce anti-treaty demonstrations. I myself am a member of the Forum now, but back in those days, I was in my third year of senior high school.

The Forum meets once a year, alternating between Japan and Korea, with members camping in a hotel for some three days. Seven sessions have been held as of summer 1999.

The first meeting was in Seoul in early December of 1993, a time when both countries were in an uproar about opening up their rice markets. It was a year of historical change, with the first civilian government in 32 years coming to power in Korea and the 38-year rule of the Liberal Democratic Party collapsing in Japan.

The second meeting took place in Gotemba, Shizuoka Prefecture, at the end of August 1994. The Murayama cabinet had just succeeded the Hata cabinet. In July, North Korean president Kim Ilsung passed away, and growing uncertainty surrounded signs of nuclear weapons development in North Korea. The third meeting was held in Cheju-do in Korea in early September 1995. That year marked the fiftieth anniversary of the war's end and the 30th anniversary of the Japan–Korea Basic Treaty, and the Forum came hard on the heels of a series of shockwaves caused by comments by Japanese politicians. Thus each of the three meetings had a slightly different tone depending on the events occurring at that time.

The debate took place in both Japanese and Korean, with simultaneous interpretation between the two languages, but what members looked forward to most were the more convivial mealtimes, where the conversation was more direct. With Japanese, Korean, and English phrases flying around the room, these were animated occasions. In the evening, everyone drank and sang karaoke together, and I enjoyed this wonderful learning experience. However, what struck me most deeply about the Forum was the very real sense that the cold war had ended. It is on this subject that I would like to report in this chapter, with special reference to discussions in the first through third sessions (1993–95).

SHARING EXPERIENCES OF CHANGE

> The reason why the LDP remained so long in power despite a succession of money-brokering scandals was that many Japanese believed that having the LDP was still better than being swallowed up by the Soviet Union. This reasoning lost its validity when the Soviet Union collapsed.

Each discussion began with a political report from both countries, and at the opening of the first meeting, this was how Kato Koichi from the LDP explained the LDP's fall. Kato belongs to the Kochikai, which has traditionally had few Korean sympathizers, but since the time of Roh Taewoo's presidency, Kato has been among the new breed of members who have consciously deepened relations with South Korea. In March that year, not only was it revealed that Kanemaru Shin, the don of Nagatacho, had stashed away an enormous amount of money received through irregular channels, but failure to enact political reform had splintered the LDP, bringing down the Miyazawa cabinet. The above statement by Kato, who had also been chief cabinet secretary in the Miyazawa cabinet, referred to these developments.

I agreed with Kato's assessment. This discussion took me back to 1980, the year when a rebellion by Fukuda Takeo and other party members had brought about a no-confidence vote against the Ohira Masayoshi cabinet, resulting in Upper and Lower House elections being held on the same day. I had rushed around gathering information in great excitement, believing that the LDP, too, would finally splinter, but the LDP was able to avoid this due to strong pressure from business, which threatened to withhold election funds in the case of a split. Thanks to the sympathy aroused by Ohira's sudden death, the LDP achieved a major election victory, with the

Suzuki Zenko cabinet subsequently emerging from a united party front as though nothing had happened.

The business world's logic was quite simply the fear that a split among the conservatives could bring about a coalition government comprising the Socialists and other opposition parties, which would mean trouble for business. This was the year of the 1980 Moscow Olympics; Japan had toed the United States line in deciding to boycott the Games because the Soviet Union had invaded Afghanistan at the close of the previous year, heightening international tensions. The cold war between the United States and the Soviet Union was at its coldest, and this was the international climate that saved the day for the LDP. By comparison, when the LDP split during the Miyazawa cabinet, Japanese business adopted an I-couldn't-care-less attitude. In retrospect, this threw into sharp relief how completely the situation had changed from cold war times.

Interestingly enough, Korea, too, put forward views emphasizing post-cold war changes. Lee Buyoung, Vice-President of the opposition Democratic Justice Party and formerly a leader of the anti-government movement who had spent considerable time in jail, noted, "If the army and corrupt bureaucrats, the business world, and politicians were all in alliance with each other before, that alliance can only dissolve now that external forces threatening the internal machinery have disappeared. It is universally observed that the melting-away of forces threatening the state from the outside leads to attempts to restore internal soundness."

Korea is still faced with a North–South cold war stand-off, but the sense of danger does not compare to the era when North Korea was backed by China and the Soviet Union. This was undoubtedly the dominant force behind the demise of Korea's military government. Kato and Lee Buyoung both saw Japan and Korea as typical examples of the political change brought about by the end of the cold war.

Such change also became the catalyst promoting Japan–Korea political dialogue. One factor which had long obstructed frank dialogue between the two countries was Japan's discomfort with Korea's military government, as well as the existence of less than transparent links between Japan and Korea. There was also, of course, the fact that the Socialist Party had long been cool toward South Korea because the Socialists were on friendly terms with North Korea. Ever since Ishibashi Masatsugu became its head, the Socialist Party had been gradually moving toward the establishment of ties with Korea, but the decisive factors behind this trend were the Socialists' decision to become more "realistic" and Korea's democratization. In this sense, the close timing of the emergence of the Kim Youngsam presidency and the Murayama cabinet was symbolic. The end of the cold war had at last created common ground for dialogue between Japan and Korea.

DISAGREEMENTS GREETED WITH RELIEF

On the other hand, another phenomenon common to both countries should also be noted: the way in which the end of the cold war led straight into turmoil. The third Forum explored the political confusion in both countries. In the case of Japan, the focus was on the dizzying changes in the coalition cabinet and the unpredictable political situation. In the case of Korea, the main subject of discussion was a return to the "three Kims" era (in addition to Kim Youngsam, Kim Daejung and Kim Jongpil were also involved with new party movements) and the bitter hostility between regions which had brought this about (for example, Kim Daejung had an overwhelming political base in Cholla-do).

The Korean side explained the historical background to this interregional animosity, which Japan found difficult to grasp, noting, for example, that the successive military governments had stressed Kyongsang-do, the President's birthplace, and neglected Cholla-do, the home of Kim Daejung. However, this was inadequate to explain the current resurgence of animosity. Lee Buyoung added that, "The reduced threat of the North allowed South Korea to break up internally. What has emerged worldwide with the end of the politics of ideology is regionalism and one-sided nationalism." In other words, this was a post-cold war phenomenon.

While contemporary Japan has not seen the same kind of regionalism as in Korea, the situation is much the same in that, with the loss of the axis of confrontation, we have entered an age *sans* ideology. The conclusion of the cold war is said to have brought nationalism and religious confrontation bubbling to the surface across the globe. Religious elements have of course been involved in the reorganization of Japan's political landscape, with fierce confrontation emerging between the ruling and opposition parties in the fall of 1995 in regard to amendment of the Religious Juridical Person Law. Listening to Lee Buyoung's analysis, I suddenly began to wonder whether religion would become a cause of violent political confrontation.

The Korean side had a somewhat complex view of the changes in Japan. At the first Forum, Korean participants noted that the Hosokawa cabinet had put thorough political reform at the top of the political agenda; since Japan had previously placed the economy in first and politics in third place, if political reform were now to seat politics in first place, would Japan no longer stand a chance of becoming an Asian superpower? Would political reform not bring about a revival in ultra-nationalism?

This was also linked to concern over the "normal country" argument being presented by the powerful Ozawa Ichiro; suspicions focused on whether becoming a normal country would turn Japan into a military power. Asked to respond, some Japanese politicians flatly denied the possibility, others indicated similar fears. The views of the Japanese side differed widely between the ruling and opposition parties. A succession of questions followed on the political reform bill and the direction of political reorganization, with different parties on the Japanese side again expressing disparate views.

Over the course of the second and third Forums, the debate between Kato Koichi and Matsuda Iwao, a member of the Shinseito (Born-Again Party) and later of the Shinshinto (New Frontier Party) on the Japanese side became particularly remarkable. These two would inevitably express diametrically opposed views on any subject, be it perceptions of the Hosokawa cabinet, the nature of the Murayama cabinet, or the merits of the small constituency system.

Ironically enough, the Korean participants were apparently comforted by, and even welcomed, these disparities in Japanese opinion. What Korea feared, in the final analysis, was a monolithic Japan.

The Korean side also had a diverse membership, ranging from key figures in the ruling party such as Kim Moonhwan, Chair of the Korea–Japan Parliamentarian League, and Kim Deogryong, a close associate of Kim Youngsam, to active opposition party members such as Lee Buyoung. At the third Forum, the opposition parties also proceeded to split along pro- and anti-Kim Daejung lines, resulting in a heated debate. In similar fashion to the reactions of the Korean side, Japanese members saw this open debate by the Koreans with some relief as a sign of the democratization of Korean politics. In other words, each side was given a wraps-off view of the other.

NORTH KOREA: NORTH–SOUTH UNIFICATION MOVES WITHIN RANGE

Was there ever before a time when the peoples of Japan and Korea shared to such an extent both interests and concerns regarding their peace and stability? Such was my feeling at the second Forum, held around the time of Kim Ilsung's death and mounting suspicions over North Korea's development of nuclear weapons. This issue was the major focus of discussion for three days.

A document on Northeast Asian security, jointly prepared by Japanese and Korean military and political science experts, was distributed at the meeting. Participants discussed Japan–Korea security cooperation, with both sides agreed on the basic position that close liaison between Japan and Korea was important in dealing with North Korea. The Socialist Party Diet member Hino Ichiro also took part in the debate. How times change! This transformation in Japan–Korean relations stirred me profoundly.

As I noted in my introduction, I first visited Korea in the summer of 1979, accompanying Yamashita Ganri, director-general of the Defense Agency. This was the first visit to Korea by a Defense

Agency head. In those days of bitter East-West confrontation, with a military government still in place in Seoul, "Japan–Korea security cooperation" was a term with a provocative and tension-creating ring, and it would be years before it became more palatable. The Koreans, too, seemed to feel some resistance to a visit by a top Japanese defense agency official, which spurred associations with the Japanese Army, and it was not until fifteen years later, in 1994, that his Korean counterpart, the Korean National Defense Director, would make the trip to Japan. Still in cold war mode, the Japanese side was somewhat allergic to the idea of Japan–Korea security, while memories of colonization created a similar allergy on the Korean side. Such were our countries' perceptions of each other.

I mentioned earlier the anecdote where Korean president Rhee Syngman, asked at the time of the Korean War how Korea would respond if the Japanese armed forces were to come to their aid, replied that the North and South would join together to throw Japan out. (see pp. 184–85) This feeling is not just a thing of the past. It was 1994 when a novel describing a nuclear attack on Japan with weapons jointly developed by North and South Korea became a bestseller in Korea.

This is symptomatic of the continued complexity of Korean feelings toward Japan, but the atmosphere at the Forum was very different. This may have been the result of an undercurrent of shared and sincere uneasiness that in a very real sense, North Korea could have a major impact on the fates of both South Korea and Japan in the near future. There was palpable irony in the fact that North Korea had turned Japan and South Korea into such bosom buddies.

Naturally, things were not so simple in terms of individual fields. While the Korean side stressed that a strong and consistent line should be taken toward North Korea, encouraging Japanese readiness in the event that the worst actually happened, the Japanese side sympathized with Korea's feelings but noted that concessions had to be made in negotiations and that a carrot rather than a stick had to be used. The two sides' views did not always coincide. As "rice support" provided to North Korea showed later, South Korea clearly had a deeply rooted fear that Japan would do a deal with North Korea without consulting the South first. Japan–Korea security cooperation still had a long way to go before anyone would suggest conducting joint exercises. The conclusion at the third Forum was that public feeling in both countries was still years from that point. Four years later, in August 1999, the Japanese Maritime Self-Defense Forces and the South Korean Navy conducted a joint military drill for the first time, cooperating in the simulated rescue of a private vessel in trouble.

Back at the first Forum, a Korean journalist had suddenly announced in connection with North Korea's development of nuclear weapons that he thought Japan, too, had its eye on possessing nuclear weapons at some point in time, a statement which suddenly brought the discussion to life. It threw into stark relief the gap between the Japanese, who backed Japan's non-nuclear policy in all sincerity, and the Koreans, who still had lingering suspicions about Japan. Flustered, Japanese politicians stressed Japan's commitment to peace, but even some on the Japanese side urged that rather than just talking, Japan needed to take objective measures that would not be misunderstood. The main cause of this gap was, of course, perceptions of the past, but I will come back to that topic later.

Participants' fears with regard to North Korea were directed toward what would happen if the current regime collapsed, a very likely scenario. Japan and Korea shared the view that the process of North Korea's collapse had already begun with the death of Kim Ilsung, and that North–South unification had now become a real possibility. Yet the road leading to that point was dark and winding, the challenges posed by actual unification overwhelming. Korean academics, seeking Japanese support, noted that unification might even take place during their lifetimes, but that Japan's understanding would be needed to overcome the immense costs and sacrifices involved. Despite the precedent of East and West Germany's unification, greater difficulties were foreseen in the case of North and South Korea, given their greater economic disparities.

A Japanese businessman asked whether actual estimates had been made and research conducted on the costs of unification. He was later to receive a number of staggeringly high totals, but at the time, a representative of Korea's finance industry simply stated his own personal opinion that the unification process should be advanced gradually (by, for example, selling North Korean state property piece by piece to investors in the South). The general impression received by the Japanese was that the Koreans' hearts were not really into the discussion.

A Japanese academic pointed out that a number of other issues would also emerge, in addition to fiscal support, including visits to Japan by Japanese spouses and the treatment of North Koreans residing in Japan. That was the least of our anxieties, of course; where was the guarantee that military chaos would not arise? The word "unification," which had seemed like a dream of the distant future, suddenly began to take on much weightier implications, but this was after all a theme simply too complex for casual discussion. I doubt that I was alone in feeling that joint research on the ins and outs of North–South unification needed to be undertaken at the earliest possible moment.

Reaching beyond the past

While Koreans' deeply rooted anti-Japanese sentiment naturally goes back to the period when Japan colonized Korea, there was no attempt on the Korean side to bring up Japan's past until the second Forum. At the first Forum, a representative from the editorial department of a major paper even noted that the Korean mass media had had a certain amount of responsibility for stirring up anti-Japanese feeling, providing specific examples and expressing his regret over these, and I was moved by such frankness. In economic debates, issues such as the trade imbalance between Japan and Korea were brought up, but the Korean side's views were astonishingly calm; my impression was that they were more interested in discussing the future of the Asia-Pacific economy.

It must not be overlooked that the Korean side accepted at face value the statements made in Kyongju by prime minister

Hosokawa, who apologized for colonial domination, mentioning specifically such wrongs as Japan's attempt to force Koreans to take Japanese-style names. On the occasion of the first and third Forums (the meetings held in Korea), Forum members paid courtesy visits at the Blue House (the Korean President's official residence) to President Kim Youngsam, who recalled his talks with Hosokawa emphasizing a "future orientation."

The tenor of the third Forum, held in 1995, the fiftieth anniversary of the end of the war, was slightly different. Korean concerns focused on the emergence of Japanese nationalism. Given their own efforts not to touch upon the past, Korean members of the Forum must have felt betrayed by the string of controversial statements made by Japanese politicians on the resolution marking this anniversary, starting with Watanabe Michio's assertion that Japan's annexation of Korea had been "achieved peacefully." In his opening comments, chairman Pae spoke pointedly of "moves by certain parties to distort or ignore the past," giving voice to the Korean participants' evident distress.

Pae, who had attended Seoul University at the same time as president Kim Youngsam, was one of those extremely concerned about how the Diet resolution would turn out. I heard participants lamenting that for Japan to win Asian confidence and become a true leader, a committed resolution was essential but unlikely. In other words, the resolution was seen as made not so much for Asia as for Japan. Forum member Choi Sangyong, a professor at Korea University and a prominent pro-Japanese academic, praised the dovishness of the Japanese government since the Murayama cabinet, expressing high hopes in regard to the realization of the Diet resolution. Forum members in general were interested in eradicating the Korean people's deeply rooted anti-Japanese feelings, and were therefore anxious that Japan should avoid treading on Korean toes. One can imagine their sense of deception at the outcome of the Diet resolution and Watanabe's statement, which spoiled all that so many had labored so long to achieve.

A Korean newspaper executive noted, for example, that his paper had been urging Korea to open its doors to Japanese culture, but the

Japanese Diet's resolution was disappointing: "Japan can become a leading nation only to the extent that it settles its accounts with the past." A Korean academic pointed out that whereas president Kim himself had chosen not to forget the past but not to cling to it either, "It would be difficult not to be skeptical of Japan's attitude." Other participants requested explanations of the re-emergence of Japanese nationalism.

Japanese politicians and members of the press came forward one after the other to acknowledge the resolution's failure and to apologize. One Japanese journalist called attention to the reconciliation between Germany and France, expressing his regret that Japan and Korea had not been able to achieve a similar reconciliation in such a milestone year. This view attracted widespread backing from both sides.

I was given the chance during this discussion to explain the reason why Japanese politicians felt such a deep-seated need to legitimize the past. I gave a very brief outline of the background as covered in this book, noting that the long and close relationship, founded on anti-Communism and a common pro-American foreign policy, between right-wing and strongly nationalistic Japanese politicians and the Korean military government had warped the Japanese political view of history. The Korean side sympathized with this view, a reflection of just how much times have changed.

On the other hand, however, I also stressed the profound changes in national consciousness compared to the thirtieth and fortieth anniversaries of the end of the war, pointing to the tide of public opinion in support of Murayama Tomiichi's August 15 comments. I felt that the massive coverage given in the Asian press to certain politicians' statements in reaction to these changes was extremely unbalanced.

One Korean academic noted that there would be no problem, provided that Japan's future actions and statements followed the lines indicated in Murayama's comments; he similarly acknowledged the prime minister's comments in the Cheju-do Statement (see the following reference), drawn up on the occasion of the fiftieth year since the end of the war and thirty years since the conclusion of the Japan–Korea Basic Treaty. However, a number of participants called attention to the repetitive pattern of apologies by prime ministers followed by controversial statements by unrepentant politicians, noting this raised doubts about Japan's sincerity. These uncertainties kept the Koreans on edge, as did the equivocal stance of Hashimoto Ryutaro, marked as the LDP's next president. The Korean side was undoubtedly deeply suspicious of Japan's continued double-dealing. Even in casual conversation on the fringes of the main discussion, participants repeatedly expressed concern over Hashimoto's chairmanship of the Japan Association of the Bereaved Families of the War Dead, a prominent group opposing the fifty-year anniversary resolution.

Reference

THE CHEJU-DO STATEMENT

. . . This year, the fiftieth anniversary of the end of World War II, was an opportunity for the Japanese people to reflect on the unhappy past in regard to Korea and for each and every citizen to deepen anew their consciousness of the past based on personal reflection. In his comments on the fiftieth anniversary of the end of the war, prime minister Murayama noted that Japan "inflicted horrific, indescribable suffering upon many people in Asia and throughout the world." He further stated: "I humbly acknowledge these irrefutable facts of history, express my deep remorse once again, and offer an apology from the bottom of my heart." This expressed the sincere feelings of the great majority of the Japanese people, and was welcomed by the Korean people.

This year also marks the thirtieth anniversary of the normalization of relations between Japan and Korea. These thirty years have witnessed enormous progress in bilateral relations in areas such as economics, politics, security, and cultural exchange and could justly be said to have established the foundations of a future-oriented relationship built upon the past. As stated by president Kim Youngsam in the Diet during his visit to Japan as a state guest in March 1994, we can be said to have reached the point where "the peoples of Korea and Japan should have dreams for new Korea–Japan relations, a new Asia-Pacific, and a new world."

I. New Japan–Korea Relations

The international environment embracing Japan–Korea relations has changed greatly. The international system has undergone structural change, as seen in the dissolution of the cold war structure. The international community is becoming increasingly interdependent, and the role played by sovereign states in international relations has become relatively small. Likewise, in terms of Japan–Korea relations, both ties between governments and direct contact between our societies and our peoples have assumed deep significance. Remarkable economic development has led simultaneously to expectations that Japan and Korea will play major roles in the international community. Japan–Korea cooperation in particular is becoming increasingly important in the further development of the Asia–Pacific region as the world's economic and political growth center, and we are also called upon to promote the Japan–Korea partnership to address such global issues such as the environment, human rights, refugees and poverty.

Looking ahead to the next thirty years, during which we will enter the twenty-first century, the goal to which our peoples should aspire is the construction of a new level of cooperative relations between Japan and Korea. As the basic recommendation of the Korea–Japan Forum in the year marking the thirtieth anniversary of normalization of relations between Japan and Korea, we suggest that joint research and dialogue should be promoted between our two countries to define the basic philosophy of these new cooperative relations and the new framework through which to realize this philosophy.

II. Recommendations in Specific Areas

[Note: Explanations of items have been omitted.]

1. Measures for the dramatic expansion of cultural and personal exchanges

   (a) Promotion of intellectual exchanges
   (b) Youth exchanges, expansion of foreign study programs
   (c) Promotion of regional exchanges
   (d) Exchanges between journalists
   (e) Simplification and waiver of visas
   (f) Expansion of artistic and cultural exchanges
   (g) Establishment of a joint committee for the promotion of Japan–Korea exchanges

2. Promotion of bilateral economic exchanges

3. Promotion of Japan–Korea security dialogue

4. Establishment of a committee for joint historical research

5. Joint hosting of the 2002 World Cup Soccer Games

Participants in the Korea–Japan Forum

There is no permanent roster of participants in the Korea–Japan Forum; participants include co-chairmen and 20-odd members from either side. Among the frequent attenders are:

Japanese side

Yamamoto Tadashi	Japanese Co-Chair and Director, Japan Center for International Exchange
Kato Koichi	LDP, House of Representatives

and other Parliamentarians

Nukazawa Kazuro   Counselor, Keidanren (Japan Federation
                     of Economic Organizations)

and other members of the business community

Okonogi Masao   Professor, Keio University

and other academics

Kojima Akira   Editor-in-Chief, Nihon Keizai Shimbun

Wakamiya Yoshibumi   Political Writer, Asahi Shimbun

and other journalists

Korean side

Ahn Byungjoon   Korean Co-Chair and Professor, Yeonsei
                     University

Kim Soonhan   Chairman, Korea-Japan Friendship
                     Association, and other Diet members

Cho Sukrae   Chairman of the Morning Star Group,

and other members of the business community

Choi Sangyong   Professor, Korea University

and other academics

Nam Siuk   President, the Dong-A Ilbo

and other journalists

PART VI

IN PROSPECTIVE PERSPECTIVE: HOW WILL JAPAN VIEW ASIA TOMORROW?

The APEC Summit, November 1994. The meeting in Bogor, Indonesia, was attended by prime minister Murayama Tomiichi (right). The arrival of a Socialist at the head of a Japanese cabinet had considerable repercussions on Japan's view of Asia.

TIME FOR A COURSE CORRECTION: LOOKING FOR A TRUE "FOCUS ON ASIA"

Thus far in this volume, by citing and examining the words and actions of my country's postwar conservative politicians, I have sought to define postwar Japan's view of Asia from various angles. Though major obstacles remain, fifty years after the end of the war, Japan seems to be shedding, finally yet ever so gradually, its unhealthy attitudes toward Asia. It is not, I hope, wishful thinking to say that Japan's view of Asia has become at least somewhat more balanced and that Japan is now entering the most peaceful and healthy period of modern times.

I feel I can say this for the following reasons.

First, as the younger generation takes over from its elders, the teaching of Japanese history in postwar Japan has corrected our previous distorted view of Asia. What is true of our young people is also true of our younger politicians.

Second, the protests awakened by various controversial statements by Japanese cabinet ministers, by the slanted coverage of history in Japan's textbooks, and by politicians' visits to Yasukuni Shrine have taught the Japanese in some fashion to see things the way other Asians do. That has not kept a good number of die-hard politicians from persisting in their ways, despite the criticism, but on the whole, there has been gradual change.

313

Third, the cold war and the age of ideological conflict are over; reforms and policies of greater openness to the outside world are visible, even in China; more fundamentally, our attitudes toward Asia are no longer dominated by rejection or acceptance of Communism as the basis of all arguments. (North Korea is one of the very rare exceptions.) The Socialist (now the Social Democratic) Party of Japan has altered its policy and now supports friendship with South Korea. The rigidity of the 1955 political structures is now a thing of the past.

Fourth, Korea and the Philippines (as well as other countries) have democratic governments. The veil that once clouded relations between Japan and Korea has been torn by South Korea's strides toward democratic rule, permitting the normalization of Japan's ties with its neighbor.

Fifth, the Vietnam war is over, and so is the war in Cambodia that followed it; though elements of instability remain on the Korean Peninsula, post-cold-war Asia is one of the most peaceful regions in the world. Vietnam has joined ASEAN and has normalized its diplomatic ties with the United States.

Sixth, the strong yen has led to greatly expanded Japanese investment in Asia, turning Asia into the region with the largest share of both imports to and exports from Japan. These closer economic ties have strengthened perceptions that Japan and Asia have shared interests.

Seventh, the rapid rise in social and economic levels in the Asian region, typified by the dynamism of "Four Little Dragons," has challenged Japanese preconceptions about Asia. Despite the subsequent severe economic crisis, the Japanese are now more motivated to nurture a sense of unity and solidarity with the rest of Asia.

Eighth, the development of satellite television and other technology is narrowing or even closing the information gap, making Asian news instantly accessible to Japan.

Ninth, local government activities and programs and private-sector contacts have widened and deepened citizen-level exchanges.

And tenth, the 2002 World Cup Soccer Games will be jointly hosted by Japan and Korea.

These changes are remarkable. In a word, they are due to something more than the succession of generations in private and public life: Asia's image as a backward region underlying and motivating Japan's historical tendency to attempt to break away from Asia and join Europe has been replaced by a much more dynamic image, again altering Japanese perceptions.

From a relatively early stage, a focus on Asia has come to occupy its rightful place beside the central US–Japan relationship and reliance on the United Nations as pillars of Japan's postwar diplomacy. The US–Japan relationship is nonetheless far and away the strongest and most important pillar of Japan's foreign policy. For too long, Asia has been perceived by Japan merely as a complementary and tactical element in the elaboration of its foreign policy toward the United States. Sino–Japanese diplomatic ties have been normalized and China's economic growth has been notable thanks to reforms and a new policy of openness to the rest of the world. The Emperor's visit to China, arranged by the Miyazawa cabinet in 1992, was a symbol of the new Sino–Japanese *entente*.

Meanwhile, now that the structure of East–West confrontation has crumbled, Asia's importance for Japan is steadily growing. The end of the cold war signals a critical juncture: it is time to correct the distorted Japanese view of Asia that has persisted since Meiji.

We have entered an era when politicians are fond of referring to Asia. Hashimoto Ryutaro, for instance, when he became prime minister in January 1996, cited the slogan "Show your stuff, Japan!" that he used in his bid for LDP presidency in September 1995, and stressed the need for Japan to adopt a foreign policy that would "capture the heart of Asia." Hashimoto, being president of the Japan Association of the Bereaved Families of the War Dead, was widely viewed as a hawk in the LDP; his move was regarded as an attempt at a course correction and public image overhaul. He was trying to compete with the dovish images of Kono Yohei, the former LDP president who backed the formation of the Socialist Murayama Cabinet, and Takemura Masayoshi, the most prominent member of and spokesman for the New Party Sakigake.

The person who had most strongly urged Hashimoto to stress a focus on Asia was the LDP party strategist Kajiyama Seiroku. Kajiyama wrote a piece in the July 1995 issue of the monthly Bungeishunju, "Coordinates for a Japan Facing the 21st Century," describing "the Kajiyama vision." Naturally, one of its central pillars was a focus on Asia.

Formerly, Japan defined itself solely on the basis of its relations with the United States; now, with the end of the cold war, Japan is opening itself again, as it were, to the rest of the world, for the third time. This time, according to Kajiyama, its action is motivated by a desire "as a member of Asia, to share both good times and bad times with fellow Asians."

Kajiyama says that the Look East slogans uttered by Japan so far have lacked creditability and that, unless something is done, Japan will isolate itself and be caught in limbo, neither part of Asia nor part of Western Europe.

As Kajiyama observes, one must not jump blindly onto the Asian boom bandwagon. Look closely at Japan's perceptions of Asia, and one will discover a variety of causes for concern.

THE GENERATION SHIFT

To begin with, whether and to what degree Japan's younger generation has a deeper understanding of and interest in Asia is questionable. Is its awareness of the war that the rest of Asia cannot forget not tenuous, at best? In March 1995, the 34-year-old Takaichi Sanae joined the Shinshinto (New Frontier Party)'s opposition to the Diet resolution expressing Japan's regret for its actions during the war. Taking to task the statement by Japanese Ambassador to the United States Kuriyama Shoichiro that it was "appropriate to express the people's regret through a Diet resolution," she said at a meeting of the House of Representatives' Foreign Affairs Committee: "Speaking for myself, I am not a member of the generation that took part personally in the war, and I have nothing to apologize for. As far as I'm concerned, I don't even think that anybody has the right to ask me to express any regrets." This outburst was, in effect, a rebuke addressed to the foreign minister, Kono Yohei. The very idea of the resolution was, to her thinking, totally preposterous. Visibly displeased, Kono countered: "I take issue with the Honorable Representative's profession of complete lack of regret with regard to the war and her claim that apologies are meaningless."

Certainly, if this were a question of individual responsibility, it would be as Takaichi says. But for this statement to come from the mouth of a member of Parliament, and worse, to be voiced in an official question session and expressed with such bluntness and utter lack of concern, is simply incredible. That is at least what I, as a member of the earlier postwar-educated generation, thought. Apparently, however, today's younger generation does not agree. A special issue (July 12, 1995) of the youth-market weekly *Spa!* titled "What's all this talk about 'responsibility for World War II'?" carried views, both pro and con, on the Japanese Diet's resolution, related opinions of non-Japanese, and reporting on the scars left by the war. I, too, was interviewed for the same issue, which was emblazoned with the following headline copy:

> The All-Too-Fuzzy Resolution on the 50th Anniversary of the War,
> Calls For Apologies From Near And Far,
> And What It Means To Apathetic Young People Like Us

In the eyes of many young people today, Japan's invasion of Asia, colonial domination, and all the rest seem like ancient history or the history of some country other than their own—nothing they have any reason to be concerned about.

DEMOCRACY'S PANDORA'S BOX

It is a fact that Asia's swing toward democracy has improved its public image in Japan, but it must not be forgotten that democracy brings with it new problems and resuscitates old ones, especially long-stifled grievances. For example, former "comfort women," especially Koreans, pressed into sexual service by the Japanese military overseas during World War II have now come forward and demanded individual compensation for their sufferings. Back in the days when Asian states kept their people under tight authoritarian control, these requests would have been unthinkable. Society's democratization, together with the victims' advanced age, has unleashed pent-up grievances and undermined the victims' previous resolve to suffer in silence. Formal complaints have now been laid at the door of the Japanese government. Similar complaints are springing up now in China. The Japanese government's official position has been that these claims were settled long ago: reparations were paid by the Japanese government to the victims' governments. The Japanese government was nonetheless so uncomfortable about the situation that it supported a "private" contribution campaign to show sympathy for the comfort women of World War II. The victims were loudly disdainful of this accommodation. This discord is symptomatic of the new problems that refuse to go away once the door is finally opened to democracy and they get their foot in. Unless these complaints are dealt with appropriately, they are certain to trigger a nationalistic backlash in Japan.

The swing to democracy also has inherent limitations. In China, where reforms and openness to the outside world are making progress in the economy and in foreign relations, strong central control continues to be wielded in government and politics. A nascent pro-democracy movement was brutally suppressed in Tienanmen Square in 1989. China is also making conspicuous moves to become a military superpower. This has quenched the ardor of Sino–Japanese rapprochement and has fueled, in some quarters, Japanese perceptions of a Chinese threat.

The Tienanmen massacre highlights the issue of human rights in China. Tokyo's criticisms are nowhere near as harsh as Washington's: by and large, Japan tends to see a measure of human rights abuses in China as an unavoidable step in the Asian development process. Prime minister Kaifu Toshiki was quick to make a visit to China, and the Emperor's visit during the Miyazawa Cabinet is further evidence of this leniency, which stems from perceptions of China that differ fundamentally from US perceptions of China. But when China resumed nuclear testing in 1995 immediately after its indefinite postponement of signing the Nuclear Nonproliferation Treaty, the Japanese began to have much more mixed feelings toward the Chinese. The Japanese came to feel more and more strongly that they could not tell what the Chinese were really thinking. Japan became increasingly worried that China was seeking to become a military superpower.

When Japan issued a strong protest against the nuclear tests and announced that it would cut back its ODA grants to China, the Chinese retaliated by lambasting the Japanese Diet's resolution on the fiftieth anniversary of the end of World War II, calling itself the victim of Japanese acts of aggression since the 19th century. The Chinese also hold that Japan's economic aid was given in exchange for China's renunciation of reparations. There is all the more potential for acrimony and distance between the two countries' positions, with the danger of fanning nationalistic sentiments in both, because nuclear warfare is among the issues that the Japanese people are most sensitive to.

Meanwhile, in Taiwan, rapid economic growth has been followed by progress toward democracy and a new image, with the abandon and renunciation of mainlanders' dictatorial control. Mainland China through its doctrine of "one China" has sought to contain Taiwan. In dealing with the issues of Taiwan's independence and efforts to improve its relations with the island, Japan faces extremely difficult choices. Japanese political conservatives continue to include a strong group of die-hard Taiwan supporters, and future dealings with Taiwan are certain to generate tumultuous repercussions.

An inkling of what is in store surfaced in the process of formulating new guidelines for the scope of Japan–US cooperation in mutual security and defense. Japan was to cooperate with the US forces in the event of "contingencies in surrounding areas"; the moot point was whether the stipulation covered a potential China–Taiwan military conflict. The Japanese government doggedly equivocated. The Treaty of Peace and Friendship between Japan and the People's Republic of China recognized the "one-China" principle, and any China–Taiwan conflict would be an internal issue of China's in which Japan had no right to interfere. That is how China sees it, and quite a few Japanese observers agree with such a reading. But Japan and Taiwan have close economic ties, and many Japanese nationals reside in Taiwan. The US and Taiwan are on the same side as allies; if the US decided to send its troops to the cross-Strait theater, what could Japan possibly do to stop them? Japanese opinion is divided over the definition of "contingencies in surrounding areas." Hence the government's painful prevarication.

The last thing the Japanese government wants to see is open hostilities between China and Taiwan. Declaring that a potential China–Taiwan conflict does not count as one of the contingencies would possibly encourage China's hawkish policy, while declaring it does count as one might give the mistaken impression that Japan supported Taiwan's independence movement. Rather than committing itself to either interpretation to the exclusion of the other, the government has chosen to walk the tightrope of ambiguity.

With China on the verge of becoming a superpower in the 21st century, naturally the wise course for Japan is to prevent China's isolation, but because the Japanese generally tend to feel that they "owe the Chinese one" because of their past actions, they find it hard to say everything they ought to say to the Chinese. Japanese right-wingers, saying they have no reason to feel guilty, brazenly defend Japan's actions in the past, further provoking the Chinese and setting in motion a vicious cycle. As I mentioned earlier, the Chinese do not hesitate to play the card of Japan's past, but it was Japan's politicians who put that card in their hands. And it was also Japan's politicians who, on the fiftieth anniversary of the war's end, when the opportunity at last presented itself to break the vicious cycle, failed to avail themselves of that opportunity. The result was the unpleasantness of Jiang Zemin's visit to Japan in 1998.

Response to the "New Asianism"

Meanwhile, with the rise and growth in prosperity of Asia's economies and the heralded advent of "the age of Asia," support is emerging for regionalism. In Southeast Asia, the United States has joined Asian-Pacific Economic Cooperation (APEC). Not content with this, some even talk of creating an East Asian Economic Caucus (EAEC) in response to the European Union (EU) and the North American Free Trade Area (NAFTA). Japan is caught uncomfortably between these nascent regionalisms and the United States. In the past, it was Japan's close cooperation with the United States that increased Japan's leverage in the Asian economy, but this tried-and-true postwar *modus operandi* no longer works as it used to, and Japan is being called on to think independently. To describe Japan's new aim, replacing "out of Asia and into Europe," a new phrase has been coined: "stay with the US and join Asia." More easily said than done.

The currency and monetary crisis that hit Thailand first in 1997 and rapidly spread to the rest of the region exposed the vulnerability of Asian economies, and amplified doubts about the US-led economic system. Japan played a major role in righting the tottering Asian economy, but in the aftermath of the burst economic bubble, Japan's economy has also had to come to terms with a perceived stinging defeat by the US economy. Looking afar and askance at the European Union, where the euro has been introduced to rival the dollar, Japan must now grope its way toward viable modes of economic leadership in Asia.

Plus, in addition to its economic might, Japan now must assume increasing responsibility as an Asian superpower politically. Japan played a part in the peace process in Cambodia; in 1992, after a fierce battle between ruling and opposition parties, Japan managed to send members of its Self-Defense Forces to Cambodia to take part in a peace-keeping mission. This was generally welcomed as a good start by other countries in Southeast Asia, who supported Japan's moves to win a permanent seat on the United Nations Security Council and are among the countries openly hoping to see

Japan play the role of Asian spokesman. This has inflated Japan's self-esteem and contributed to calls for a more aggressive Japanese role in international diplomacy and for expanded military contributions overseas (via amendment of the Japanese constitution).

Malaysia's Mahathir, as I mentioned before, is probably the best example of an inflator of Japan's self-esteem. As the initiator of the EAEC concept, he called loudly for Japan to align itself with his initiative and to play a role, distinct from that of the United States, as a leader of Asia. Mahathir is a new breed of Asianist who is calling for a clear line of demarcation with respect to Asia's "white states," Australia and New Zealand. Ishihara Shintaro, then an LDP Diet member, now Governor (mayor) of Tokyo, was so sympathetic to Mahathir's call that he resorted to action, resigning his Diet seat in April 1995 to protest Japan's (and his party's) lukewarm response to the EAEC. One can argue that a burgeoning anti-American Asianism is present in Japan—and also that Japan's indecisiveness is causing mounting irritation in Southeast Asia.

Asia is no monolith: perceptions of Japan differ vastly between Southeast and Northeast Asia. Chinese and Korean wariness was not eliminated when Japanese Self-Defense Forces took part in a United Nations peace-keeping operation. The truth of the matter is that both nations have serious reservations about allowing Japan to have a permanent seat in the UN Security Council.

At the root of it all is undoubtedly their mistrust of Japan. According to an opinion poll conducted by the *Asahi Shimbun* in major Asian cities in June 1995, the question "Do you think today's Japan has become a country that other Asian countries can trust?" was answered in the following way in seven Asian cities:

	Japan is trusted in Asia	Japan is not trusted in Asia
Beijing	15%	85%
Shanghai	20%	79%
Seoul	28%	61%
Bangkok	79%	10%
Manila	55%	43%
Singapore	62%	31%
Jakarta	85%	14%

(Data include only answers: invalid or missing answers were not counted. Published in the *Asahi Shimbun*, August 13, 1995)

How much Japan has cooperated in different countries' national development is likewise variously appreciated: in Jakarta 88% and in Bangkok, Manila, and Singapore about 70% of respondents state that Japan has been cooperative in their country's economic development; yet in Seoul 66% and in Beijing 57% of respondents say Japan has not. In Seoul 92% and in Beijing and Shanghai more than 70% say that Japan has not done enough to recompense their country for the damage it did during the war; the response was the same in Southeast Asia, even in Singapore (where 55% of respondents said Japanese reparations were insufficient).

One must also take into account Asia's very diversity. Despite divisions between Protestants and Catholics in Western society, Christianity is a unifying force, whereas in Asia, a multiplicity of religions—Buddhism, Islaam, Hinduism, Christianity, and many others, including Confucianism—wield great influence. Add to this linguistic and cultural diversity and differing degrees of exposure to Western influences. And while democracy has made inroads everywhere, Asia has countries like North Korea and Myanmar that are still ruled by military dictatorships.

In his memoirs (*Kaisojunen*), Yoshida Shigeru wrote: "Today's Japan, whether you look at its domestic politics or its economy or its industry or its social situation, is more Western European than Asian."[1] This assessment betrays a deeply rooted ideological tendency to place Asia lower than Europe and the United States and a desire to get "out of Asia and into Europe." Culturally and economically, many of Japan's values have undergone westernization, and it is doubtful whether Japan still belongs to Asia or really finds its identity there. Having acquired economic might virtually on a par with the United States and become the only non-Western member of the G7 Summit nations, Japan's Asian identity has, perhaps, been diluted.

This is apparent in the way non-Japanese Asian residents of Japan are received by Japanese society: by no means are they welcomed warmly; indeed, they encounter humiliating discrimination. The strong yen has boosted Japanese investment in Asia but it has led at the same time to deindustrialization and unemployment in

Japan; meanwhile, a flood of Asian workers is pouring into Japan. There are few grounds for optimism about the changes that this tendency will generate in Japanese attitudes toward Asians. Japan's legislators have contributed to dismantling discrimination, little by little, in response to strong demands from Japanese residents originating from North and South Korea, but they can scarcely be said to be facing the issue squarely. The difficulties faced by Asian foreign students when they look for a place to stay in Japan are indicative of how cold this country, even today, can be to Asians.

NOWHERE ELSE TO GO TO

The Japanese are doubtlessly sensitive to developments on the Korean Peninsula. Normalization of diplomatic ties with North Korea is on the agenda for the 21th century, but the moment negotiations between North Korea and Japan bigin, however, they will set in motion a process necessitating solutions to many thorny issues: What to say about the colonial period? Was the Japan–Korea Annexation Treaty of 1910 valid? Should Japan pay reparations for colonial rule? Japan must now go over questions that were settled in the Treaty on Basic Relations Between Japan and the Republic of Korea (Japan–Korea Basic Treaty) through political compromises, but North Korea can be expected to adopt a harsher, less compromising attitude than did South Korea.

With Japanese prime ministers now apologizing for Japan's colonial past and with changes taking place in the Japanese people's awareness of these issues, it is inappropriate for Japan to continue to adopt the old attitude. But if Japan makes more concessions to North Korea than it did to South Korea in the Japan–Korea Basic Treaty, South Korea is unlikely to remain silent. Already there are calls in South Korea for a revision of the Japan–Korea Basic Treaty; talks between Japan and North Korea are likely to touch off very strong feelings in the South. And should the Korean Peninsula ever be engulfed in war again, Japan is certain to feel the repercussions.

The Japanese government will be forced to make tough decisions, not only about support for American troops, but also about whether to send its own forces. Refugees are very likely to pour into Japan. *Nolens volens*, Japan will be forced to respond to the situation on the Korean Peninsula, and a chauvinistic Japanese nationalism may erupt from dormancy.

Even the opposite scenario, in which North and South Korea manage to reunite peacefully, would be a mixed blessing. Reunification is expected to be immensely costly, and Japan is certain to be asked to contribute. Whether Japan cooperates willingly and to the best of its ability will be a major determinant of its future image in Asia.

Some years ago, I introduced an influential member of the LDP to a Korean journalist. We agreed that the occasion called for getting right to the point and speaking openly. The LDP member said, "While we Japanese want the Korean Peninsula to be reunited, we are at the same time, deep down inside, somewhat wary of this happening." Some Japanese fear that the dynamism of South Korea, flush with its economic achievements, will be given a new impetus by reunification with the North, and that a reunified Korea may become so strong as to become a military threat to Japan.

The LDP member went further, and cited the Rangoon bombing incident and the bombing of a Korean Air Lines plane, terrorist acts for which the North Koreans are held responsible, and acknowledged that some Japanese politicians wonder whether these incidents stem not so much from the nature of the North Korean regime but perhaps from character traits of Koreans in general. The Korean journalist was startled, and revealed in turn that some Koreans believe that the Japanese are monsters, citing the Japanese assassination of Korea's Queen Min and the massacres of Korean residents in Japan immediately following the Great Kanto Earthquake. This memorable exchange was typical of the yawning perception gap between Japanese and Koreans. When the Japanese think about Asia, I believe they are often unaware of this abyss.

I remember the celebrated phrase of prime minister Ohira Masayoshi on the difficulty of Japan–Korea relations: "Yes, but even so, we can't exactly just pack up and move." Similarly, applying this to a wider geographical scope, no matter how much the Japanese regard themselves as different, they simply can not, with so much in common with Asia, pack up and move out. Today, now that the world is a smaller place, talk of Japan's transcending Asia and "belonging to the world" is natural. It is hoped in particular that Japan can play a role of go-between, "bridge" between Asia and the West. But before Japan readies itself for that role, it must first become a trusted community leader in its local neighborhood—that is, in Asia—and make everybody feel at home in its company. Only then can it become a go-between with people from outside. The first thing it must do is break its habit of thinking of itself as "Asia's leader" or "first in Asia" in every domain. It is crucial for Japan to act as a member of the Asian team with as much humility as possible, conscious of its militaristic stigma. In recent history, Japan brought untold misery to people throughout Asia (and brought ruin on itself). That is why it must teach its history as it is, without convenient excuses or omissions, to coming generations. To strive to "share history" with the people of Asia—that is the most fundamental of the obligations that Japanese statesmen and leaders must assume today.

In the summer of 1995, taking office as minister for education and referring to the fact that two-thirds of the Japanese population was born after the end of World War II, Shimamura Yoshinobu asked: "Why should we still be rehashing the past to a generation that knows nothing about the war?" How absurd, utterly absurd! Precisely because the younger generation knows nothing about the war, educators and political leaders bear a weighty responsibility to ensure that a bigoted nationalism can never rear its head again.

Though we may have entered "the age of Asia," many difficulties lie ahead. As we have seen, Japanese politicians' attitudes, especially with regard to Asia, are behind the times compared with recent Japanese attitudes in general, and compared in particular with people in Japanese business and finance, who are already diligently at work finding an economic *modus vivendi* with Asia.

It is politicians' job to steer and decide the orientation of the nation's ties with other Asian countries. I sincerely hope that Japan's political leaders henceforth will come to realize the immensity of their personal responsibility.

APPENDIX

CHRONOLGY OF POLITICAL EVENTS IN POSTWAR JAPAN AND ASIA

Prime Minister Yoshida Shigeru represented Japan in September 1951 at the San Francisco peace conference, where neither China nor South or North Korea were in attendance. Japan's rehabilitation in Asia would take many years.

Year/Month	Major events	Cabinet (term in office)
1945		
August	The Second World War ends. With Japan's defeat, its colonies and occupied territories are liberated.	Prince Higashikuni Naruhiko (Aug.–Oct. 1945)
October		Shidehara Kijuro (Oct. 1945–May 1946)
1946		
May	The International Military Tribunal for the Far East opens (Tokyo Trials).	Yoshida Shigeru (May 1946–May 1947)
1947		
May		Katayama Tetsu (May 1947–March 1948)
1948		
March		Ashida Hitoshi (March–October 1948)
August	The Republic of Korea is founded.	
September	The People's Democratic Republic of Korea is founded, dividing the Korean Peninsula into North and South Korea.	
October		Yoshida Shigeru (Oct. 1948–Dec. 1954)
1949		
October	The People's Republic of China is founded; Chiang Kaishek and the remainder of the Kuomintang flee to Taiwan.	

Year/Month	Major events	Cabinet (term in office)
1950 *June*	Outbreak of the Korean War.	
1951 *September*	Peace treaty is signed in San Francisco; China, Taiwan, North and South Korea, Burma, and India do not attend. The U.S.–Japan Security Treaty is signed.	
1952 *February*	First talks begin between Japan and South Korea.	
April	The San Francisco Peace Treaty comes into effect. Japan signs a peace treaty with Taiwan.	
June	Treaty is signed with China on private-sector trade.	
October	Prime Minister Yoshida calls for closer economic ties with Southeast Asia in a policy speech.	
1953 *January*	At the invitation of U.N. Forces, President Rhee Syngman of Korea visits Japan, where he holds talks with Prime Minister Yoshida.	
July	Truce agreement ending the Korean War is signed.	
October	The third session of talks between Japan and South Korea is broken off because of a statement by Kubota Kenichiro, the chief of the Japanese negotiating team.	
1954 *September*	The National People's Congress elects Chairman Mao Zedong and Prime Minister Zhou Enlai.	

Year/Month	Major events	Cabinet (term in office)
1954 *(continued)*		
November	A reparations agreement is signed with Burma.	
December		Hatoyama Ichiro (Dec. 1954–Dec. 1956)
1955		
April	The Bandung Conference of Asian and African Countries, the first such meeting, is held in Indonesia.	
1956		
July	A reparations agreement is signed with the Philippines.	
October	Normal diplomatic relations with the Soviet Union are restored by a joint declaration.	
December	Japan joins the United Nations. Prime Minister Ishibashi expresses willingness to improve relations with China.	Ishibashi Tanzan (Dec. 1956–Feb. 1957)
1957		
February		Kishi Nobusuke (Feb. 1957–July 1960)
May	Prime Minister Kishi makes his first tour of Southeast Asian countries.	
June	Prime Minister Kishi holds talks with President Chiang Kaishek in Taiwan. Kishi agrees to the resumption of talks between Japan and South Korea.	

Year/Month	Major events	Cabinet (term in office)
1957 *(continued)*		
October	India's Prime Minister Nehru visits Japan, issues a joint declaration.	
November	Prime Minister Kishi makes his second tour of Southeast Asian countries.	
1958		
January	A peace treaty and an agreement on reparations with Indonesia are signed.	
April	The fourth series of talks with South Korea is reopened.	
May	An incident involving the Chinese flag at a stamp exhibition in Nagasaki worsens relations with China. Prime Minister Kishi sends Yatsugi Kazuo as a special personal envoy to South Korea.	
1959		
March	Japan Socialist Party First Secretary Asanuma Inejiro visits China and declares that "American imperialism is the joint enemy of Japan and China."	
May	A reparations agreement and a loan agreement are signed with South Vietnam.	
1960		
January	The US–Japan Security Treaty is revised and extended.	
April	Student protests force South Korean President Rhee Syngman to resign.	
July		Ikeda Hayato (July 1960–Nov. 1964)

Year/Month	Major events	Cabinet (term in office)
1961 *May*	Coup d'etat in South Korea.	
November	Park Chunghee, Chairman of the Supreme Council for National Reconstruction (President of the Republic of Korea after 1963), visits Japan and holds talks with Prime Minister Ikeda. Trade agreement engineered by Liao Chengzhi and Takasaki Tatsunosuke is signed between Japan and China.	
1964 *December*		Sato Eisaku (Nov. 1964–July 1972)
1965 *February*	The United States begins bombing North Vietnam. Foreign Minister Shiina Etsusaburo visits South Korea and expresses his regrets for Japan's past actions.	
June	The Japan–Korea Basic Treaty is signed.	
November	The "Great Proletarian Cultural Revolution" begins in China.	
1966 *November*	The Asian Development Bank holds its inaugural meeting in Tokyo.	
1967 *June*	Prime Minister Sato visits Korea. The leaders of Japan, the United States, South Korea, and Taiwan hold a summit in Seoul.	

Year/Month	Major events	Cabinet (term in office)
1967 *(continued)* *August*	The Association of South East Asian Nations (ASEAN) is established.	
1971 *July* *October*	U.S. President Nixon announces plans to visit China. China decides to join the United Nations; Taiwan withdraws.	
1972 *July*		Tanaka Kakuei (July 1972–Dec. 1974)
September	Prime Minister Tanaka visits China; Japan–China diplomatic ties are normalized with the China–Japan joint Communiqué. Diplomatic ties with Taiwan are cut off.	
1973 *January* *August* *September*	A peace treaty is signed with Vietnam. Korean opposition leader Kim Daejung is kidnapped in Tokyo. Diplomatic relations are established with North Vietnam.	
1974 *January* *August*	Prime Minister Tanaka tours five Southeast Asian countries. Students hold anti-Japanese demonstrations in Bangkok. Anti-Japanese riots break out in Jakarta. The wife of Korean President Park is assassinated by a Korean resident of Japan.	

Year/Month	Major events	Cabinet (term in office)
1974 *(continued)* *December*		Miki Takeo (Dec. 1974–Dec. 1976)
1975 *April* **1976** *December*	With the fall of Saigon, South Vietnam surrenders and the Vietnam War ends.	Fukuda Takeo (Dec. 1976–Nov. 1978)
1977 *August* **1978** *August* *December*	Prime Minister Fukuda visits ASEAN and proclaims the Fukuda Doctrine. The Treaty of Peace and Friendship between Japan and the People's Republic of China is signed.	Ohira Masayoshi (Dec. 1978–June 1980)
1979 *June* *October* **1980** *May* *July*	The first Tokyo Summit is held. President Park is assassinated in South Korea. Kwangju uprising in South Korea.	Suzuki Zenko (July 1980–Nov. 1982)

Year/Month	Major events	Cabinet (term in office)
1982 *July*	China and South Korea protest revisions of Japanese history textbooks.	
November		Nakasone Yasuhiro (Nov. 1982–Nov. 1987)
1983 *January*	Prime Minister Nakasone makes the first official visit of a Japanese prime minister to South Korea.	
1984 *September*	South Korea's President Chun Doohwan visits Japan. At the official banquet held in his honor, Emperor Hirohito expresses his "deep regret for the countries' unfortunate past."	
1985 *August*	Prime Minister Nakasone makes an official visit to Yasukuni Jinja shrine on the anniversary of the end of World War II. China, Korea, and other Asian countries protest vehemently.	
1986 *March*	A revolution in the Philippines deposes President Marcos, who flees to the United States; Mrs. Corazon Aquino becomes President.	
September	Education Minister Fujio Masayuki is removed for publishing a statement justifying Japan's annexation of Korea. Prime Minister Nakasone visits South Korea to apologize.	

Year/Month	Major events	Cabinet (term in office)
1987 *November*	A Korean Air Lines jetliner is destroyed in flight by a bomb.	Takeshita Noboru (Nov. 1987–June 1989)
1988 *May*	Okuno Seisuke, Director General of the National Land Agency, is ousted because of a statement he made justifying Japan's actions in World War II.	
1989 *January* *May*	Emperor Hirohito dies. Tienanmen Incident in Beijing.	
June		Uno Sosuke (June–Aug. 1989)
August		Kaifu Toshiki (Aug. 1989–Nov. 1991)
1990 *May*	South Korean President Roh Taewoo visits Japan. Emperor Akihito expresses his "feeling the deepest regret."	
August	Iraq invades Kuwait, precipitating the Gulf Crisis.	
September	A joint delegation of the Liberal Democratic Party and the Socialist Party led by Kanemaru Shin visits North Korea; the two countries agree to begin talks on normalizing their ties.	

Year/Month	Major events	Cabinet (term in office)
1991		
January	The Gulf War breaks out in the Mideast.	
September	Emperor Akihito visits Thailand, Malaysia, and Indonesia.	
November		Miyazawa Kiichi (Nov. 1991–Aug. 1993)
1992		
September	Members of Japanese Self-Defence Force are sent to co-operate for United Nations peacekeeping and other operations in Cambodia.	
October	Emperor Akihito visits China.	
1993		
August	The Liberal Democratic Party loses its majority and becomes an opposition party for the first time in decades; Prime Minister Hosokawa Morihiro expresses his view that "the last war was a war of aggression."	Hosokawa Morihiro (Aug. 1993–Apr. 1994)
November	Prime Minister Hosokawa Morihiro visits South Korea and apologizes for Japan's colonial rule, specifically mentioning the Japanese attempt to make the Koreans adopt Japanese names.	
1994		
April	Justice Minister Nagano Shigeto resigns after proclaiming that "talk of the Nanking Massacre is a fabrication."	Hata Tsutomu (Apr.–June 1994)

Year/Month	Major events	Cabinet (term in office)
1994 *(continued)*		
June	A coalition is formed, consisting of the Liberal Democratic Party, the Democratic Socialist Party, and the New Party Sakigake.	Murayama Tomiichi (June 1994–Jan. 1996)
July	North Korea's Chairman Kim Ilsung dies.	
August	Prime Minister Murayama visits South Korea.	
	A joint communiqué by the United States and North Korea announces their agreement to establish diplomatic representation.	
	Environment Agency Director General Sakurai Shin resigns over his statement that Japan had had "no aggressive intentions."	
1995		
March	The Korean Energy Development Organization (KEDO) is established by Japan, the United States, and South Korea to provide North Korea with energy.	
	A delegation of representatives from the three parties of the governing coalition headed by Watanabe Michio visits North Korea and agrees to resume Japan–North Korea talks.	
June	A resolution on the fiftieth anniversary of the end of the war is passed by less than a majority of the lower house of the Diet.	

Year/Month	Major events	Cabinet (term in office)
1995 *(continued)*		
August	Prime Minister Murayama releases a fiftieth anniversary statement apologizing for Japan's invasion of Asia. Management and Coordination Agency Director General Eto Takami resigns over his statement that Japan also did good for Korea during the colonial period.	
November	The APEC Summit is held in Osaka.	
December	Former South Korean President Roh Taewoo is arrested for taking bribes during his presidency.	
1996		
January		Hashimoto Ryutaro (Jan. 1996–July 1998)
March	China holds missile maneuvers off Taiwan. In Taiwan, Lee Tenghui is elected President in the country's first direct presidential election.	
May	Announcement that the World Cup Soccer Games of 2002 will be held under the co-sponsorship of Japan and Korea.	
1997		
February	On his way back from Japan, North Korea's Workers' Party Secretary Hwang Jangyop seeks asylum in Beijing and defects, via the Philippines, to South Korea.	

Year/Month	Major events	Cabinet (term in office)
1997		
July	A severe monetary crisis strikes Thailand.	
	Myanmar and Laos join ASEAN.	
September	Prime Minister Hashimoto visits China in commemoration of the 25th anniversary of the normalization of diplomatic relations with China, and he makes the first official visit of a Japanese Prime Minister to the Marco Polo Bridge where the Manchurian Incident took place.	
	The Japanese and U.S. governments agree to set up new guidelines for defense cooperation.	
October	In North Korea, Kim Jongil becomes chairman of the Workers' Party.	
November	Japanese women married to North Koreans are allowed to make temporary visits to Japan.	
	Chinese Prime Minister Li Peng visits Japan.	
	Korea asks the International Monetary Fund to help it overcome the financial crisis.	
1998		
February	In South Korea, Kim Daejung becomes President.	
May	In Indonesia, in the throes of an economic crisis, the Suharto regime is forced to step down.	

Year/Month	Major events	Cabinet (term in office)
1998 *(continued)*		
July		Obuchi Keizo
August	North Korea experimentally launches the long-range missile Taepodong.	(July 1998 to present)
October	South Korea's President Kim Daejung visits Japan.	
November	China's Chairman Jiang Zemin visits Japan.	
1999		
March	Japan's Maritime Self-Defense Force ship pursues a North Korean spy ship off the Niigata coast.	
April	Japan–US defense cooperation guidelines bill is approved by the Japanese Diet.	
July	Prime Minister Obuchi visits China.	
December	Former prime minister Murayama Tomiichi leads a nonpartisan delegation of Diet members to North Korea; it is agreed to resume talks on the normalization of diplomatic relations.	

Postface

Sometime in June of 1994, a person I know and admire, Japan Center for International Exchange Director Yamamoto Tadashi, presented me with an unexpected challenge, asking me out of the blue: "Would you mind writing up for us an organized report on how Asia has been perceived in postwar Japanese politics?"

The theme of the US–Japan Shimoda Conference, coming up in October, was US–Japan relations in the Asian context. His request meant writing a report for presentation at the conference.

I remember gasping in alarm. Yamamoto was the guiding force behind the Korea–Japan Forum: only he would have thought of such an apposite topic, and indeed, if I knew of such a report, I would want to read it as soon as I could. But it was a task so far beyond my ability that I could not give him an answer straight away.

Still, knowing how much I wanted to read such a report gave me the impetus I needed to undertake the task. I was further encouraged by the famous Japanologist and participant in Shimoda Conferences, Columbia University Professor Gerald Curtis, whose encouragement finally decided me. I spent my entire summer vacation writing a report entitled "Perceptions of Asia in Japan's Postwar Politics."

I attempted to put down on paper my own feelings and impressions day to day, backing them as I could with whatever reference materials I found. My report was well received, fortunately, and the monthly *Chuo Koron* decided to publish it with almost no changes in their February 1995 issue. The Shimoda Conference's English version, "Asianism in Japan's Postwar Politics," was included in the Japan Center for International Exchange collection *Japan and the United States in Asia Pacific: : The Challenges for Japan in Asia* (Background Papers for the Shimoda '94).

Despite this success, I still didn't dream that the editorial board of Asahi Sensho would present yet another virtually impossible request: They asked me to expand the concept and turn the report into a book. "Now I've got myself into another fine fix," I thought. This time, it was the rising chorus of shrill opposition to the Diet resolution on the fiftieth anniversary of the war that gave me the impetus to undertake the task. I realized that it was a once-in-a-lifetime opportunity to delve into the depths of Japanese feelings about Asia and what lurks beneath the surface of Japan's postwar politics at a time when Japanese politicians seemingly never tired of provoking Asia with their comments. Despite my lack of expertise in the field, I decided to accept this difficult challenge and entered an excruciating race against the clock.

To begin with, I am neither a historian nor a political scientist. All I had to draw on was my experience and reminiscences as a newspaper reporter. The rest had to come from politicians themselves, or from academics and more experienced political reporters' writings. This book is simply the product of my agonized or elated research, involving much groping in the dark.

It is therefore full of citations from a number of sources, both specialized and academic publications, from which I have chosen the most recent and most easily obtainable. I have leaned toward easy-to-read materials, and I hope that this will give many readers an accessible guide to the subject. Among the references cited are old documents with old spellings and typographical conventions, which I have modernized for this book. The pronunciations of Korean and Chinese proper nouns in the English translation are of course the Korean and Chinese, not the Japanese, pronunciations.

At the start, I planned to address the views on Asia of the entire spectrum of Japanese politics, including the progressive camp, but there was not time enough to cover that much. Hence the reference only to the political right in the title of this book. I feel, nevertheless, that the outlook on Asia of the conservative politicians covered in this volume is generally representative of the postwar Japanese public's attitudes as well. For example, a look at the tone of newspaper articles at the time of the talks between Japan and South Korea on normalizing diplomatic relations shows that the political world and the press saw things in roughly the same terms. The other side of the coin, however, is the painful realization that Japanese journalism (including the *Asahi Shimbun*) sided with the apologists of prewar colonial domination and aggression against Asia.

In this sense, I consider that I'm risking considerable embarrassment by venturing to write this book. I beg the reader's indulgence to recognize that I am admonishing myself at the same time, as someone who has spent his life as a reporter of the postwar school of journalism. Though much of this was written 'fresh' for these pages, Part I was partly based on material in the monthly *Ronza* (the June 1995 issue), and parts of Part II and V on articles I wrote for the *Asahi Shimbun*. Part IV was first published in *Chuo Koron*'s September 1993 issue.

I wish to express my deep gratitude to the authors who allowed me to quote their works and to the many people who shared their views with me. I benefited greatly from many other works that I did not quote directly, including Goto Motoo et al.'s *Sengo hoshuseiji no kiseki* (The tracks of postwar conservative politics),[1] and Yui Daizaburo's *Nichibei sensokan no sokoku* (Conflicting US and Japanese views of the war).[2] In Part IV, I also borrowed from reporting by my contemporary and junior colleagues in the Political Department of the *Asahi Shimbun*. In Part V, I draw on the views of participants in the Korea–Japan Forum; the forum's rules do not allow me to reveal the names of participants, but exceptionally I quoted the statements of a number of politicians. I wish also to acknowledge my deep gratitude to the late Shiba Ryuji, who gladly gave me the opportunity to study the Korean language in Korea when he headed the *Asahi Shimbun*'s Political Department.

The present work was translated into Korean and published in April 1996 under the title of "The View of Asia in Japanese

Politics—Undercurrents of Gaffes and Apologies" (The *Dong-A Ilbo* Press). I am very happy to see its English version included now in the LTCB International Library Selection. Perceiving Japan's position in Asia is a difficult task for us Japanese, and it is my hope that the English version will offer some food for thought to Japan and Asia watchers across the world. I am grateful to Anzai Takashi, Soga Yoshiki, and Murakami Ichiro of the LTCB International Library Foundation for the privilege.

I am also indebted to Mitsunobu Meiyo, Christopher Holmes, Marie Speed, Tachibana Junko, Ikeda Naoki and their associates for the care with which they have translated and edited the Japanese text, with all its elusive and highly nuanced turns of expression, into a readable English version. Last but not least, I am grateful to Saji Yasuo for performing the Herculean task of collating, page-making, citation-verifying, and performing myriad nerve-wracking chores of editorship.

I am also indebted to Mitsunobu Meiyo, Christopher Holmes, Marie Speed, Tachibana Junko, Ikeda Naoki, and their associates for the care with which they have translated and edited the Japanese text, with all its elusive and highly nuanced turns of expression, into a readable English version. Last but not least, I am grateful to Saji Yasuo for performing the Herculean task of collating, page-making, citation-verifying, index-generating and performing myriad nerve-wracking chores of editorship.

And to my readers, those who have read this far, I would like to say thank you: now you deserve a rest. There were undoubtedly many things I should have thought of, but didn't, and my assessment is off the mark in places, I am sure. I would very much appreciate any suggestions or further information about facts or any passages requiring corrections or improvements.

Wakamiya Yoshibumi

Notes

INTRODUCTION

1. Textbook Incident of 1982, *see* pp. 19, 183, 196–98, 280 of this book; for the second Textbook Incident of 1986, *see* pp. 177–78, 200 of this book.

PART I THE FIFTIETH END-OF-WAR ANNIVERSARY RESOLUTION OF 1995 AND ITS SHORTCOMINGS

1. This is the translation issued by the Lower House secretariat of the Diet resolution that the Lower House passed to commemorate the 50th anniversary of the end of World War II, as published in the *Asahi Evening News*, June 10–11, 1995.

2. *Asahi Shimbun*, April 26, 1988.

3. Greater East Asia Co-Prosperity Sphere, *see* part III, chapter 3 of this bok (pp. 71–78).

4. *Sekai* magazine, May 1995.

5. *Mainichi Shimbun*, May 5, 1994.

6. *Asahi Shimbun*, August 13, 1994.

7. *Asahi Shimbun*, August 10, 1995.

8. *Dong-A Ilbo*, June 6, 1995.

9. *Bungei shunju*, October 1995.

10. Unno Fukuju, *Kankoku heigo* (Annexation of Korea), (Tokyo: Iwanami Shoten, 1995).

11. Japan–Korea Treaty of 1965 (formally known as the Treaty on Basic Relations Between Japan and the Republic of Korea).

12. Hayashi Kentaro, *Rekishi kara no keikoku* (Warnings of history), (Tokyo: Chuo Koronsha, 1995), 100.

13. Kuroha Kiyotaka. *Taiheiyo senso no rekishi* (The history of the Pacific War), (Tokyo: Kodansha, 1985), 7–35.

14. *Asahi Shimbun*, November 22, 1994.

15. Hashimoto Ryutaro, *Seiken dakkairon* (To win back the seat of power), (Tokyo: Kodansha 1994), 99.

16. *LDP Monthly*, October 1993.

17. Yoshida Yutaka, *Showa Tenno no shusenshi* (Emperor Showa's history of the end of the war), (Tokyo: Iwanami Shoten, 1992), 197–99.

18. *Asahi Shimbun*, June 25, 1995.

19. Comments of the Press Secretary, Chinese Foreign Ministry, reported in *Asahi Shimbun*, August 23, 1995.

20. *Asahi Shimbun*, August 8, 1995.

21. Yokoyama Hiroaki, *Nitchu no shoheki* (The Invisible Wall Between Japan and China), (Tokyo: The Simul Press, 1994), 71.

Part II "The Wrongs Committed by Ito Hirobumi": On the Trail of an Apology and a Cover-Up

1. Kim Dongjo, *Kan–Nichi no wakai* (Korea–Japan Reconciliation: Seoul's Negotiator Recalls Normalization Talks), (Tokyo: The Simul Press, 1993).

2. Ibid., 144.

3. Ibid.

4. Kishi Nobusuke, *Kishi Nobusuke kaikoroku* (Memoirs of Kishi Nobusuke), (Tokyo: The Kosaido Publishing Co., 1983).

5. Kishi Nobusuke, Yatsugi Kazuo, and Ito Takashi, *Kishi Nobusuke no kaiso* (Reminiscences by Kishi Nobusuke), (Tokyo: Bungei Shunjusha, 1981), 222.

6. Kim Dongjo, *Kan–Nichi no wakai*, 115.

7. Hara Yoshihisa, *Kishi Nobusuke* (Tokyo: Iwamani Shoten, 1995), 16.

8. Yatsugi Kazuo, *Waga ronin-gaiko o kataru* (The story of my maverick diplomacy), (Tokyo: Toyo Keizai Shinposha, 1973).

Part III Pieces of the Past in Retrospect

Chapter 1. The Tokyo Tribunal and Why Kishi Nobusuke Wasn't Hanged

1. *Asahi Shimbun*, November 22, 1994.

2. Hara Yoshihisa, *Kishi Nobusuke*, 29.

3. Ibid.

4. Yamamuro Shinichi, *Kimera—Manshu-koku no shozo* (Chimera: A portrait of Manchukuo), (Tokyo: Chuokoronsha, 1993), 10.

5. Manshu Kaikoshu Kankokai, *Aa Manshu* (Oh Manchuria), (Tokyo: Manshu Kaikoshu Kankokai, 1965), preface.

6. Hara Yoshihisa, *Kishi Nobusuke,* 41.

7. Abe Yoko, *Watashi no Abe Shintaro* (Abe Shintaro as I remember him), (Tokyo: Bungei Shunjusha, 1992), 67.

Chapter 2. Yoshida Shigeru Before and After the War

1. Wakamiya Yoshibumi, *Wasurerarenai kokkai ronsen* (Unforgettable debates in the diet), (Tokyo: Chuokoronsha, 1994), 4–29.

2. Shimokobe Motoharu, and Shindo Eiichi eds., *Ashida Hitoshi nikki* (The Ashida Hitoshi diary, 1986), 7 vols. (Tokyo: Iwanami Shoten, 1986).

3. Kosaka Masataka, *Saisho Yoshida Shigeru* (Yoshida the Prime Minister), (Tokyo: Chuokoronsha, 1968), 11–12.

4. John Dower, *Yoshida Shigeru to sono jidai* (Yoshida Shigeru and his times), translated by Ookubo Genji (Tokyo: Chuo Koronsha, 1991); originally published as *Empire and Aftermath: Yoshida Shigeru and the Japanese Experience, 1878–1954* (Cambridge, Mass.: Council on East Asian Studies, Harvard University: distributed by Harvard University Press, 1979).

5. Kosaka Masataka, *Saisho Yoshida Shigeru*, 12.

6. John Dower, *Empire and Aftermath*, 64–65.

7. John Dower, *Yoshida Shigeru to sono jidai*, 118.

8. Kosaka Masataka, *Saisho Yoshida Shigeru*, 15.

9. Fukuzawa Yukichi, "Datsu A ron" (Out of Asia into the West), in *Fuluzawa Yukichi zenshu*, (Tokyo: Iwanami Shoten, 1980), VII: 221–24.

10. Yoshida Shigeru, *Kaiso junen* (Ten years in retrospect), (Tokyo: Shirakawa Shoin, 1957), I: 36–38.

11. Tanaka Hiroshi, *Zainichi gaikokujin* (Resident aliens in Japan), (Tokyo: Iwanami Shoten, 1995), 70–71.

12. MacArthur Archives. Courtesy of Sodei Rinjiro, Professor Emeritus, the University of Tokyo.

13. Igarashi Takeshi, *Tainichi kowa to reisen* (Peace with Japan and the Cold War), (Tokyo: The University of Tokyo Press, 1986), 145–46.

14. Kosaka Zentaro, *Giin gaiko yonjunen* (Forty years of parliamentary diplomacy), (Nihon Keizai Shimbunsha, 1994), 80.

Chapter 3. The Tangled Roots of "Out-of-Asia" and "Greater Asianism"

1. Fukuzawa Yukichi, *Bunmeiron no gairyaku* (An Outline of a Theory of Civilization), translated by David A. Dilworth and G. Cameron Hurst, A Monumenta Nipponica Monograph (Tokyo: Sophia University English Press Society, 1973).

2. Fukuzawa Yukichi, *Seiyo jijo* (An Introduction to the West and Its Conditions)

3. Keio Gijuku ed., *Fukuzawa Yukichi zenshu* (The collected works of Fukuzawa Yukichi), (Tokyo: Iwanami Shoten, 1926), 5: 186–87.

4. Ibid., 10: 239–40.

5. Kim Liangji, "Kan–Nichi kan no rekishi ninshiki no gyappu" ("Korea–Japan conflicts and gaps in historical perceptions"), in *Ajia kara mita Nihon* (Japan as viewed from Asia), ed. Kim Liangji (Tokyo: Kawade Shobo Shinsha, 1994), 10–39.

6. Inoki Masamichi, *Gunkoku Nihon no kobo* (The rise and fall of militarist Japan), (Tokyo: Chuokoronsha, 1995), 4.

7. Ibid., 265.

8. Irie Akira, *Shin Nihon no gaiko* (New Japanese diplomacy), (Tokyo: Chuokoron-sha, 1991), 4.

9. Ibid.

10. Fujimura Hisao, *Kakumeika Son Bun* (Sun Wen the Revolutionary) (Chuokoron-sha, 1994), 182–83.

11. Sun Wen, "Dai Ajia shugi" ("Greater Asianism"), in *Son Bun senshu* (The selected works of Sun Wen), translated by Imazato Tei, (Tokyo: Shakai Shisosha, 1989), 3: 375.

12. Okakura Tenshin, *Toyo no riso* (The Ideals of the East with Special Reference to the Art of Japan), translated by Tomihara Yoshihisa, (Tokyo: Kodansha, 1986); originally published as *The Ideals of the East with Special Reference to the Art of Japan* by Kakasu [sic] Okamura (London: John Marray, 1903).

13. Okawa Shumei, *Nihon seishin kenkyu* (Studies in the spirit of Japan), in Okawa Shumei zenshu, vol. 1, (Tokyo: Iwasaki Shoten, 1961).

14. Irie Akira, *Shin Nihon no gaiko*, 26–27.

15. Chiang Kaishek, *Bo o motte bo ni mukuyuru nakare* (Return not violence for violence), translated by Yamada Reizo (Tokyo: Hakuyosha, 1947).

16. Inoki Masamichi, *Gunkoku nihon no kobo*, 261.

Chapter 4. The Tragedy of Ishibashi Tanzan

1. Kyo Kokujitsu (Jiang Keshi), *Ishibashi Tanzan* (Tokyo: Maruzen, 1994).

2. Sataka Makoto, *Ryo-Nihonshugi no seijika—ima naze Ishibashi Tanzan ka?* (Statesman of sane Japanism—Why Ishibashi Tanzan now?), (Toyo Keizai Shinposha, 1994).

3. Masuda Hiroshi, *Ishibashi Tanzan* (Tokyo: Chuokoronsha, 1995).

4. Hando Kazutoshi, *Tatakau Ishibashi Tanzan* (Ishibashi Tanzan the fighter), (Toyo Keizai Inc., 1995).

5. Matsuo Takayoshi ed., *Ishibashi Tanzan hyoron shu* (Selected papers of Ishibashi Tanzan), (Iwanami Shoten Publishers, 1984).

6. Jiang Keshi, *Ishibashi Tanzan*, 5.

7. *Ishibashi Tanzan zenshu* (The collected works of Ishibashi Tanzan), (Tokyo: Toyo Keizai Shinposha, 1970–72), I: 111–13

8. Ibid., 375–81.

9. Masuda Hiroshi, *Ishibashi Tanzan* (Chuokoronsha, 1995), 72–73.

10. *Toyo Keizai Shimpo*, Editorial dated July 23, 1921.

11. Ishida Hirohide, *Ishibashi seiken nanajuichinichi* (Seventy-one days of the Ishibashi administration), (Tokyo: Gyosei Mondai Kenkyujo [Institute of Administrative Issues], 1985).

12. Masuda Hiroshi's *Ishibashi Tanzan*, 127.

13. Takeuchi Yoshimi, *Nihon to Chugoku no aida* (Japan and China: betwixt and between), (Tokyo: Bungei Shunjusha, 1973), 357.

14. Masuda Hiroshi's *Ishibashi Tanzan*, 252.

Chapter 5. Scant Awareness of Having Been Defeated by Asia

1. Irie Akira, *Shin Nihon no gaiko*, 29.

2. Ibid., 28–29.

3. Awaya Kentaro et al., "Postwar Settlements at the Tokyo Tribunal" in *Senso sekinin sengo sekinin* (Responsibility for War and its aftermath), (Tokyo: Asahi Shimbun Publishing Co., 1994), 109–111.

4. Miyazawa Kiichi, *Shin goken sengen* (New declaration of defense of the constitution), (Tokyo: Asahi Shimbunsha, 1995), 172.

5. *Takeuchi Yoshimi zenshu* (The collected works of Takuchi Yoshimi) (Tokyo: Chikuma Shobo, 1981), 5: 110.

6. Yoshida Yutaka. *Showa Tenno no shusenshi*, 196–207.

7. Ibid., 216.

Chapter 6. The Context of Postwar Diplomacy: Options Under Cold War Conditions

1. Masuda Hiroshi, *Ishibashi Tanzan* (Chuokoronsha, 1995), 174–87.

2. Yoshida Shigeru, *Kaiso junen* (Ten years in retrospect), (Tokyo: Shinchosha , 1957), I: 270–71.

3. Yoshida Yutaka, *Showa Tenno no shusenshi* , 192.

4. Sataka Makoto, *Ryo-Nihonshugi no seijika* (Statesman of sane Japanism) (Tokyo: Toyo Keizai Shinposha, 1994), 196.

5. Ishida Hirohide, *Ishibashi seiken nanajuichinichi*, 1985), 159.

6. *Yomiuri Shimbun*, February 3, 1995.

7. Tominomori Eiji, *Sengo hoshuto shi* (The postwar history of Japan's conservative parties), (Tokyo: Shakai Shisosha, 1994), 117.

8. Kishi Nobusuke, *Kishi Nobusuke kaikoroku* (Memoirs of Kishi Nobusuke), (Tokyo: The Kosaido Publishing Co., 1983), 312.

9. Yoshimoto Shigeyoshi, *Kishi Nobusukeden* (Kishi Nobusuke biography), (Tokyo: Toyo Shokan, 1957), 291–92.

10. Kishi Nobusuke, *Kishi Nobusuke kaikoroku*, 320.

Chapter 7. The Pro-Taiwan Faction and "Repaying Violence with Virtue"

1. Kaya Okinori, *Taiwan kirisute no bokyo o imashimeru* (Remonstrance against the recklessness of abandoning Taiwan), in *Senzen sengo hachijunen* (Eighty years before and after the war), (Tokyo: Keizai Ourai Sha, 1976), 337–54.

2. Kaya Okinori, *Senzen sengo hachiju nen*, 345–46.

3. Sankei Shimbunsha, *Sho kaiseki kiroku* (Memoirs of Chiang Kaishek), (Tokyo: Sankei Shuppan, 1985), II: 411.

4. *Asahi Shimbun*, June 4, 1957.

5. Ibid.

6. Kishi Nobusuke, et al., *Kishi Nobusuke no kaiso*, 174–75.

7. *Asahi Shimbun*, June 21, 1957

8. Kishi Nobusuke, et al., *Kishi Nobusuke no kaiso*, 176.

9. Ibid.

10. Tagawa Seiichi, *Nitchu koryu to Jiminto ryoshutachi* (Japan–China exchange and LDP leaders), (Tokyo: Yomiuri Shimbunsha, 1983), 25–29.

11. Fukuda Takeo, *Kaiko kyujunen* (Ninety years in retrospect) (Iwanami Shoten, 1995), 204.

12. Ibid., 52–53.

13. Ibid., 204.

Chapter 8. The Pro-China Faction and Nostalgia for the Continent

1. Tagawa Seiichi, *Nitchu koryu to Jiminto ryoshutachi*, 15.

2. Tagawa Seiichi, *Matsumura Kenzo to Chugoku* (Matsumura Kenzo and China), (Tokyo: Yomiuri Shimbunsha, 1972), 207–27.

3. Ibid.

4. Ibid.

5. Furukawa Mantaro, *Nitchu sengo kankeishi* (A history of postwar Japan–China relations), (Tokyo: Hara Shobo Press, 1988), 129.

6. Endo Kazuko, *Matsumura Kenzo*, (Tokyo: KNB Kosan Shuppanbu, 1975), 226.

7. It is reprinted in *Kako-Getsuen—Matsumura Kenzou ibunsho* (A selection of writings by the late Matsumura Kenzo), (Tokyo: Seirin-Shoin Shinsha, 1978).

8. Ikeda Masanosuke kankoiinkai ed., *Hankotsu no seijika Ikeda Masanosuke* (Ikeda Masanosuke—A statesman with a spirit of defiance), (The Ikeda Masanosuke Memorial Publication Committee, 1995).

9. Ikeda Masanosuke, *Nazo no kuni—Chugoku tairiku no jittai* (The realities of a mysterious country: communist continental China), (Tokyo: Jiji tsushin-sha, 1969).

10. Ikeda Masanosuke, *Shina minzoku no kaimei* (Explorations into the ethnicity of the Chinese), (Tokyo: Naigaijijyo Kenkyujo, 1971).

11. Kishi Nobusuke, et al., *Kishi Nobusuke no kaiso*,

12. Fujiyama Aiichiro, *Seiji wagamichi* (My way in politics), (Tokyo: Asahi Shimbunsha, 1976), 167.
13. Ibid., 168.
14. Ibid., 169–70.

Chapter 9. Yoshida's Disciples' Cool and Calm View on China: From Ikeda Hayato to Miyazawa Kiichi and Tanaka Kakuei

1. *Kako-Getsuen—Matsumura Kenzou ibunsho* (A selection of writings by the late Matsumura Kenzo), (Tokyo: Seirin-Shoin Shinsha, 1978),
2. Fukuda Takeo, *Kaiko kyujunen*, 204.
3. Ito Masaya, *Ikeda Hayato to sono jidai* (Ikeda Hayato and his age), (Tokyo: Asahi Shimbunsha, 1985), 220.
4. Tagawa Seiichi, *Nitchu koryu to Jiminto ryoshutachi*, 41.
5. Tominomori Eiji, *Sengo hoshuto shi*, 169–70.
6. Tagawa Seiichi, *Nitchu koryu to Jiminto ryoshutachi*, 40–41.
7. Miyazawa Kiichi, *Shakaito tono taiwa* (Dialogues with the Socialist Party), (Tokyo: Kodansha, 1965), 125.
8. Ibid., 153–54.
9. Ibid., 165.
10. Ishida Hirohide, *Myogonichi eno michishirube* (Signpost to the day after tomorrow), Tokyo: Daikosha, 1970)
11. Hayasaka Shigezo, *Seijika Tanaka Kakuei* (Tanaka Kakuei, politician), (Tokyo: Chuo Koronsha, 1987), 324–25.

Chapter 10. Nakasone Ysuhiro's Worshipful Visit to Yasukuni Shrine

1. *Asahi Almanac*, 1986 edition.
2. Yokoyama Hiroaki, *Nitchu no shoheki*, 62–81.
3. *Mainichi Shimbun*, September 4, 1986.
4. Yoshida Yutaka, *Nihonjin no sensokan* (The Japanese people's view of the war), (Tokyo: Iwanami Shoten, 1995), 167–70.
5. *Asahi Shimbun*, August 11, 1993.
6. Yokoyama Hiroaki, *Nitchu no shoheki*, 79.
7. Nakasone Yasuhiro and Miyazawa Kiichi, *Tairon: Kaiken/Goken* (Constitutional revision or preservation: A debate), (The Asahi Shimbunsha, 1997).
8. Ibid., 126.

Chapter 11. The Internal Inconsistencies of the Pro-Koreans

1. Japan–Korea Treaty of 1965 (formally known as the Treaty on Basic Relations Between Japan and the Republic of Korea).

2. Takasaki Soji, *Mogen no genkei* (The archetype of thoughtless remarks), (Tokyo: Mokuseisha, 1990), 224–251.

3. "Isseiki no Kan-Nichi kankei—kaiko to tenbo" (The Century's Korea–Japan Relations, Review and Overview) in *Ajia kara mita Nihon* (Japan viewed from Asia), (Tokyo: Kawadeshobo Shinsha, 1994), 54.

4. Ibid., 54–55.

5. Ibid.

6. Fujita Yoshiro, *Kiroku Shiina Etsusaburo* (The Shiina Etsusaburo record), 2 vols., (Tokyo: Shiina Etsusaburo tsuitoroku kankokai, 1982).

7. Fujita Yoshiro, *Kiroku Shiina Etsusaburo*, II: 22–23.

8. Ito Masaya, *Ikeda Hayato to sono jidai*, 207.

9. Fujita Yoshiro, *Kiroku Shiina Etsusaburo*, 25.

10. Ibid., 27.

11. Ito Masaya, *Ikeda Hayato to sono jidai*, 207.

11. Ishihara Shintaro and Morita Akio, *No! to ieru Nihon* (A Japan that can say no!), (Tokyo: Kobunsha, 1989).

Chapter 12. The Anti-Pro-South Koreans and the Diet Delegation to North Korea

1. This information is found in Utsunomiya Tokuma's book *Ajia ni tatsu* (Standing in Asia), (Tokyo: Kodansha, 1978).

Chapter 13. Japanese Leaders' "Ego Trips" to Southeast Asia

1. *Asahi Shimbun*, August 28, 1994.

2. *Asahi Shimbun*, December 31, 1994.

3. Kishi Nobusuke and Ito Masaya, *Kishi Nobusuke kaikoroku*, 311–13.

4. Hara Yoshihisa, *Kishi Nobusuke*, 190.

5. Kishi Nobusuke, *Kishi Nobusuke kaikoroku*, 315–316.

6. Ibid., 388.

7. Ibid., 389.

8. Fukuda Takeo, *Kaiko kyujyunen* (Reminiscences of ninety years) (Iwanami Publishing Co., 1995), 281.

9. Ito Masaya, *Ikeda Hayato to sono jidai*, 164.

10. Ibid., 165.

11. Ibid., 166.

12. Ibid.

13. Ibid., 167.

14. Ibid., 167–68.

15. Ibid., 168.

16. Fukuda Takeo, *Kaiko kyujyunen*, 280–81.

17. Miyazawa Kiichi, *Shakaito tono taiwa* (Dialogue with the Socialist Party), (Tokyo: Kodansha, 1981), 171–73.

Chapter 14. The Political History of Japan's Apology Diplomacy

1. *Asahi Shimbun*, February 17, 1965.
2. Fujita Yoshiro, *Kiroku Shiina Etsusaburo*, II: 43–44.
3. Ibid., 46–51.
4. Ibid., 72.
5. Shiina Etsusaburo, *Dowa to seiji* (Fairy tales and politics), (Tokyo: Toyo seiji keizai kenkyujo [the Toyo Political and Economic Research Institute], 1963).
6. Ibid., 58–59.
7. *Asahi Shimbun*, September 7, 1984.
8. Ibid.
9. *Asahi Shimbun*: Evening edition. September 7, 1984.
10. *Asahi Shimbun*, May 25, 1990.
11. *Asahi Shimbun*, November 7, 1993.
12. *Asahi Shimbun*, September 29, 1990.
13. Hayasaka Shigezo, *Seijika Tanaka Kakuei*, 362.
14. *Asahi Shimbun*, September 26, 1972.
15. Ibid.
16. *Asahi Shimbun*, September 29, 1972.
17. *Asahi Shimbun*, October 24, 1992.
18. *Asahi Shimbun*, May 15, 1991.
19. *Asahi Shimbun*, Evening edition, August 15, 1994.
20. *Asahi Shimbun*, Evening edition, August 15, 1995.
21. *Asahi Shimbun*, Evening edition, October 8, 1998.
22. *Asahi Shimbun*, November 27, 1998.
23. *Asahi Shimbun*, November 27, 1998.

PART IV. THE EMPEROR'S ROAD TO CHINA

PART V. REPORT: THE POST-COLD WAR ERA AS SEEN IN THE KOREA–JAPAN FORUM

PART VI. IN PROSPECTIVE PERSPECTIVE: HOW WILL JAPAN VIEW ASIA TOMORROW?

1. Yoshida Shigeru, *Kaiso junen*, I: 37.

POSTFACE

1. Goto Motoo and et al., *Sengo hoshuseiji no kiseki* (The tracks of postwar conservative politics), (Iwanami Shoten, 1994).

2. Yui Daizaburo, *Nichibei sensokan no sokoku* (Conflicting US and Japanese views of the war), (Iwanami Shoten, 1995).

Index

The LTCB International Library Foundation
Statement of Purpose

The world is moving steadily toward a borderless economy and deepening international interdependence. Amid this globalization of economic activities, the Japanese economy is developing organic ties with the economies of individual nations throughout the world via trade, direct investment, overseas manufacturing activities, and the international movement of capital.

As a result, interest in Japan's politics, economy, and society and in the concepts and values that lie behind Japan's socioeconomic activities is growing in many countries.

However, the overseas introduction and dissemination of translations of works originally written in Japanese lags behind the growth of interest in Japan. Such works are not well known outside Japan. One main reason for this is that the high costs involved in translating and publishing materials written in Japanese hinder the undertaking of such activities on a commercial basis. It is extremely important to overcome this barrier to deepen and broaden mutual understanding.

The LTCB International Library Foundation has been founded to address this pressing need. Its primary activity is to disseminate information on Japan in foreign countries through the translation of selected Japanese works on Japan's politics, economy, society, and culture into English and other languages and the publication and distribution of these translations. To commemorate the completion of The Long-Term Credit Bank of Japan, Ltd.'s new headquarters and its 40th anniversary, LTCB has provided the LTCB International Library Foundation with an endowment.

We sincerely hope that the LTCB International Library Foundation will successfully fulfill its mission of promoting global understanding and goodwill through enhanced cultural exchange.

March 1, 1994

The founders of the
LTCB International Library Foundation